Haiku 61 Revisited

Haiku 61 Revisited

~ THE SONGS OF BOB DYLAN,
INTERPRETED AS HAIKU ~

Robert MacMillan

ISBN: 0692753303
ISBN 13: 9780692753309
Library of Congress Control Number: 2016911554
Windswept Atlantic Publications, New York, NY

Introduction

B ob Dylan released his first album on March 19, 1962. He has written and performed more than 1,000 songs in the 54 years since then. Among them are some of the most enduring, profound and beloved songs in the history of the world. Included in the approximately 700 songs that he has released are classics such as "Blowin' in the Wind," "A Hard Rain's a-Gonna Fall," "The Times They Are a-Changin'," "Mr. Tambourine Man," "My Back Pages," "Like a Rolling Stone," "All Along the Watchtower" and "Knockin' on Heaven's Door." Many of his songs have invited thousands of pages of commentary as people sought to decipher the symbols and meaning in his lyrics. This book tries to tease out the meaning, or at least the flavor and events happening in each song in a new way – as haiku.

Haiku is a kind of poetry that flourished in Japan hundreds of years ago, and has proven a resilient, entertaining form of expression. A haiku in its classical English-language structure is built like this: it has three lines. Lines one and three contain five syllables. Line two contains seven. Not all English-language haiku follow this structure. Some wander off the trail as they seek to capture the spirit of Japanese-language haiku, in which sounds, rather than syllables (there is a difference) determine the outcome of the poem. The themes of haiku obey more rules. So do the rhythm of the lines and the relationship of each line to the next. Haiku typically are poems that use nature as a topic and as a metaphor for our emotions. The middle line often contains a "cutting word" that makes an inexact boundary between a first thought in the haiku and a second thought.

I have thrown away those rules and introduced new guidelines. Half of my inspiration for this project came not from Dylan or Japanese poetry, but from the album collection produced by scholar and album collector Harry Smith, "The Anthology of American Folk Music." Smith wrote newspaper-style headlines in the collection's liner notes to introduce listeners to the essence of each song, using the brevity of a copy desk editor to bring a lighthearted comedy or grim humor to the tales that these old-time American singers shared. Applying a similar approach through the space constraints of haiku seemed like a new way to boil down Dylan's songs to their essence, whether in meaning or failing that, in summary, and to present them in a way that would make them an entertaining complement to the songs. What you read here are the results. I do not intend this to be an academic treatise, nor do I expect those familiar with Dylan's work to find results with which they always will agree. In some cases, I have drawn my conclusions as an enthusiastic listener, though I have consulted many texts and have not ignored them in the final product.

"Haiku 61 Revisited" began in 2009 as a lark. I work at an international news service, and was a reporter then. We used a DOS-based computer program to publish our news and to communicate with colleagues in our office and in bureaus around the world. Our message screens for these communications provided a finite number of characters, similar to Twitter's 140-character count. Sometimes we would joke around by rendering our comments and questions to one another as haiku. A colleague and I were wasting time one day by changing rock n' roll lyrics into haiku, and he challenged me to try my luck at some Dylan songs, so notable for their length, verbosity and complexity. I said I could do it, and that is how I came up initially with "Blowin' in the Wind" and "Lay Lady Lay." I enjoyed the process enough to toy around with some more Dylan songs when I got home that evening, and found that I couldn't stop. In a month or so, I wrote haiku for every song that Dylan had released through his latest albums at the time, "Together Through Life" and "Christmas in the Heart." Another colleague asked whether I would write a book. Who would buy such a thing? Then I thought, "who cares? Just write it."

And that is what I did.

A note on the contents

The first draft of this book was a shaggy mess. The deeper I got into writing, the more I realized how prolific Dylan is. Not knowing where to stop, I began spelunking for Dylan performances that he recorded but never released. At the time, that included the complete "Basement Tapes" recording sessions, now available commercially. Then there were the multiple songs from recording sessions that he left off his albums and that did not (and still in some cases do not) appear on the "Bootleg Series" and other compilations. And still there was more… the songs that he performed in concert but nowhere else, the songs that he contributed to tribute albums and soundtracks, the songs that he wrote, but that only other musicians performed. At one point, I was juggling some 1,300 haiku, many of them offering little in the way of entertaining returns. Subsequent drafts of this project limit the songs that I covered only to those that Dylan commercially released on albums or singles under his own name. I made this decision at a time when that brought the haiku count down to about 500. More recently, to my delight and dismay, Sony has been releasing multiple recordings from the vaults, either in wide or limited editions, and since 2012, when I thought this project was finished, the haiku count grew by about 200. Nevertheless, this collection is fairly clean and organized under its present limits. Any unintentional omissions are my errors alone.

How to read this book

I have arranged "Haiku 61 Revisited" in a way that I hope will prove accessible to Dylan fans and new-comers alike. Finding the proper way to order Dylan's songs can be hard because of the variety of studio and live albums as well as archive albums and singles that he has released. I determined that the easiest way to present his songs was to list them chronologically by the release date of the album on which they appear. That means a song that Dylan recorded in 1962, for example, that didn't appear in commercial form until 2012 would appear on the album that debuted in 2012. In the case of songs that appeared on singles and later on other albums, such as "Positively 4th Street" or "George Jackson," I included them on the date of the single's release. Songs that appeared only as singles, such as "Trouble in Mind," also appear in chronological order. (Sharp Dylan fans will notice that I broke this rule with at least two songs. "Spanish Is the Loving Tongue" appeared in 1971 on the single, "Watching the River Flow." I chose to include "Watching the River Flow" under the second greatest-hits album entry, and moved "Spanish Is the Loving Tongue" to 1973 where another take that Dylan recorded appeared on the album "Dylan." Similarly, "Corrina, Corrina" first appeared on the 1962 single "Mixed Up Confusion," but I included it on "The Freewheelin' Bob Dylan" album in 1963. Any other discrepancies I likely committed by accident.)

I tried to make the text as easy to read as possible. I list each album and single, and underneath those the names of the songs on the album. After that, the title of each song appears, and following that, the haiku, and then a short essay about the song as well as the building blocks that I used or considered while writing the haiku.

A final note on the text: It is inevitable in an undertaking requiring this much research, not to mention writing and rewriting and more rewriting, that there will be some errors of fact, grammar, usage and so on. I thank my friend and colleague Derek Caney for applying his prodigious knowledge of music, journalism and writing to saving me from some big errors. Any others that remain are my responsibility.

Bob Dylan

You're No Good; Talkin' New York; In My Time of Dyin';
Man of Constant Sorrow; Fixin' to Die; Pretty Peggy-O;
Highway 51; Gospel Plow; Baby, Let Me Follow You Down;
House of the Risin' Sun; Freight Train Blues; Song to Woody;
See That My Grave Is Kept Clean.

You're No Good

You're sweet and evil.
You please me and tease me too.
What am I to do?

This is a song by Jesse Fuller, who was born in 1896, but
didn't make a career as a full-time singer until the 1950's.
It's part of the expansive "hard-headed woman" canon
of songs written by guys who think their girlfriends and
wives boss them around. Fuller was a one-man band.
He played guitar, harmonica, kazoo, cymbals and the
"fotdella," a device he invented that allowed him to play
bass and percussion with foot pedals. He's probably best
known for "San Francisco Bay Blues," which was covered
by everyone from The Weavers to Eric Clapton to Paul
McCartney.

Talkin' New York

I went to New York,
Tried to be a great singer.
Now I'm in Jersey.

This song is a farcical chronicle of Dylan's early adventures in New York City when he was hungry, cold and looking for gigs. He comes out of the West, the Midwest, that is. He sees the tall buildings, the wind blows him around, he freezes to the bone. He finds Greenwich Village. A club owner doesn't like his sound. Too much hillbilly, Dylan explains in the punch-line, not enough folk. He gets a dollar a day for playing the harmonica for other people. Small-time music nabobs take advantage of him, and he leaves for the very western East Orange, New Jersey.

In My Time of Dyin'
I'm going to die.
Heaven awaits, but I'm bad.
Meet me halfway, God.

"In My Time of Dyin'" is a dirge that sounds like it has been around for ages. It has. The first known recording was by Reverend J.C. Burnett in 1926, but it was Blind Willie Johnson's version, released in 1928, that became the hit. The best-known version these days probably is the one by Led Zeppelin on their 1975 album "Physical Graffiti." Its alternate title is "Jesus Make Up My Dying Bed." This line is thrilling in its evocation of the grotesque visions of Hieronymus Bosch or Matthias Grünewald: "Well, meet me Jesus, meet me, meet me in the middle of the air. If these wings should fail to me, Lord, won't you meet me with another pair."

Man of Constant Sorrow
A woman hurt him
He left her, but she haunts him.
Now he's going home.

The original, so far as I can determine, was by Dick Burnett, a fiddler from Kentucky who also was partially blind, in the best tradition of mysterious folk and blues singers. There is some evidence that elements of the song date back to 1850 and perhaps even earlier by another century or two.

- He's leaving Colorado where he was born and raised.
- He says to his child: "Your mother says that I'm a stranger, a face you'll never see no more." He promises to meet him or her "on God's golden shore," one of those vast and epic lines that speaks of eternity in the minds and in the landscapes of America.
- Going back to Colorado – a return, a defeat.

Fixin' to Die
This man will die soon
And will leave his kids alone.
He doesn't like that.

This is a shorter version of a 1940 blues song by Bukka White, who was inspired to write it by seeing a man die in prison.

Pretty Peggy-O
Captain falls for girl.
Lieutenant suddenly leaves.
Captain dies for girl.

While the soldiers are marching to Fennerio, the captain falls in love with a "lady like a dove." Meanwhile, a lieutenant who hasn't made an appearance before has gone to Texas and joined the rodeo. And of the captain? He died for a woman's love, and is buried in Louisiana. The song is based on an old Scottish folk song called "The Bonnie Lass o' Fyvie," and the song's lyrics call Fennerio "Fyvie-o." (Fyvie is the name of the town if you look for it on the map.) The song says there are many beautiful women in the Howe (valley) of Auchterless, Garioch and Aberdeen, but the prettiest one is Peggy in Fyvie. In this version, the captain promises her fine things, but she won't go away with him because she says she was never meant to be a soldier's wife. He goes away and is killed in battle.

Highway 51
Bob's baby lives there.
If she dumps him, he won't go
Down that road no more.

This song takes place along Route 51, which runs from west of New Orleans north to the Michigan-Wisconsin border. (Laplace, Louisiana nearly to Ironwood, Michigan)

It was one of the major routes of black migration after the Civil War as people sought jobs in the industrialized north. The song has been ascribed to Curtis Jones. You can hear the seeds of the song "It's Alright Ma (I'm Only Bleeding)," which appeared four years later, in the music.

Gospel Plow
Keep your hand on it.
(I'm talking about your plow.)
Think about heaven.

The title is a reference to Luke 9:62 in the Bible:

"And Jesus said unto him, No man, having put his hand to the plow, and looking back, is fit for the kingdom of God."

Jesus has just spent some quality time extracting a demon from a child. The disciples are arguing. Jesus seems irritated (or so it seems to me). John tells Jesus that they prevented another exorcist from joining their band because the exorcist was doing his work while invoking Jesus's name. Jesus says, he who is not against us is for us, so what is your problem? Jesus decides to take the whole show to Jerusalem, since he's already told the gang that he's going to be delivered into the hands of the law. They pass through villages in Samaria where he and the disciples are unwelcome. James and John suggest asking

God to rain fire on their houses and burn the people to death. Jesus tells them to knock it off. They find another guy who wants to follow them. Jesus complains that he has nowhere to sleep that night, while others are made for the place that they are meant to be. Another guy wants to join up, but says he has to bury his father first. Jesus says, are you kidding? Let the dead bury their dead. You're with me or not with me. Another guy says he wants to join up, but he needs to say goodbye to his family first. Jesus lectures him about the man with the plow. Keeping a steady hand on the plow means training your eyes on the heavenly reward and navigating a straight line. Looking backward or away from the path of faith makes you screw up the straight line, and not just in the pasture of your life. In the man's case, it means that he must commit or not commit, and taking time to say goodbye to his family is the opposite of commitment.

Baby, Let Me Follow You Down
I'll do what you want.
I'll follow you to your house.
Be my future wife.

Guitarist Eric von Schmidt reworked this song from what at one time was known as "Don't Tear My Clothes," a 1935 song by the State Street Boys. Von Schmidt attributes it to Blind Boy Fuller and the Reverend Gary Davis. Dylan introduces the song by saying he took it from von Schmidt.

House of the Risin' Sun
Girl from poor family
Falls in with drunken gambler
And ruins her life.

"Woman to woman," as Joe Cocker and Chris Stainton would put it. A prostitute tells the sad tale of how she ended up in a New Orleans whorehouse, thanks to a case of misdirected wanderlust and a no-good drunken gambler for a boyfriend. She tells her story to her mother, urging her not to let her little sister take the same course. Then she gets back on the train, doomed to resume her role at the Rising Sun.

Freight Train Blues
I'm a train person.
When the freight trains start moving,
I do the same thing.

"Freight Train Blues" is the template for songs about men who can't stay home and maintain healthy relationships because they're always catching a train somewhere.

Song to Woody
Bob finds out how big
Woody Guthrie's shoes are, and
Prepares to fill them.

You have to admire Dylan's ability to decide what he wants, and then beg, borrow or steal to get there. He knew he wanted to be a famous pop singer, and he went for it. He took what he needed along the way, whether it was other people's songs, shticks or personalities. I wonder if that's why he seemed so embarrassed by and contemptuous of Donovan in the "Don't Look Back" documentary when Donovan did his best Dylan impression in front of Bob, and Dylan looked like he couldn't get rid of the kid fast enough. Donovan must have reminded him of an earlier version of himself, trying on costumes and disguises to advance. Dylan decided that he could see a persona in Woody Guthrie that would suit him, and he made sure to spend time around the dying Guthrie, study his method and study his songs, and finally left him with this sort of thank-you note, which is also a promise that he plans to equal and surpass the folk master.

See That My Grave Is Kept Clean
Once I'm dead, I'm dead,
And I won't care about much.
But please clean my grave.

How will he be judged? By those left behind. And by the Lord.

Single: **Mixed Up Confusion**

Mixed Up Confusion
Mixed up and confused
Man keeps walking and searching
For mixed-up women.

"Mixed Up Confusion" is Dylan's first single, issued on the other side of the song "Corrina, Corrina." These two were the only songs from the sessions for the 1963 album "The Freewheelin' Bob Dylan" that were released with electric instruments backing him. The song feels like a conscious attempt at an easy-going hit single, though it didn't perform that way. The song is a compact lament:

- I have mixed-up confusion. It's killing me. It's hard to please so many people.
- I'm walking around with my hat in my hand, looking for a woman who's as mixed up as I am.
- I have lots of questions and a fever. I don't know whom to ask for answers.
- I'm still walking. Every time I see my reflection, "I'm hung over, hung down, hung up!"

The Freewheelin' Bob Dylan

Blowin' in the Wind; Girl From the North Country; Masters of War; Down the Highway; Bob Dylan's Blues; A Hard Rain's a-Gonna Fall; Don't Think Twice, It's All Right; Bob Dylan's Dream; Oxford Town; Talkin' World War III Blues; Corrina, Corrina; Honey, Just Allow Me One More Chance; I Shall Be Free

Blowin' in the Wind

Bob knows so little.
He asks where the answers are.
He has a strong hunch.

You have questions, the wind has answers. The song is a series of unanswerable questions about life, peace, war, mankind and the whole damned thing, with the answer being, as Douglas Sirk put it, written on the wind – everywhere and nowhere, always within reach and not close enough to grab. Or as Yoko Ono sang, "Who has seen the wind? Neither you nor I, but when the trees bow down their heads, the wind is passing by." The melody comes from the slavery song "No More Auction Block," but the catchy, wistful lyrics are Dylan's.

Girl From the North Country

If you go up north,
Check on my former girlfriend.
She might get chilly.

Singer pines for his former lover, presumably in Minnesota's north country where Bob came from. She originally hails from "Scarborough Fair," as do the origins of this song.

Masters of War

The masters of war,
They are killers and scoundrels.
Let's dance on their graves.

A hate note to the haters. The difference between this and many other protest songs is its lack of peace as an antidote to war. This song is about killing the enemy.

Down the Highway

You cross the country,
You miss a girl, you hitch rides,
You gamble, you die.

I've always been partial to this lesser-known song. It's a standard blues song with the usual ingredients – walking and loneliness, and wouldn't you know it, there's a woman to blame. Dylanologists would say that the song is about Bob's girlfriend at the time, Suze Rotolo, who left New York to study in Perugia and left their relationship up in the air.

Bob Dylan's Blues
Bob has some troubles.
The Lone Ranger and Tonto
Won't help him fix them.

This is one of Bob's melancholy-go-lucky walking songs. It's the first time in his recorded work that we see him introduce pop culture characters in relation to something he's doing or some problem that he's having. He also ruminates on cheap women who seek his attention when he already has a perfectly good girlfriend, his lack of a sports car and how he doesn't need one anyway, the wind that blows him up and down the block, and his advice to another guy: if you want to be like him, pack a six-shooter and rob every bank you see. Tell the judge that Bob said it was OK.

A Hard Rain's a-Gonna Fall
Well, it's all right, ma.
I went for a walk and saw
The end of the world.

This song captured the fearful mood of a nation at a time when, historians say, we came closer than ever to a nuclear war. Sad people, racists, riches ignored, signs of the apocalypse, death and loneliness and self pity, and the path that the human race is taking that will lead to oblivion, and the voice of one poet who will do his best to tell the story until he drowns in the murk.

That's what the blue-eyed boy says he saw when he went out for a ramble.

Don't Think Twice, It's All Right
No no, please do go.
I loved you, you hurt my pride.
That's fine; I hate you.

Assigning fault to a failed relationship can be like try-ing to determine who caused a fender bender. Parties rarely agree on the events that led to the accident. This is Bob's version so it's all we have to go by. He castigates his former lover, saying she's why he's leaving and there's no point in trying to figure out why. Then he explains anyway: She is the reason. He gave her his heart, but she wanted his soul. She could have done better by him. She wasted his time. Now she's trying to act like she still loves him, but the words he can't hear and the light of her love he can't see.

Bob Dylan's Dream
I miss all my friends.
We were each other's whole world.
Then we sought paychecks.

This dose of nostalgia could have veered into mawkish territory, but I find it affecting and sincere. I've always thought that the song "The Last Time I Saw Richard" by Joni Mitchell was a natural sequel to this one – several affairs, jobs and a few thousand cocktails later, only this time in a suburban desert:

> "Richard got married to a figure skater
> And he bought her a dishwasher and a coffee percolator
> And he drinks at home now most nights with the TV on
> And all the house lights left up bright."

Oxford Town
They lynch black people
In Oxford, and they tear gas
Protesting white folks.

Here's a Dylan postcard from hell during the Civil Rights movement, focusing on Mississippi.

Talkin' World War III Blues
Bob tells his doctor,
"I dreamed about a world war."
"So did I," Doc says.

"Talkin' World War III Blues" is a fascinating, funny and dark song about a dream life in New York City after a nuclear war, or about getting nervous while waiting for one to begin.

Corrina, Corrina
Bob misses a girl.
He has a bird that can sing.
That don't mean a thing.

People talk about the time when Dylan "went electric," but he already was performing in the studio with plugged-in instruments in 1962. "Corrina, Corrina" is one such song. As for Corrina, she appears to have been bailing out on men since Thomas Edison turned electricity into a commodity. Various versions of the song have appeared since 1918, referring to Corrine, Corrina and Maggie. Country-and-western versions as well as the folk music boom brought the song into Dylan's orbit.

Honey, Just Allow Me One More Chance
You know what I like?
Women who like worried men
And second chances.

"Honey, Just Allow Me One More Chance" offers respite from the grim humor, the just plain grim, and the tragedy that mark many of the songs on this album. The origin of the song might be desperate; the title is a decent indicator, but the treatment is much lighter.

I Shall Be Free
Bob dates tough women
And helps JFK solve the
Nation's big problems.

This is the first of two talking-blues songs that Dylan
did over two years that share nearly identical titles. A
more descriptive title might be, "I Shall Free-Associate."
It seems like an introduction to the more hallucina-
tory songs that he would deliver a few years later on
"Bringing It All Back Home," "Highway 61 Revisited"
and "Blonde on Blonde." Here, he delivers his barely
related verse-long short stories as a talking blues song,
similar to songs from the "Anthology of American Folk
Music" like "The Cuckoo Is a Pretty Bird." Much of the
song focuses on the crazy woman he loves who toler-
ates his own unacceptable and foolish behavior, though
there is a great moment in which he imagines cuckolding
Richard Burton with Elizabeth Taylor. The girlfriend
could be an early version of the title character of "Ugliest
Girl in the World" whom he sang about on the "Down
in the Groove" album 25 years later. The standout line
must be his conversation with JFK. The president asks
Bob what will make the country grow. "Brigitte Bardot,"
Bob answers. "Anita Ekberg. Sophia Loren… Country'll
grow." Even better, in the printed lyrics, he inserts "Put
'em all in the same room with Ernest Borgnine."

The Times They Are a-Changin'

The Times They Are a-Changin'; Ballad of Hollis Brown; With God on Our Side; One Too Many Mornings; North Country Blues; Only a Pawn in Their Game; Boots of Spanish Leather; When the Ship Comes In; The Lonesome Death of Hattie Carroll; Restless Farewell

The Times They Are a-Changin'

Change is coming soon
Whether you like it or not.
Don't be left behind.

If ever there were an anthem in the Bob Dylan catalogue, this is it. A twinning of the folk music "movement" and calls for social change and justice for all people, particularly minorities and everyone else who's on the wrong end of the power structure in America. More broadly, it's about accepting change because you have no choice.

Ballad of Hollis Brown

Hollis kills wife, kids
And himself. They were starving.
Better dead than poor.

Brown's plagues are like those that God visited on Job to keep good on his wager with Satan. Whereas Job accepted faith, Hollis tried to make a change on destiny.

With God on Our Side
The bad things we do
Are OK, we say, because
God is on our side.

I quote John Cale:

> "Read and destroy everything you read in the
> press
> Read and destroy everything you read in books
> It's a waste of time
> It's a waste of energy
> It's a waste of paper
> And it's a waste of ink
> Whatever you read in the books, leave it there."

- I was raised in the Midwest, learning to obey the law because my country has God on its side.
- In the history books, they say the Indians died by our hands because the country was young and had God on its side.
- Spanish-American War, Civil War: they were fighting and dying with God on their side.
- World War I: Who knows why they fought it, but I sure was proud, as we had God on our side.
- The Germans murdered 6 million in the camps, but now we're friends because they more recently have gotten God on their side.

- If we have to fight the Russians, we'll do it with God on our side.
- If we have to fight a nuclear war, we'll do that with God on our side too.
- I keep wondering if Judas Iscariot had God on his side.
- If God's on our side, he will stop the next war before it happens.

One Too Many Mornings

Couple has a fight.
Man thinks about leaving town.
He's torn. What to do?

Many of Dylan's narrators in his early years can't help but wander, particularly when the emotional demands of their ladies run hot and the arguments begin. The singers regret leaving, but they have no choice because they're outlaws, wanderers and hobos at heart. And because they're not so different from Goethe's young Werther, they feel bad about the choices they've made, usually once it's too late to take them back.

North Country Blues

Miners get priced out.
Mine shuts down, cripples the town,
Men drink, the kids leave.

Here's a depressing song about the collapse of a mining town in northern Minnesota, sung from the point of view of a miner's wife whose children abandon her when they get out of town for their own good. Dylan likely is drawing on memories of his youth growing up in Hibbing in that region.

Only a Pawn in Their Game
They killed a black man.
They too are caught in a web.
Someone pulls their strings.

This is a song about the assassination of civil rights leader Medgar Evers. It examines the idea of individual responsibility versus collective evil and the agenda of a wily and powerful few in the perpetuation of racism in the United States, similar to the idea of individual operators in the Nazi death machine. Are the individual criminals to blame? Were they following orders? Or were they brought up by entrenched powers to act in a way that they couldn't control? Dylan seems to conclude that it's a mixture. He makes an interesting defense of the poor, white, uneducated man who's manipulated by forces bigger than he is to behave in accordance with their ambitions. It would be interesting to get this song out there in public more than 50 years after it appeared to see what modern audiences would make of it.

Boots of Spanish Leather
Bob stays home alone.
Girl offers guilt gifts. She's sailed
Far from him for good.

Usually it's Dylan who's doing the wandering, the walking and the rambling. This time the girl sails away and offers him gifts, presumably from the guilt she feels because she left him. He asks only for her to return, saying that's worth more than "the stars from the darkest night and the diamonds from the deepest ocean." She's not feeling guilty enough to change her plans for an indefinite expatriate life, and once she makes this clear, our hero asks for boots of Spanish leather. These boots are, after all, made for walking. (It's the opposite of "Blackjack Davey," the old folk song about a woman who leaves her husband for a young rake. In that version, he chases after his wife, only to have her throw back in his face all his curdled love.)

When the Ship Comes In
When our ship arrives,
We'll drown our enemies and
Everyone will laugh.

Note to hoteliers, maitre d's and other gatekeepers: the next time you refuse Dylan service, remember what happened to the last guy. This song, according to Joan Baez and others, was a reaction to a hotel employee refusing to offer a room to Dylan because of his unkempt appearance. He got mad and wrote this song, which has a lot more than hotel tyranny on its mind.

The Lonesome Death of Hattie Carroll
White man kills Hattie.
He serves six months and gets out.
Isn't that a bitch?

"The Lonesome Death of Hattie Carroll" tells the story of Maryland tobacco farm owner Billy Zantzinger who got drunk at a Baltimore party, and beat a black hotel employee with a toy cane. The employee, Hattie Carroll, died of a brain hemorrhage hours later. Zantzinger first was charged with murder, with the charge later downgraded to manslaughter and assault, seeing as it was unclear whether hitting her with the cane actually killed her. He said that he was too drunk to remember the incident. He was found guilty and sentenced to six months in jail. Dylan suggests that Zantzinger's society and political connections got him off easy. Zantzinger later said he should have sued Dylan and gotten him sentenced to jail. He also characterized Dylan as "a scum of a scum bag of the earth."

Restless Farewell
Upset by gossip
And jerks, Bob slinks off until
His next record comes.

More of a testy farewell.

- Money: So much for that, we spent it on good times. It's closing time now, so I'm off.
- Girls: I never meant to harm any of them, and I wanted to stay friends, but to do that you need to take time.
- Enemies: It was never personal, and I never regretted the battle. Thoughts: I've expressed my art for the sake of myself and my friends, not for every Tom, Dick and Harry (despite being a hit recording artist for a major music label). Maybe it's time to leave all that behind.
- Distractions: I don't want to be stuck on someone's notion of what I should be doing and when. Doing my own thing means I'll be the subject of gossip. But you'll see by my work that the "arrow of my intent can pierce the dust of rumors that cover me," and in the meantime I'll do whatever the hell I want, and "bid farewell and not give a damn."

Another Side of Bob Dylan
All I Really Want to Do; Black Crow Blues; Spanish Harlem Incident; Chimes of Freedom; I Shall Be Free No. 10; To Ramona; Motorpsycho Nitemare; My Back Pages; I Don't Believe You; Ballad in Plain D; It Ain't Me Babe

All I Really Want to Do
Bob will befriend you.
But there are 46 things
He won't do to you.

- Baby, you can trust me. I just want to be your friend. Maybe with benefits, but just maybe.
- My adoring fans, you must have me confused with someone else. I am here to be your friend, not your protest leader. This is, after all, "another side" of Bob Dylan.

Here are the 46 things that Bob mentions in this song that he is not trying to do to you:

- Compete.
- Beat.
- Cheat.
- Mistreat.
- Simplify.
- Classify.
- Deny.

- Defy.
- Crucify.
- Fight.
- Frighten.
- Tighten.
- Drag down.
- Drain down.
- Chain down.
- Bring down.
- Block up.
- Shock up.
- Knock up.
- Lock up.
- Analyze.
- Categorize.
- Finalize.
- Advertise.
- Straight-face.
- Race.
- Chase.
- Track.
- Trace.
- Disgrace.
- Displace.
- Define.
- Confine.
- Meet kin.
- Spin.

- Do in.
- Select.
- Dissect.
- Inspect.
- Reject.
- Fake out.
- Shake out.
- Forsake out.
- Feel like me.
- See like me.
- Be like me.

Black Crow Blues
Bob wants his babe back.
He wanders, disconsolate,
And suffers mood swings.

This song makes me think of Van Gogh's wheat field with the crows, but long after the harvest, maybe well into December or some other winter month. Black crow's in the meadow, sort of like Churchill's black dog. As for Dylan, he doesn't feel scarecrow enough to chase it away. That's a fancy way of saying he has the blues, the special kind of blues of walking on a frozen fallow field on a cloudy day far from the city.

Spanish Harlem Incident
Bob wants gypsy girl
To tell him his fortune and
Then hook up with him.

Here is the story of a sexy gypsy fortune teller and the singer's designs on her. He uses sophisticated poetry to woo her with this ultimate aim: "I got to know, babe, will you surround me? So I can tell if I'm really real."

Chimes of Freedom
The chimes of freedom
Flash for the world's losers
And make lots of noise.

"Chimes of Freedom" was a big hit for the Byrds, and that's the version that most people know. Dylan's recording is a denser affair, and one of the first to slide into the realm of the surreal where he was to pay the rent for the next two or three years. It's a haunting song, and the repetition of the slow, spare melody skirts the border between hypnotic and annoying, but the end product is undeniably a strong, intelligent work about bondage, liberation and freedom.

For whom they toll:

- Warriors whose strength is not to fight.
- Refugees on unarmed road of flight.

- Underdog soldier at night.
- Rebel.
- Rake.
- Luckless.
- Abandoned.
- "Forsaked."
- Outcast.
- Burnt at stake.
- Gentle.
- Kind.
- Guardians.
- Protectors of mind.
- Unpawned, derivative painter.
- Tongues with no place for their thoughts.
- Deaf.
- Blind.
- Mute.
- Mistreated.
- Single mother.
- Mistitled prostitute.
- Misdemeanor outlaw.
- Chased.
- Cheated.
- Searching.
- Unharmful, gentle prisoners.
- Aching with terminal wounds.
- Countless confused.
- Countless misused.
- Countless accused.

- Countless strung outs.
- Worse.
- Hung-up people.

I Shall Be Free No. 10
Bob gets strange notions
To box Ali and Goldwater.
His woman is mean.

Another side of "I Shall Be Free."

- He's just like everyone else. There's no point talking to him because it's just the same as talking to yourself.
- He's shadow-boxing, dreaming of a bout with Muhammad Ali, then known by his given name, Cassius Clay. Bob intends to knock him out of his spleen.
- If the streets of heaven are lined with gold, what happens if the Russians get there first?
- He's liberal, but come on, people have their limits. No way would he let Barry Goldwater move in next door and marry his daughter, not "for all the farms in Cuba."
- He puts his monkey on the log, asks him to do the Dog. He does the cat instead. Weird monkey.
- He goes to play tennis with a wig hat and high-heeled sneakers. He's not allowed onto the tennis court.

- His woman is mean. Evidence: she puts his boots in the washing machine, shoots him with buckshot when he's naked, puts gum in his food, wants his money, calls him honey.
- His friend spends all his time stabbing Bob's picture with a Bowie knife. He wants to strangle Bob with a scarf, and he vomits whenever someone mentions Bob's name. There are nearly a million other people out there just like his friend.
- The sorority sisters invite him over to read his poetry. They knock him down and send him to the dean of women. He must be a real poet.
- He plans to wear his hair in the style of a mountain range, horseback ride to Omaha, go to the golf course at the country club, carry a copy of The New York Times with him, and blow everybody's minds while he plays the links.

To Ramona
Bob lets a girl down.
He tries to make her feel good,
But it might not work.

"To Ramona" is supposed to be a song about Joan Baez, so they say. I don't know. My friend Derek tells me that the melody might come from Rex Griffith's 1937 single

"The Last Letter," a maudlin suicide note. Griffith was an alcoholic and a diabetic, and he died of tuberculosis. Which is to say, he was a country singer.

Suggestions and encouragement:

- Stop crying.
- You won't be sad for long.
- Even the flowers in the city can't keep from drooping sometimes.
- Don't bother with the dying. There's no point. I'm having trouble expressing this.
- I still want to kiss you.
- The world you want to be part of doesn't exist. It's just a con job that makes you feel bad.
- You've been listening to idle chatter. No need for that.
- You don't have to leave here. You're your own worst enemy.
- You say that everybody's equal, but trust me, it's not true. You can be better than others, or else why are you doing what you're doing?
- Friends can be a drag on your ambition and feelings.
- I realize I can't help you though I keep trying.
- You know what? I'm sure that one day I'll be where you are and come to you for advice.

Motorpsycho Nitemare
Right-wing farmer hosts
Bob for the night. His saucy
Daughter flirts with Bob.

- Tired traveler reaches farmhouse. Farmer points a gun at him.
- Farmer asks if he's the infamous traveling salesman. Bob says no, he's a doctor and college educated at that.
- His daughter Rita looks like Anita Ekberg. Bob tells the farmer what a nice farm he has. Farmer is suspicious.
- Farmer offers him a bed under the stove as long as he doesn't touch Rita and milks the cow.
- He goes to sleep. Rita wakes him up, looking like Tony Perkins in "Psycho." She offers to give him a shower. He's afraid.
- He realizes he can't leave without breaking his promise to milk the cow, so he figures he needs to say something that the farmer will not like. He shouts, "I like Fidel Castro and his beard." Good choice. The farmer loses his temper. Rita looks offended.
- The farmer tries to hit Bob. Rita mumbles something mysterious about "her mother on the hill." The farmer calls Bob an "unpatriotic rotten doctor Commie rat."

- Farmer throws a Reader's Digest at Bob as Bob somersaults through the window and lands in the garden. Rita asks him to come back. The sun rises and Bob's running down the road.
- Bob decides not to return to that part of the country for a while. The farmer's still waiting for him, while Rita moved away and got a job at a motel just like Norman Bates.

My Back Pages

It's easy to preach
When I think I know it all.
But I know nothing.

Dylan spent two notable periods of his songwriting life as a preacher. The second was his three-year, three-album journey into born-again Christianity, while the first was the period for which he is best remembered, that of a protest singer. "My Back Pages," so the interpretations go, is his renunciation and rejection of those kinds of songs, and the realization that the world is a complex place and the abandonment of unquestioned ideals is a sign of maturity. He goes one step further and shows how maturity and acceptance are signs of a youthful soul – a meeting of innocence and experience. People should grow wise as they age, but they often become set. This is the cautionary tale against that. I've read various descriptions of these words as being like those of

William Blake, though with the songs of experience coming first, then the songs of innocence.

I Don't Believe You
Girl sleeps with guy, then
Pretends she doesn't know him.
Two can play that game.

Saturday night:

- "We kissed through the wild blazing nighttime."
- "She said she would never forget."

Sunday morning:

- "Something has changed, for she ain't the same."

Ballad in Plain D
Relationship dies
From family interference.
Bob kisses and tells.

Here is an uncomfortable, intimate and venomous eight-minute-plus reconstruction of Dylan's quarrel with Carla Rotolo, sister of his ex-girlfriend Suze Rotolo and the breakup of his and Suze's relationship. It's raw and mean and condescending, and Dylan has indicated that he probably should have let that song stay in the dark. It's undeniably interesting and engrossing, but it does feel a little bit like reading someone else's mail.

It Ain't Me Babe
You need someone else,
A defender, a doormat.
I am not that guy.

If you think Dylan's version is good, you should try listening to Johnny Cash and June Carter do it with a mariachi band.

Bringing It All Back Home
Subterranean Homesick Blues; She Belongs to Me; Maggie's Farm; Love Minus Zero/No Limit; Outlaw Blues; On the Road Again; Bob Dylan's 115th Dream; Mr. Tambourine Man; Gates of Eden; It's Alright, Ma (I'm Only Bleeding); It's All Over Now, Baby Blue

Subterranean Homesick Blues
Instructions for life:
Nothing but fine print designed
To keep you guessing.

Dylan stuffs a lot of material into this song, which starts the album off at high speed. It's his first album to feature songs with a full rock 'n' roll band, and the first side barely slows down with the exception of two "love" songs. While Dylan spent a lot of time saying he wasn't a protest singer, this song makes you wonder. Dylan's protest is against the struggle of staying alive in the land of plenty. "Subterranean Homesick Blues" is a mixture of unrelated portraits and complaints. (The codeine maker in the basement, watching out for the DA, as well as cops who use fire hoses on Civil Rights workers, and so on.) But taken in total, it sounds like a description of the futility of the modern-day, white-collar rat race – a grim road map for middle-class Americans striving for prosperity, house, wife, husband, kids, dog, car and on and on. This is where the man in the gray flannel suit begins to burn out before he drops out. Following the map leads to the conclusion that none of it was worth it once it's too late to turn back. You have to be crazy to want to work like a dog ("20 years of schooling and they put you on the day shift"), constantly risk failure ("join the Army if you fail"), never knowing if you're doing things the right way ("you're doing it again"), never having enough money (11 dollar bills when you've only got 10), and not knowing why the hell you're doing it. (Get born, dressed, blessed, try to be a success, please her, please him....) The song's influences include Jack Kerouac's writing, as well as a Woody Guthrie and Pete Seeger song, along with, as Dylan said, Chuck Berry's "Too Much Monkey Business."

She Belongs to Me

I love an artist.
But I belong to her. I'm
Not sure she loves me.

The artist in this song has everything she needs, and she definitely doesn't need her man, though he tries to please her. She's above the law, beyond reproach and she can make men rob and steal.

Maggie's Farm

Bob hates his farm job.
He's tired of pleasing his fans.
He has other chores.

Many see this as Dylan's protest against protest songs, or even a complaint about being the singer that his record company or his fans want him to be. Or maybe he's a serf in a Turgenev novel who is sick of the farm, that is to say, all of us who are working on somebody's farm. Some say that "Maggie's Farm" is a pun on "McGee's Farm," a place where he performed a memorable version of his protest song, "Only a Pawn in Their Game." I would also note that "farm" meant "prison" to a lot of old-time blues singers and prisoners in southern jails. Another antecedent for the song is "Down on Penny's Farm."

Love Minus Zero/No Limit
Girlfriend with an edge:
She's above petty concerns
And she's very smart.

The qualities of Bob Dylan's girlfriend:

- No ideals, no violence, faithful, laughs, and has a different definition of success and failure than the rest of us.
- She speaks softly whereas other people babble nonsense about what they read.
- Departure from the song for the sake of adding some imagery to trip up college students and their professors: dangling cloak and dagger,

madams with candles, ceremonies of the horse-
men and grudge-holding pawns, and matchstick
statues crumbling together.

Outlaw Blues

Bob needs some good luck.
He speaks the truth and they treat
Him like an outlaw.

This song has some terrific, raucous, noisy playing, and
it produced that great line, "Don't ask me nothing about
nothing, I just might tell you the truth." As the song
"The Wicked Messenger" suggested a few years later,
that's not what people want to hear. Then there's the cu-
rious aside in which he says he looks like Robert Ford,
but feels like Jesse James. He also notes that he doesn't
plan to hang a picture frame. James decided to dust a pic-
ture frame as it hung over his living room mantle. It was
while he was doing this that Robert Ford shot him dead.
Ford was in cahoots with the governor of Minnesota to
betray his fellow outlaw, so he was pardoned after he and
his brother Charley were sentenced to death by hanging
for first-degree murder.

On the Road Again

Your crazy family
Is unbearable, and you –
How do you stand it?

I've always appreciated this weird little song. Dylan describes the miserable state of affairs in a woman's house, most of which are brought on by her eccentric and intolerable family. The brown rice and seaweed hint at the family's "Bohemian" ways.

Bob Dylan's 115th Dream
Bob's friends in New York:
Jailed for harpoon possession.
That's the least of it.

Bob discovers the New World with a gang of lusty sailors aboard the Mayflower. They're promptly jailed, though Bob breaks out and encounters a variety of freaks and geeks all over lower Manhattan while trying to spring his crew. As he passes Christopher Columbus on his three ships heading in while he's on his way out of town, he wishes them a cynical "good luck."

Mr. Tambourine Man
Set me free tonight,
The sea and sky my fences.
I'll follow your song.

Attempts to analyze "Mr. Tambourine Man" can make something beautiful and light into something ponderous and heavy. It is a crystalline song that sees the singer follow the beat of the tambourine player into a borderless world of freedom and inspiration where anything is possible.

Many people associate the song with drug use as a way to slip through the gates of our minds, but I think that the psychotropic fascination is a fixation that weighs on the song. The poignancy rests in the trip on the swirling ship through the smoke rings of his mind and dead time, down to a beach and the sea, dancing free beneath a "diamond sky," coupled with Bob's plea to the tambourine man to let him "forget about today until tomorrow." Sooner or later, the most beautiful flight must return to earth.

Gates of Eden
Nothing is good here.
The only hope lies beyond,
Where it's unlikely.

Dramatis personae:

- Curfew gull.
- Four-legged forest clouds.
- Cowboy angel.
- Lamppost.
- Wailing babies.
- Savage soldier.
- Shoeless deaf hunter.
- Hound dogs.
- Aladdin.
- Utopian hermit monks.
- Golden calf.
- Kings.

- Bob.
- Lonesome sparrow.
- Motorcycle black Madonna.
- Two-wheeled gypsy queen.
- Silver-studded phantom.
- Gray-flannel dwarf.
- Birds of prey.
- Paupers.
- Princess.
- Prince.
- Friends and other strangers.
- Free men.
- Bob's lover.

There are many bad things happening outside the gates of Eden. Twisting truth, a black-waxed candle lit into the sun, the wailing babies in holes, the crash of "all in all," the complaining soldier, the barking dogs, the city, machinery, Aladdin and the monks on the golden calf (idolators), promises of paradise which must be false, people condemned to suffer succeeding kings, the screaming dwarf, wicked birds of prey who snap up the dwarf's tiny sins, rotting kingdoms, jealous poor people, the royalty taken up with the discussion of what's real (they are wasting their time), Bob's inability to ever find a home, and finally Bob's lover, who doesn't bother to analyze her dreams. This is all what's outside the gates of Eden. Inside sounds like it should be a paradise, but it doesn't sound like Bob is giving you a hard sell. We end up with a false promise of paradise, keeping in mind that the original sin happened inside those gates.

It's Alright, Ma (I'm Only Bleeding)
Everything you hear
Is a lie, including this.
You are a target.

"It's Alright, Ma (I'm Only Bleeding)" is seven-and-a-half minutes of electrifying bile and scorn. I used to think that as I grew older, I would begin to find the aggression and the hatred of "the way things are" immature. I was wrong. The song has become sharper over the years. Dylan radiates in all directions on this song, but he hits each target. The message is that life is a lie, that we're aiming for the wrong ends, we've been conned, and in fact we've conned ourselves and been a party to our own futility. Action means nothing, there's no point in trying. But, as he says at the end of every verse, it's all right.

It's All Over Now, Baby Blue
Guy leaves a lover
Who can't face reality.
He takes his carpet.

This song is about abandoning a life that you can't live anymore. Sooner or later, the signs become more than signs – we all must be forced from our old lives into something new, and usually at a point where we would rather stay still. If you want to be portentous, you can call it death, but I think the death here is more about transformation or transfiguration, or just the end of something old and the beginning of something new. Whoever "Baby Blue" is, the clock has run out and it's time to move on, even with no help or sign that you're going the right way. Attempts to keep things as they were mean you stay behind even as all your support vanishes – think of the seasick sailors all rowing home in the song, or Bob's admonition to "forget the dead you've left, they will not follow you." The vagabond says to me that there's always someone who will take what you've been forced to lose, and it's shameful to see things that don't belong to you anymore in the hands of others, but that's the old line about everything that once was solid melting into air. And yet, there are new things, as Bob notes when he says, "Leave your stepping stones behind, there's something that calls to you."

Highway 61 Revisited

Like a Rolling Stone; Tombstone Blues; It Takes a Lot to Laugh, It Takes a Train to Cry; From a Buick 6; Ballad of a Thin Man; Queen Jane Approximately; Highway 61 Revisited; Just Like Tom Thumb's Blues; Desolation Row

Like a Rolling Stone

Now you feel like a
Stone alone without a home
Because of your tone.

It's a one-size-fits-all poison-pen letter. The subject of the song went to the finest schools and lived a charmed life, but lost the trappings of money and the support of friends, ending up destitute, desperate and in the thrall of people who have their own needs on their minds. One odd twist: the nearly envious tone about having nothing left, nothing to lose and no secrets to hide. He sounds like he's singing not just about the object of his scorn (popularly thought to be the late actress and model Edie Sedgwick), but one of the Christian saints (Francis of Assisi, for example), or various beggars who forsake everything on the path to enlightenment. Only in this case, that path seems hard because the subject of the song wasn't looking for enlightenment. Every time Dylan strips away another layer of possession, comfort and faith, you can feel the cruelty increase, the haplessness and folly of the subject, her (or his?) refusal to see that the situation is getting a little worse with each second, and the suspicion that Dylan feels sadness and pity along with his revulsion and his satisfaction that yesterday's big winner is today's big loser.

Tombstone Blues
Murderers, toadies
And quacks run the country. Bob
Is feeling their blues.

"Tombstone Blues" features a grand assortment of nefarious characters doing bad things to themselves and others, while Dylan gets the tombstone blues, his father skulks in an alley and his mother (without a pair of shoes on her feet) works in a factory. There's an indictment of business and government going on here.

- The city fathers endorse a reincarnation of Paul Revere's horse, the one that helped spread the word to the colonial militias to take up arms against the invading Brits.
- Outlaw Belle Starr shares her world view with false prophet/whore Jezebel who is busy knitting a wig for Jack the Ripper, head of the local chamber of commerce.
- Doctor and medicine man offer quack advice to a hysterical bride and tell her to relax.

- John the Baptist tortures a thief and expresses remorse to his boss, the president. The president tells him to get over it.
- A philistine king, which to me is the same as the president, flatters his dead soldiers while getting slaves ready to go out and do some fighting in the jungle. (Vietnam?)
- Gypsy Davey, the eternal wife stealer of old British folk songs, burns the soldiers to death while currying favor with his uncle.
- Innocence forces Galileo, the man of experience, to throw a math book at the calculating Delilah, now scorned and alone, but she's weeping tears of laughter.
- Culture goes for a toss as a marching band plays patriotic music around a flagpole in the same place that Ma Rainey and Beethoven used to make real music.
- The bank makes its money by selling maps to the soul to impressionable young and old people.

It Takes a Lot to Laugh, It Takes a Train to Cry
If she doesn't climb
On top of your train, she might
Miss it when it's gone.

This surreal title grabbed at me when I was young because I couldn't figure out what it meant, and because of the surreal juxtaposition of two phrases in symmetry – one resting on an adverb and one resting on a noun. I still don't know, but I think I found the thread that runs through the song. What we have to play with are three verses:

- He's riding a train and "can't buy a thrill." He's been leaning on her windowsill. He might die on top of the hill, but if he does, his baby will still make it.
- The moon looks good through the trees. The brakeman looks good on the train track. Baby from verse 1 looks good when she's in the mood for the singer.
- Winter's coming, the windows are getting frosty. He tries to tell everyone, but they don't understand him. He tells his baby that he wants to be her lover, not her boss, then reminds her that he's warned her before that she might lose her train.

I'm going with the Alfred Hitchcock "North by Northwest" solution, which ends with a passionate embrace between Cary Grant and Eva Marie Saint as the train they're riding on thrusts itself into a tunnel as it speeds down the track... In other words, it must be a song about not getting any. But to conclude this ignores three things: she seems to want him in verse 2, but not in verses 1 and 3; and the brakeman and the frost. Or maybe they're just there because the song is partially a collection of older blues lyrics, and Dylan wanted something to sing.

From a Buick 6
The wife has the kid.
But the mistress has the fun.
She is resourceful.

Graveyard woman:

- Keeps his kid.

Soulful mama:

- Keeps him hid.
- Gives him bread.
- Sews him up with thread.
- Doesn't talk too much.
- Doesn't make him nervous.
- Walks like Bo Diddley sans crutch.
- Keeps a loaded gun.
- Brings him everything (and more).
- Ready to put a blanket on his deathbed.

Ballad of a Thin Man
Hopeless square shows up,
Acts like he's above it all.
We know otherwise.

This chronicle of a square foretold is mean. The song appears to be Dylan's reaction to people who were asking him what his songs meant and "what it was all about" when he was exploring surreal territory in his music and confounding people's expectations of him. At the time, journalists and others questioned him about the meaning of his lyrics, and his responses became surly. In the song, he places one of the journalists in a room full of freaks.

- Mr. Jones enters room, pencil in hand. Asks who that man is. He doesn't know what he's going to write when he gets home.
- Something is happening here, but Mr. Jones doesn't understand it.
- He asks if this is "where it's at." Someone else asks him sarcastically what he's talking about.
- He gawks at a geek who asks him what it feels like to be a freak. Impossible, he says.
- He has contacts among lumberjacks who back up his arguments when someone attacks what he writes. They expect him to write tax-deductible checks to charity.
- He grew up widely admired by academics and lawyers, discussing all the big issues of the world. He's well read, particularly on F. Scott Fitzgerald.
- Male sword swallower in high heels asks Mr. Jones how "it" feels and gives him back his throat.

- Mr. Jones engages in pointless repartee with a midget who tells him he's a cow, and should give some milk or else go home.
- Mr. Jones looks like a camel when he looks around the room. There should be a law against him showing up.

Queen Jane Approximately

Queen Jane's a pain, but
Prince Bob wants to see her when
Her schedule frees up.

"Queen Jane Approximately" is an entreaty to a woman, or, as Dylan once said to Nora Ephron, a man, who is a little too busy for real people, and is spending too much time in wasteful pursuits with wasteful people. Unluckily for the subject, many of those people are about to be done with Queen Jane, but at that rock-bottom moment, Dylan would be happy to see him/her.

Highway 61 Revisited

We know just the place
For sacrificing sons and
Other strange requests.

Dylan makes Highway 61 the location for a number of symbolic acts by inhospitable, greedy and opportunistic people, ranging from unwilling Abraham's attempt to sacrifice his son Isaac, to a world war. The real

Highway 61 runs from Duluth, Minnesota to New Orleans. It travels along the mighty Mississippi River for most of its nearly 1,407 miles. It was a major transportation route for the African-American migrations from south to north after the abolition of slavery, and carries with it a mystical association with blues music. It also evokes the myth of Robert Johnson, the blues singer who supposedly went to the crossroads and sold his soul to the devil in return for his supernatural ability to play the guitar. There is more than one version of that legend, though some people like to say it happened at midnight at the crossroads of highways 49 and 61 in Clarksdale, Mississippi. That Dylan added a "Revisited" to the name of the song and the album at a time when he was tearing down and rebuilding the blues and rock music speaks to his overt intent as a radical musician. Or maybe he just liked the name. The road also appeared in "Highway 61 Blues" by Roosevelt Sykes and "Highway 61" by Sunnyland Slim.

Just Like Tom Thumb's Blues
Bob goes to New York.
He might make it there, but he
Makes it nowhere else.

The runaway imagery that sometimes obscures the clarity of Dylan's songs remains at a manageable level in

"Just Like Tom Thumb's Blues." The fractured narrative from verse to verse that can turn a song into a pond disturbed by ripples from a rock here makes a series of related if discrete episodes. The music rolls along with resignation, but it's punchy instead of bloated.

- Lost in the rain in Ciudad Juarez on Easter Sunday. Rue Morgue Avenue with hungry, aggressive women.
- Saint Annie: Tell her thanks. I can't move. Doc doesn't know what's wrong with me.
- Melinda: Goddess of gloom. Also a prostitute.
- Housing Project Hill choices: fortune or fame. It's a trick. By the way, you should leave if you want to get silly. The cops don't need your trouble.
- Boasting authorities who blackmailed the sergeant-at-arms. Then there's the story of Angel who showed up from Los Angeles and didn't take well to New York.
- Round one: burgundy. Round two: harder chaser. Game got rough. Joke was on me. I couldn't handle it. Back to New York.

Desolation Row
Famous lovers and
Doomed geniuses find a place
They can call their own.

Whatever Desolation Row might be, it **is** a state of mind, a place that Bob might prefer to wherever he was stuck at the time he wrote the song. Nearly everyone in the song who achieved fame for something seems to be doomed to a circle of hell where they become parodies of themselves.

The people of Desolation Row:

- People who sell postcards at the hanging and paint the passports brown.
- Beauty parlor/sailor.
- Circus.
- Blind commissioner. (In a trance. One hand on tightrope walker, other in pants.)
- Riot squad.
- Lady and Bob.
- Cinderella, acting like Bette Davis. (Virgin princess turns out to be Jezebel.)
- Romeo. (Makes entrance with a claim on a woman. Someone else sends him on his way.)
- Fortune-telling lady.
- Cain and Abel. (Along with the Hunchback of Notre Dame – the only ones not making love or expecting rain.)
- The Good Samaritan. (He's too busy to be helpful tonight.) Ophelia. (Old before she's had a chance to be young, she spends her time peeking at the fun going on where she isn't.)

- Einstein, disguised as Robin Hood. (Intellectual as thief, speaking incoherently, bumming cigarettes and maybe getting high.)
- Dr. Filth and his sexless patients and his nurse.
- The Phantom of the Opera. (As a priest.)
- Casanova. (Starts out timid, later overestimates his prowess.)
- Skinny girls.
- Agents.
- Superhuman crew.
- Everyone who knows more than the crew does.
- Insurance men.
- Nero's Neptune.
- Everybody on the Titanic who asks you your political affiliation. (Doomed to drown while arguing about party lines.)
- Ezra Pound and T.S. Eliot. (Fighting in the captain's tower of the Titanic.)
- Calypso singers.
- Fishermen with flowers.
- Lovely mermaids.
- You.
- Lame people with new faces and names.

Single: **Positively 4th Street**

Positively 4th Street
Rage, jealousy, scorn:
Negatively 4th Street is
Where this guy must live.

- You're not really my friend. You took pleasure in my earlier distress.
- You don't really want to help me. You just like me because I'm a winner right now.
- You say I let you down? Nonsense. If you have a problem, bring it.
- You don't have any faith to lose so stop saying you have done so.
- You talk behind my back because we used to socialize together.
- Why would I seek you out when you don't know anything to begin with?
- You act cool on the street and ask me small-talk questions. Liar, you don't mean them.
- You don't like me. You'd like it if I were paralyzed. Don't be afraid to tell me the truth.
- I don't like the losers you hang out with. I wish I were a thief so I could rob them.
- You don't like your station in life? Too bad. Not my problem.
- I wish we could switch places just once. You would realize just how much it sucks to run into you.

Single: **<u>Can You Please Crawl Out Your Window?</u>**

Can <u>You</u> Please Crawl Out Your Window?
You're with a loser.
Are you one too? Why don't you
Come date me instead?

"Can <u>You</u> Please Crawl Out Your Window?" is a tale of
Romeo seducing Juliet from the window, but by mocking
her even as he makes clear that he has lustful thoughts.
The man she's dating? Dylan can barely talk to him.
He just harangues her about him. It's great to be young,
smart, wanted and admired, but you get the impression
that for a year or two, the singer couldn't stand to be
around anyone because they were bunch of jerks. And
there's a saying about the company that you keep.

Blonde on Blonde

Rainy Day Women #12 & 35; Pledging My Time; Visions of Johanna; One of Us Must Know (Sooner or Later); I Want You; Stuck Inside of Mobile With the Memphis Blues Again; Leopard-Skin Pill-Box Hat; Most Likely You Go Your Way and I'll Go Mine; Temporary Like Achilles; Absolutely Sweet Marie; 4th Time Around; Obviously 5 Believers; Sad Eyed Lady of the Lowlands

Rainy Day Women #12 & 35

Don't feel so alone –
You cannot escape stoning.
It's a fact of life.

The song that brought us the famous phrase "Everybody must get stoned" is so clearly not a drug song that it has given Dylan plenty of room to grouse about never having written a drug song. But you can't write a song with that line in every verse and give it a brass marching band arrangement without having a good idea of how people are going to react. I read it as stoning like in the Bible or in "The Lottery" by Shirley Jackson, but also as a more metaphorical stoning, the idea that you're going to be compelled by society to do what they do whether you like it or not.

Pledging My Time

Pay attention, girl.
Bob has time for you. It's *you*
He's not sure about.

Johnny Ace pledged his love. This is an altogether more ambiguous, transactional song.

- Got a headache all day and night, though I feel all right. "I'm pledging my time to you, hopin' you'll come through too."
- Hobo steals girlfriend, then steals me.
- Baby, come with me. Though our success is not guaranteed, you'll be the first to know in the event of failure.
- Stuffy room. Everybody gone. We're still here, but you'll have to leave before I do.
- Somebody needed an ambulance, and they got one.

Visions of Johanna
On a late-night trip
Through the shadows of New York,
And Johanna's ghost.

There's a hint of place, a loft apartment in New York City, maybe the Chelsea Hotel. It's cold outside, it's night. There are people in the loft, Louise and her lover, and there's a night-watchman nearby, as well as some ladies in a vacant lot and girls on the subway, a mysterious "little boy lost," the primitive wallflower, jelly-faced women and the peddler and the countess and the fiddler. They do stuff, they say stuff, they drift muffled and quiet through the frozen Manhattan night, and Dylan lades the symbolism on board like he's getting ready to float the world's largest literary container ship. Taken separately, the parts are nearly nothing, but they add up to everything. Through it all, the singer falls prey to visions of a woman who's somewhere else.

One of Us Must Know (Sooner or Later)
There are eight million
Girls in the Naked City.
This was one of them.

This is another one of Dylan's breakup songs, fitting in well with the dyspeptic but majestic sound of the album.

- Don't take it personally that he treated you poorly. He didn't mean to make you feel sad. He would have done it to anyone in your place. You just did what you were supposed to do, but don't forget that he made an effort to get close to you.
- You said you could know him despite his misgivings. You wanted to know if he was going to be with you or her. You betrayed your tender age with such a question.
- He followed you through doubt and bad weather, but later when he left and you tried to hurt him,

you failed to perceive that he didn't mean to hurt you.

I Want You
A bunch of symbols
Waste their time symbolizing
While I just want you.

Here's a list of the other characters you'll find in this ensemble performance:

- Guilty undertaker. (Sighing.)
- Lonesome organ grinder. (Crying.)
- Silver saxophones.
- Cracked bells.
- Washed-out horns.
- Drunken politician. (Leaping into the street.)
- Weeping mothers.
- Sleeping saviors.
- Fathers without true love.
- Daughters who don't like Bob because he doesn't think about true love.
- The Queen of Spades.
- The Chambermaid.
- Dancing child with Chinese suit and flute. (Some say this is meant to portray Brian Jones. Dylan notes that he "wasn't very cute to him, was I?")
- Me. (I want you so bad.)

Stuck Inside of Mobile With the Memphis Blues Again

Bob's stuck in Mobile,
But it feels like Tennessee.
Happens all the time.

It all works the way it should in this song. It doesn't take itself too seriously, and is mellow in a way that many of his other fever-dream songs are not. Maybe it was the Nashville studio musicians. For me, it is the highlight of the album.

- The ragman won't tell us what's wrong as he draws circles up and down the block.
- The ladies are kind and give Bob tape.
- Shakespeare's wearing pointed shoes and bells in an alley where he's chatting up a French girl who says she knows Bob. She hasn't said anything else though it's unlikely that Bob can prove this because the mailbox was locked and someone stole the post office. (One of the absurdities that creeps into the song. The other is the brakeman in the next verse who smokes Bob's eyelid and punches his cigarette.)
- Mona says stay away from the brakemen because they drink your blood like wine. Bob says he wasn't aware of this, and that his only brakeman encounter was the one just mentioned.

- Grandpa died. It had to happen after he built the fire on Main Street and shot it with a gun.
- The senator is in town for his son's wedding. He has a gun too. Bob didn't get a ticket to the wedding and ended up under a truck.
- Bob shows the preacher that they're not too different from one another. The preacher, curiously, is wearing 20 pounds of headlines stapled to his chest.
- He asked a rain man for a cure. He got Texas medicine and railroad gin. His outlook has been fairly dim ever since.
- He gets an invitation to watch her dance under the Panamanian moon in her honky-tonk lagoon. He protests – he's dating a debutante, but Ruthie suggests that she knows better than the debutante what Dylan wants.
- Neon madmen climb on bricks lying on Grand Street. Bob wonders what it would take to get out of having to do all this stuff again.

Leopard-Skin Pill-Box Hat

That's a nice new hat.
But I wish you would not let
Your lovers wear it.

The pill-box style is classy, the leopard-skin is not. The lady in question wears the hat and charms her admirer, all while behaving poorly toward him.

- The doctor told me I shouldn't see you because it's bad for my health. I went anyway. I found him there. You were cheating on me with him, and the bugger was wearing your hat.
- You have a new boyfriend. I saw you and him doing it in the garage because you forgot to shut the door. You think he wants you for your money, but I know that he wants you because of the hat.

Just Like a Woman
How does she take, fake
Love and ache? Like a woman.
But see how she breaks.

A man spends some time describing a woman, presumably rich, befogged by drugs and doing just fine, until she breaks down like a little girl. He also reminds her to please not tell anyone the next time they meet that there was a time when he needed her when he was hungry and it was her world.

Most Likely You Go Your Way And I'll Go Mine
You say you love me,
But you don't. You love him,
Though you say you don't.

"Most Likely You Go Your Way And I'll Go Mine" is a prelude to a breakup. He jokes, bitterly, that she says she wants to hold him, but she knows she isn't that strong. He accuses her of trying too hard to act like she loves him, all while she's entertaining another man. Dylan suggests that they know where this is going, and time will tell who won this war. Musically, it's well known for its distinctive trumpet flourish between verses.

Temporary Like Achilles
Achilles stands guard
Over my true love. I wish
I knew his weak spot

Some women are hard to get, even if you're one of the most prominent rock n' roll stars on the planet.

- He wants her loving, but she's not giving. He's standing on her window, where he has stood before, and wondering why she doesn't send him any regards.
- He's beneath her ceiling, significantly kneeling, and trying to read her portrait. He can't because he's helpless "like a rich man's child." She sends someone out to prevent him from entering.
- Is her heart made from lime, stone or solid rock?
- He leans on her "velvet door," though it seems like she won't let him in. He watches her scorpion and wonders what she is guarding.

- She's gotten Achilles to guard her. He doesn't seem know how to best him.

Absolutely Sweet Marie
Marie vanishes,
Leaves Bob beating his trumpet
In a traffic jam.

He suffers through traffic, illness, hatred, a prison sentence, the delivery of half-a-dozen horses, a drunk Iranian guy and other bad company as well as one omniscient riverboat captain, only to discover that Marie stood him up. All he has to console himself is his trumpet, which needs a good beating. As Jackson Browne once sang, "When you turn out the light, I've got to hand it to me. Looks like it's me and you again tonight, Rosie."

4th Time Around
The grass doesn't grow
Under Bob's feet. One girl down,
He finds another.

Another in the "peevish lovers" edition of the Dylan catalogue, "4th Time Around" is widely seen as a response or a parody or an affectionate love tap in return for John Lennon's song "Norwegian Wood," itself an expression of Dylan's style. The singer takes selfish positions against his lovers even as he knows that it pisses them off.

Obviously 5 Believers
Please don't let me down.
I'm sad despite my jugglers
And five believers.

- Early in the morning, he's calling you to come home. He could make it without you, but it would make him lonely.
- He won't let you down if you don't let him down. He *would* let you down if you did let him down, but all the same, it would be better if you didn't.
- His black dog is barking in the yard. He could translate the dog's remarks, but it's too much effort.
- Your mother is crying while working. He could translate your mother's remarks, but he doesn't speak in her mother tongue.
- Fifteen jugglers and five believers are dressed like men. Your mother appears concerned about them, but she shouldn't be because they are his friends.

Sad Eyed Lady of the Lowlands
Tougher than metal,
No one can understand you,
But I know you best.

Some people consider "Sad Eyed Lady of the Lowlands" to be an epic, classic ode to love. And it is. That still doesn't change my view that it's an interminable song stuffed full of references to things and people that most of us can't be expected to get. Still, Dylan scholars have spent lots of time breaking this one down. It is commonly seen as a wedding song for his then-wife Sara. The song stretches over 11 minutes and 22 seconds, and is divided into five verses. This amounts to a detailed portrait of an ethereal woman with her own unknown motives and desires, and is misunderstood by all who try to co-opt her into supporting their various causes.

What she's like, what she has:

- Mercury mouth.
- Eyes like smoke.
- Prayers like rhymes.
- Silver cross.
- Voice like chimes.
- Well-protected pockets.
- Streetcar visions that she places on the grass.
- Silky flesh.

- Glassy face.
- Sheets like metal.
- Belt like lace.
- Incomplete card deck. (Fifty cards, no jack and no ace.)
- Basement clothes.
- Hollow face.
- Moonlight swims in her eyes.
- Gypsy hymns.
- Childhood flames.
- Midnight rug.
- Spanish manners.
- Mother's drugs.
- Cowboy mouth.
- Curfew plugs.
- Sheet-metal memories of Cannery Row.
- On a thief's parole.
- Saint-like face.
- Ghost-like soul.

Other people who show up in the song:

- A sad-eyed prophet.
- The kings of Tyrus who wait in line for a geranium kiss, though they don't just want to kiss her. (Tyrus as in Tyre, the Lebanese city and ancient city of the Phoenicians, founded by Herodotus.)

- Farmers and businessmen who show her the dead angels that they used to hide, though it's hard to understand why they picked her to sympathize with them.
- The child of a hoodlum in her arms.
- The ex-husband in publishing.

Single: **If You Gotta Go, Go Now**

If You Gotta Go, Go Now
He gives her options:
He'll let her leave, but if not,
He gets to do her.

This is Dylan doing his version of the guy who corners the girl at a party and puts one hand up against the wall so she has to duck under his arm to leave. "If You Gotta Go, Go Now" ("Or Else You Gotta Stay All Night") is a 1965 song that was left off the album "Highway 61 Revisited," but released as a single along with "To Ramona," but only in the Netherlands.

John Wesley Harding

John Wesley Harding; As I Went Out One Morning; I Dreamed I Saw St. Augustine; All Along the Watchtower; The Ballad of Frankie Lee and Judas Priest; Drifter's Escape; Dear Landlord; I Am a Lonesome Hobo; I Pity the Poor Immigrant; The Wicked Messenger; Down Along the Cove; I'll Be Your Baby Tonight

John Wesley Harding

He's a wanted man,
Armed too. But poor folks love him,
And he's innocent.

The real John Wesley Hardin (no "g" at the end) was a lawbreaker. Murder, horse theft, helping prisoners escape... but Dylan's character is more of a Robin Hood, guilty of crimes that don't hurt the rich and do help the poor. And "stand" that he takes with his lady by his side? "And soon the situation there was all but straightened out." Since when did gunslingers settle their problems with the law by calling everything that happened until that moment a silly misunderstanding? Is this a parody of outlaw songs like "Pretty Boy Floyd?" Or did Dylan leave it all half resolved because, as he said, he planned a longer story, but decided shorter felt better? "John Wesley Harding" sets the tone for the rest of the album, with its meanderings through the Old West, Appalachia and other dark, lonely and allegorical corners of the old, rural, wild America. Dylan's Harding is the idealized lawbreaker in that he's just, prefers simple solutions to sticky situations, and earns the respect of the people though he lives outside the law. Finally, let's not forget that this was Dylan's first musical offering since his motorcycle accident and reclusive summer in upstate New York. After the rage and fire and noise of his previous three albums, putting this out in the dark winter that followed the summer of love must have been a shock to his fans.

As I Went Out One Morning
Tom Paine says sorry
For letting daughter seduce
Bob with ideals.

It might be my imagination, but nearly every song on "John Wesley Harding" resembles a collapsed star. The area and volume are limited, and their density is astounding. "As I Went Out One Morning" is just such a song, The story is simple and ends quickly, but there is much to dig into:

- Dylan goes out for a walk to "breathe the air around Tom Paine's." He meets a "damsel" in chains. She suggests slyly that they escape to the South. South as in the cradle of slavery, and this comes from a woman who's occupying space around Tom Paine, one of the architects of the American dream.

- Dylan isn't having it. Get away, he says. I don't want to, she says. I insist, he says.
- Tom Paine arrives and tells the girl to knock it off. Then he apologizes to Dylan for her.

There's a list of old songs including "Seventeen Come Sunday," "As I Roved Out," "One May Morning" and "The Soldier and the Maid" that sound similar to this song, though in those, a soldier seduces a teenage girl by promising marriage, then returns to his ranks. There's also a W.H. Auden poem called "As I Walked Out One Evening" that has a similar meter.

Bob steps out to get a breath of fresh common sense, also the name of the pamphlet that Paine wrote on the civil liberties that guide America in theory. The woman, and this is just a guess, is the America we have today. Bob offers her his hand, but she grabs him and tries to trap him with cajolery and her good looks – but she is in chains. Oddly, Tom Paine intervenes, like Marshall McLuhan making his gag appearance in "Annie Hall," but even as the champion of liberty sets Bob free, he shows a base attitude by commanding the woman to yield, almost like a dog or a master commanding a slave.

I Dreamed I Saw St. Augustine
Martyr in waiting,
Augie consoles the people.
Of course, they kill him.

Bob dreams of his complicity in the martyrdom of a saint.

- St. Augustine: alive, frenzied and miserable. He has his blanket (like a wandering mendicant) and a coat of gold (spiritual riches). He's looking to save souls, but they've been sold.
- He tells the rich: You have no martyr to make your saint, so keep doing your thing, but know that you're not alone. I'm assuming that he means he is prophesying his death at their hands.
- Bob dreams that he's one of the people who put the saint to death, that he is part of the mob. Bob wakes up, alone and terrified. He cries.

The real St. Augustine of Hippo was born on November 13, 354 and died on August 28, 430. He lived to be an old man, and he wasn't martyred. The Christian theologian and philosopher left the world behind at the age of 76 during the Vandal siege of Hippo in Roman Africa. He asked the church library that his books be preserved. The Vandals lifted the siege, but later came back and burned the city to the ground – except for his cathedral and library. Augustine is well known for his shaping of Medieval Christian thought, and for undergoing a conversion into a pious man after living a life that some might describe as dissolute – drinking, philandering, that sort of thing. Could Dylan, reborn since his motorcycle accident and his decision to lead a quieter life than he had been leading, have seen a reflection of himself in the confessions? Augustine had solid notions about redemption and the grace of Christ, and if it's not applying too vulgar a term, he seemed like a decent guy.

As for other Augustines, the first archbishop of Canterbury was named Augustine. He died in 604, and was not martyred. Then there was Augustine Webster, the prior of Our Lady of Melwood in Epworth, Lincolnshire. He and three other Carthusians were tried and executed for refusing to take the Oath of Supremacy to King Henry VIII, an operation overseen by Thomas Cromwell. They were hanged, beheaded and quartered on May 4, 1535. Pope Paul VI canonized him in 1970. (Cromwell got his later because of backroom machinations that backfired. King Henry had him beheaded in 1540 on the same day that Hal married Catherine Howard. His head was put on a spike and set on London Bridge for everyone to see. Henry later regretted the decision, saying that his ministers put him up to it.)

The song echoes the labor union song "I Dreamed I Saw Joe Hill Last Night."

All Along the Watchtower
The joker can't cope.
Chill, says the thief, life's a joke.
Princes wait, wind howls.

Two stories in one, making this a 2-1/2 minute epic of inscrutability:

- The joker is sick of being exploited by business-men and farmers, while the thief adjusts the joker's vantage point to the longest-term view that there is: when you're dead, you won't care.
- The princes walk along a watchtower, attended by women and barefoot servants. It's nasty outside: howling wind, cold weather, a growling wildcat and two unidentified horsemen. Are they the joker and the thief?

As usual, the atmosphere is the key here, I've read the word "apocalypse" many times as a key association with this song, and it's not hard to see why. Chapter 1 opens with despair and fatalism, chapter 2 provides peripatetic princes on a parapet, presumably in peril.

The likely story of the second half of the song is the prophet Isaiah's vision of the messenger who brings news that the empire of Babylon has fallen. In chapter 21, Isaiah relates his vision. God says to Isaiah, "go, set a watchman, let him declare what he seeth." The watchman waits on the watchtower, and a man in a chariot, accompanied by horsemen, approaches. One tells the watchman that Babylon is gone, "and all the graven images of her gods he hath broken unto the ground."

Try reading the two verses of the song in reverse order, by the way...

The Ballad of Frankie Lee and Judas Priest
Frankie Lee wants what
Judas has. He scrounges, which
Proves his undoing.

This is a cautionary tale about temptation, charity, friendship, greed, betrayal, lust, taking advantage of kindness and a few other things.

- Frankie needs some money. Judas offers him a bunch of $10 bills and says take your pick. Frankie's ready to take, but he doesn't like Judas watching him do it.
- Judas winks and says, sure, fine, OK, I'll be down the road in "eternity," and they'll meet up in some time. Frankie says he doesn't believe in eternity.
- Frankie is counting his money when a stranger says Judas is calling him from a house down the road. Clearly Judas's generous offer was more than an offer; it was a test of Frankie's character.
- Frankie sees the house and notes that there are 24 women in there, presumably hot ones.
- He goes on a 17-day tear inside the house, most likely a brothel, then dies in Judas's arms.

- They bury Frankie Lee, and a little "neighbor boy," unmentioned until now, says nothing is revealed.
- Bob digs into the 10 commandments, noting that you should not covet what belongs to others, but should always help them if they need you.

Drifter's Escape
Drifter goes on trial.
He's probably not guilty
So God lets him go.

It's the story of a hobo who falls into the clutches of the law, and seems to be heading for some rough justice at their hands, though no one tells him what crime they accused him of committing. God, or maybe some other power, intervenes on the drifter's behalf. The drifter is one of several characters on this album who might or might not be guilty of sins, but are in need of holy redemption.

- The judge, though sympathetic, abdicates his primacy in the courtroom. The jury bays for the trial to continue. They are a mob.
- An attendant and his nurse sympathize as well, and wish the jury would hush.
- Lightning strikes the courthouse. The people in their religious gullibility kneel and pray. The drifter knows an exit when one presents itself.

Dear Landlord
It's a simple ask:
Don't raise my apartment rent.
I have commitments.

- Don't put a price on his soul. Burden heavy, dreams beyond control. He'll pay when the steamboat whistle blows, and he hopes you take the pay.
- You're not the only one who has suffered. Sometimes we work too hard and spend time on things that aren't meaningful.
- Please don't dismiss his case. He's not moving. He won't underestimate you if you don't underestimate him.

The less glib reading on this song is that Dylan is begging his manager or even his listeners, or perhaps a more divine listener, to please take him and his work seriously, and to not minimize it. On a spiritual level, the song rebukes the landlord for seeking material gain, when there are more eternal prizes to seek.

I Am a Lonesome Hobo
Hobo warns people
Not to covet or distrust,
Lest they become him.

- Hobo has no family or friends. He has bribed, blackmailed and deceived. He's done time for everything except begging.
- He used to be rich, but failed to trust his fellow man. His accusations of others drove him to doom and shame. You could argue that it was the money and its effect on his character that did it.
- Lesson: don't be jealous, don't live as others think you should, and don't judge lest you be judged.

I Pity the Poor Immigrant
Pity the people
Who live evil, selfish lives
And cannot repent.

One of Dylan's most gray, dense morality tales, it spends its short running time with the narrator expressing pity for bad people, and them pitying them all the more when everything they believe falls apart. It's possible that this is a straightforward lament for the white people who ruined America for the Indians. I've also seen an argument that this is God singing about mankind come to earth only to fail to see what they have and to ruin all they touch. Lawrence J. Epstein, who wrote an essay on this idea in 2009, refers to lines from the Book of Leviticus that are similar to Dylan's words, notably Leviticus, chapter 26: "Ye shall eat, and not be satisfied." Look there for other passages that wound up in this song.

The immigrant:

- Wishes he would have stayed home.
- Works hard to do evil.
- Is always left alone.
- Cheats.
- Lies. (Constantly)
- Hates his life, but fears dying.
- Wastes his strength.
- Heaven like Ironsides. (The paraplegic police consultant Ironside from the TV show? The USS Constitution? Oliver "Old Ironsides" Cromwell ? Or maybe see Leviticus 26:19-20.)
- Cries a lot.
- Hears, but can't see.
- Falls in love with wealth.
- Ignores other people.
- Tramples in the mud.
- Laughs while building towns of blood.
- Doomed to failure.

The Wicked Messenger
Man learns a lesson:
They *do* shoot the messenger.
He gets a new job.

The interpretation I like best is that the messenger is Bob, who discovers through his abrasiveness that there is more to delivering messages than making them harsh, blunt and mean, and bitter truths conceal a message by making people close their ears instead of opening them.

Words that opened up my heart:

There was a wicked messenger.

- Bob Dylan, protest singer, scourge of the bourgeoisie and the squares. Via Proverbs 13:17: "A wicked messenger falleth into mischief: but a faithful ambassador is health."

He came from Eli.

- High Priest of Shiloh. Sent a message to Hannah that she would get pregnant by her husband, despite previous infertility and subsequent mocking by her husband's other wife. He trains Samuel on how to be a religious judge. Eli's sons are wicked: they take prime cuts of meat from sacrifices and have sex with the women who serve at the sanctuary. God tells Samuel to tell Eli that his sons will die on the same day. Samuel tries to hold back specifics of the bad news, but Eli insists on getting the whole story. Messenger recognize messenger.

He always made something out of nothing.

They asked who sent him, but he could not be honest because his tongue was made for nothing else than flattery, and he knows that doing this now, when confronted, would be wrong. "Words disobey me," as Mark Stewart sang.

- His very body disobeys him because it disavows his bitter truths.

He stayed behind the assembly hall.

- Stage performer.

One day, he appeared with a note. We don't know who wrote it. "The soles of my feet, I swear they're burning."

- From the Book of Malachi: "And ye shall tread down the wicked; for they shall be ashes under the soles of your feet in the day that I shall do this, saith the LORD of hosts." Either the messenger or someone else is getting that feeling of ecstasy for doing the right thing.

- And, especially given the next verse of the Dylan song, consider this line from the Book of Habakkuk, in which God gets pissed off, having a proper "don't make me come down there" moment: "God came from Teman, and the Holy One from mount Paran... His glory covered the heavens, and the earth was full of his praise. And his brightness was as the light; he had horns (sun rays) coming out of his hand: and there was the hiding of his power. Before him went the pestilence, and burning coals went forth at his feet."

Leaves fall, seas part. The people confront the messenger, and tell him, "If ye cannot bring good news, then don't bring any." Despite his mission to tell the truth and to do right and to turn away from flattery, the people prefer it. And that is OK. These are the words, as Dylan says, that open up the messenger's heart. Compassion? It's a big change from "Outlaw Blues" in 1965, in which he warned people not to ask him anything because he just might tell them the truth.

- Enlightenment is hard. Or to quote Carl Jung: "There is no coming to consciousness without pain. People will do anything, no matter how absurd, in order to avoid facing their own Soul. One does not become enlightened by imagining figures of light, but by making the darkness conscious."

Down Along the Cove
Bob meets his girlfriend
Down along the cove. And then
They take a short walk.

After the sere and mysterious cavalcade of the first 10 songs on "John Wesley Harding" come this song and "I'll Be Your Baby Tonight." This one is clear and bright. Bob and his girl go for a walk along the cove. They're in love, and everybody knows it, and what's more, everybody understands why.

I'll Be Your Baby Tonight
Bob promises you
He's gonna be your sweetheart
As soon as tonight.

"Down Along the Cove" is the bright walk in the meadow near the water on a warm day. "I'll Be Your Baby Tonight" hovers on the intersection of sleep and canoodling. Dylan has suggested that maybe it's a good-night song from a baby's point of view. He seems to be trying hard to shed his reputation for writing songs with deep lyrics – something that the fans were expecting from the master of the surreal. Consider, "That big fat moon is gonna shine like a spoon. We're gonna let it."

Bedtime ritual:

- Close eyes.
- Close door.
- No worry no more.
- Shut light.

- Shut shade.
- No be afraid.
- Forget sail-away mockingbird.
- Let be shine-like-spoon fat moon.
- Kick off shoes.
- No fear.
- Bottle bring here.

<u>Nashville Skyline</u>

Girl From the North Country; Nashville Skyline Rag; To Be Alone With You; I Threw It All Away; Peggy Day; Lay Lady Lay; One More Night; Tell Me That It Isn't True; Country Pie; Tonight I'll Be Staying Here With You

(Note: There is no haiku in this section for "Girl From the North Country," as Dylan performed it first on the album "The Freewheelin' Bob Dylan." This version is a duet performance with Johnny Cash. There is no haiku for "Nashville Skyline Rag," an instrumental.)

To Be Alone With You
Hang with me, baby.
That's my favorite thing to do:
Be alone with you.

"Is it rolling, Bob?" Dylan asks producer Bob Johnston at the start of this sweet country-music love song. The song continues the use of the standard blues line, "Night time is the right time to be with the one you love," with Dylan nodding to Ray Charles, Roosevelt Sykes and others by prefacing it with, "They say..."

I Threw It All Away
Bob tossed them away –
The girl, the mountains, rivers.
Now he feels awful.

This is a lesson song. If you find someone who loves you, take it to your heart and don't throw it away. "Take a tip from one who's tried."

Peggy Day
Peggy Day and Night
Make Bob feel more than all right.
What two girls can do.

A tale of two Peggies.

Lay Lady Lay
Bob wants you in bed.
He has balls and beds of brass.
You're lying on them.

I've never tried such a direct approach to get someone to fool around with me. Maybe I was doing it wrong. Dylan wrote the song for the film "Midnight Cowboy," but didn't file in time. It became a big country and pop hit all the same.

- Lie across my big brass bed. I'll show you what's in your mind.
- Stay with me until dawn, make me smile.
- "Why wait any longer for the world to begin?"
- Let's have our cake and eat it too.
- I want you at night. I want you in the morning. Let's not delay our amorous adventures.

One More Night
Girlfriend left her man.
That was a big, bad mistake.
Now he's all alone.

A splendid song of heartbreak, set to a bouncy country-and-western arrangement.

Tell Me That It Isn't True
They say she's cheating.
He suspects they might be right.
He hopes that they're wrong.

"Tell Me That It Isn't True" sparkles with melancholy. It's charming and affecting and perfect. Try to find Robert Forster's version, which appears on his album "I Had a New York Girlfriend." It's nearly as good.

Country Pie
Bob loves all the pies.
Show him a pie, he'll eat it.
Give him some more pie.

A one-minute-and-37-second slice of perfection à la mode. Pies potentially consumed include raspberry, strawberry, lemon, lime, blueberry, apple, cherry, pumpkin and plum.

Tonight I'll Be Staying Here With You
Bob won't take that train.
He's given his seat to someone
And stays home with you.

Whoever she is, the singer has found her worth canceling his plans to take the train. He throws out his ticket, he throws out his suitcase and he throws out his troubles. All he needs is her. He was supposed to go this morning, but her love proved too strong. He tells the station master to give his seat to a poor boy.

Self Portrait

All the Tired Horses; Alberta #1; I Forgot More Than You'll Ever Know; Days of 49; Early Mornin' Rain; In Search of Little Sadie; Let It Be Me; Little Sadie; Woogie Boogie; Belle Isle; Living the Blues; Like a Rolling Stone; Copper Kettle; Gotta Travel On; Blue Moon; The Boxer; The Mighty Quinn (Quinn the Eskimo); Take Me As I Am; Take a Message to Mary; It Hurts Me Too; Minstrel Boy; She Belongs to Me; Wigwam; Alberta #2

(Note: There are two versions of "Alberta" on this album, but one haiku. "In Search of Little Sadie" and "Little Sadie" contain identical lyrics, so there is one haiku. "Woogie Boogie" and "Wigwam" are instrumentals, so there is no haiku. "Like a Rolling Stone" and "She Belongs to Me" are concert performances. The haiku appear in "Highway 61 Revisited" and "Bringing It All Back Home.")

All the Tired Horses

The horses are tired.
How can we ride them? PS:
The horses are tired.

Two women sing, "All the tired horses in the sun, how'm I supposed to get any ridin' done? Hmmmmm....." They sing that several more times over a pretty guitar chord and lush strings. Then the song ends. We hear the question a lot, but we never find out how the ladies are going to get the riding done. One singer whose voice we don't hear on the song: Dylan's.

Alberta

Bob would pay this girl
To let down her long, long hair
And improve his mood.

This is an old Leadbelly standard, and he liked it enough to record it four times. It's a fun little song, considering that all the singer wants is for Alberta to let her hair down, to the extent that he will pay her to do it (more gold, in fact, than her apron can hold). Not only that, Alberta keeps the singer worried and bothered and reportedly treats him unkindly. I suppose you could read some innuendo into lines like that, especially as one of Leadbelly's versions asks Alberta to "take him down" into her rocking chair, and I suspect that rocking chairs aren't always rocking chairs.

I Forgot More Than You'll Ever Know

Man tells other man
How his ex dumped him, and says
The other guy's next.

"I Forgot More Than You'll Ever Know" gets the saccharin treatment. There's nothing wrong with it. It's just pure musical sugar, and plenty of people don't care for listening to Dylan croon. The original version from 1953, sung by Skeeter Davis and Betty Jack Davis, is a typical country-and-western lament about losing in love and telling off the next guy (or gal) who takes your place. It topped the country charts for eight weeks. It was the only single the pair would record. Shortly afterward, Betty Jack was killed in a car accident. Skeeter survived the crash and went on to become a solo star and a member of the Grand Ole Opry.

Days of 49
Gold miner recalls
His saucy crew and the ways
They met early graves.

This is a faux-folk song, or maybe it's not even faux as I don't know how old a song has to be to be considered an antique. It's by John and Alan Lomax as well as Frank Warner. It's the tale of a derelict gold miner reminiscing about the good old days with his crew during the California gold rush. Or maybe they were the bad days. It seems like everyone winds up dead, usually because they were drinkers, gamblers and malingerers, and prone to violence.

Early Mornin' Rain
Woman hops a plane.
Her lover can't come with her.
He pines on the ground.

"Early Mornin' Rain" is full of the melancholy that singer-songwriters slathered into their songs in the countrified interim between the oldies of the '60s and the more modern-sounding oldies of the '70s. The 707 plane and the majesty of the phrase "silver bird on high," and the weird techno-sentimentality of the line, "Out on runway number nine," not to mention that unique feeling of an early morning rain in the United States, gray and cold and final, work for me.

- It's raining, he's outside, he has a buck to his name and an ache in his heart. He misses his girl, who presumably is on the plane.
- He's watching a 707 set to take off on the runway. He's at the fence. It's cold. He was at a party and there were lots of hot women there, but that was yesterday.
- The plane takes off. In a few hours, it and his lady will fly over his home.
- He hates the airport. He's cold and drunk. He wishes he could hop a freight train. He leaves.

In Search of Little Sadie
Man murders Sadie.
He tries to flee and is caught.
He goes to prison.

"In Search of Little Sadie" has many antecedents in American music, including the songs,

"Bad Lee Brown," "Cocaine Blues," "Transfusion Blues," "East St. Louis Blues," "Late One Night," "Whiskey Blues," "Chain Gang Blues," "Bad Man Ballad," "Bad Man's Blunder," "Ode to Bad Bill" and "Penitentiary Blues." The story is simple and grim: A man shoots his lover, flees, is caught, returned and sentenced to prison, and feels really bad about it.

Let It Be Me
Don't break up with him.
There's no life without your love.
Don't leave him lonely.

This is an English version of the song "Je t'appartiens" by Gilbert Bécaud and Pierre Delanoë. It's one of the numerous cover versions of middle-of-the-road pop music on this album that people see as Dylan's confounding attempt to shed his status as a seer and a musical visionary, and to take on the guise of just another singer who's not beset by batshit-crazy fans.

Belle Isle
Man in a disguise
Tempts his girlfriend to cheat, but
She proves quite faithful.

Ireland: a guy spies a good-looking woman. He notes that she's hot, but stops short of suggesting that they get together. She says she's a poor, hard-working lass, and more's the point, she can't entertain untoward suggestions from strange men because she's promised to another and waiting for him to return from a journey. At this point, he reveals that he has come in disguise and is that man. He was testing her loyalty. What a creep.

The song is known in Newfoundland, where it is called "The Blooming Bright Star of Belle Isle," a line that appears in Dylan's version, and is adapted from an old Irish song. There is an island off the northern tip of Newfoundland called Belle Isle, but it is uninhabited, cold and not the kind of place where a lovely maiden ever was likely to live.

Living the Blues
They all let him know
His gal has a new lover.
Now he has the blues.

A relaxed country blues song that tells a familiar tale:

- My head's been down to my shoes since you've left. In fact, I've been living the blues.
- I know where you are and what you're doing because strangers tell me what you're up to.
- I need to forget my pride and take some time off to recover, but I still have feelings.
- If you knew just how upset I was because of your departure, you surely would come back.

Copper Kettle
Here's a good date night:
Let's make illegal moonshine
And cuddle outside.

The song was written by Albert Frank Beddoe and pop-
ularized by Joan Baez. On an album that many people
couldn't stand, "Copper Kettle" was regarded as one of
the standout tracks.

Instructions for date night:

- Get kettle, coil.
- Fill with corn mash.
- Lie with me by the juniper in the moonlight.
- Watch the jugs fill.
- Preserve tradition since 1792 of not paying whis-
  key taxes.

Gotta Travel On
My feet itch again.
Time to hit the road. I might
Go home forever.

"Gotta Travel On" is a shuffling, slightly funked-up ver-
sion of an earlier folk song by Paul Clayton, who killed
himself in 1967, reportedly by adding an electric heater
to his bath. The song is basic enough:

- I've been around this town too long. Winter's coming.
- Going home to stay.
- I'll catch a train and go home hobo-style.

Blue Moon
Thanks to the blue moon,
Lonely man gets the woman
He was hoping for.

This is Dylan's rendition of the 1934 song by Richard Rodgers and Lorenz Hart. The original version was intended for Jean Harlow to sing in the movie "Hollywood Party," expressing her hope to become a movie star. The song went unused in the film, and was copyrighted as "Prayer (Oh Lord, make me a movie star)." The current lyrics, the fourth set that Hart wrote, were in place by 1935. I like its repeated use of the songs by various singers in the John Landis film, "An American Werewolf in London."

The Boxer
Having decided
He's a tragic boxer type,
A loser goes home.

Dylan's version of this Simon and Garfunkel song borders on parody. As Jimmy Guterman and Owen O'Donnell wrote in "The Worst Rock 'n' Roll Records of All Time: A Fan's Guide to the Stuff You Love to Hate," Dylan's voice is double tracked and neither voice is on time or on key or in sync with the other. It sounds to me like an intentionally horrible take on the soaring original. As with most of Dylan's lesser moments, this one grew on me, if only because I like seeing how far you can go with a song before you break it.

The Mighty Quinn (Quinn the Eskimo)
Quinn the Eskimo
Makes people doze, run and jump.
He attracts pigeons.

"The Mighty Quinn (Quinn the Eskimo)" is the bizarre breakout hit from the Basement Tapes sessions, though not for Dylan. Manfred Mann scored with it in 1968. Dylan's versions appeared on "Self Portrait" (a live version recorded at the Isle of Wight festival with the Band) and his "Greatest Hits Vol. II" album (same version). There are more takes on volume 11 of the Bootleg Series, the multi-volume series of albums of previously unreleased Dylan studio and live performances. The song is about as silly as they come, but that's part of the charm:

- What people are doing: building big ships and boats and monuments, writing their notes, being in despair, feeding pigeons on a limb, not sleeping, wondering who's on their toes. Jumping for joy after Quinn shows up. There's nothing like this Eskimo. After that, he'll make them want to doze.

- Bob: likes his sugar sweet like other people do. Doesn't like guarding fumes or being in a hurry. It's not his "cup of meat." He knows how to meow like a cat and moo like a cow. He can refer you to someone who can help you if you're in pain.
- The pigeons: they run to Quinn.

The title character apparently is a vague reference to Anthony Quinn's role as an Inuit in Nicholas Ray's 1960 film, "The Savage Innocents."

Take Me As I Am
When we date people,
They want to change us. Please don't.
I am who I am.

This Boudleaux Bryant song is a complaint about a lover who keeps trying to reshape the singer's image to suit him (or her). It sounds like it was boiled down from the plot of "Vertigo."

Take a Message to Mary
Frontier lad gone bad
Goes to jail, and hopes Mary
Doesn't find out why.

"Take a Message to Mary" is an Everly Brothers song, written by the songwriting team of Felice and Boudleaux Bryant. Dylan and producer Bob Johnston give the song a sappy arrangement typical of the times with saccharine female backup vocals and accoutrements that you would expect from a TV variety show special from those days. In short: frontier boy turns bad, robs a stagecoach, presumably shoots someone by accident, goes to jail for life, and asks someone to please not tell his girlfriend Mary what he did because he's ashamed of himself. He would rather she believe that he abandoned her, which to me seems at least as bad as saying you turned into a criminal. At least a prison sentence would convey the idea that he's still in love with her, but a victim of his own stupidity, whereas leaving her because he had wandering feet makes him sound like an ass.

It Hurts Me Too
I can feel your pain.
You should be with me. If not,
You will hurt us both.

Emotional blackmail, courtesy of Tampa Red.

- Don't change your mind about me.
- I want to be your lover, baby, I don't want to be your boss.

- Come back to me.
- I wouldn't mistreat you.

"When things go wrong, so wrong with you, It hurts me too."

Minstrel Boy
Minstrel sings for cash
While Lucky's stuck on a hill,
Lonely with ladies.

"Minstrel Boy" is not the same song as "The Minstrel Boy," an Irish song written by Thomas Moore in the late 18th or early 19th century to commemorate the men from Trinity College in Dublin who fought in and were killed in the Irish Rebellion of 1798. This is a stranger song whose words to me are unclear and disjointed. Dylan sang it with the Band at the Isle of Wight festival in 1969, and it's that version that appears on the album.

The chorus asks who will throw the minstrel boy a coin, and "let it down easy to save his soul."

Then we have:

Story 1: Lucky
Lucky has 12 gears on his rig, and he's been driving a long time. He's stuck on top of a hill now with a bunch of

ladies, yet he's lonely. It reminds me of Dylan's comment in 1965's "It Takes a Lot to Laugh, It Takes a Train to Cry" that if he should die on top of the hill, his baby will make it without him. Then there's Jesus who died on top of a hill, but that's taking things too far.

Story 2: Mighty Mockingbird
Mighty is "deep in number and heavy in toil," and he has a large load to bear. Dylan says he's underneath his own boundaries and that there's no more to the story other than his traveling. And then he changes the words to first person, saying "I'm still on that road."

New Morning

If Not for You; Day of the Locusts; Time Passes Slowly; Went to See the Gypsy; Winterlude; If Dogs Run Free; New Morning; Sign on the Window; One More Weekend; The Man in Me; Three Angels; Father of Night

If Not for You

If you weren't around,
It would be cold and rainy.
Life would be pointless.

If not for you:

- No find door.
- No see floor.
- Yes sad blue.
- Awake all night.
- Morning light no new.
- Sky fall through.
- Rain gather too.
- Lost but for you.
- No winter spring.
- No robin sing.
- No have clue.
- No ring true.

Day of the Locusts

Bob takes a road trip
After getting a degree
That he didn't want.

Dylan's songs don't usually add sound effects to underscore a literal point, but "Day of the Locusts" is an exception. (As is "Man in the Long Black Coat" 19 years later, done with crickets.) It opens with the "trill" of locusts before he sings about a trip to Princeton that he didn't want to make to accept an honorary degree that he didn't want. This is one of the first Dylan songs that I ever heard, and it's stuck with me for years as a favorite. I don't like the idea that he is so turned off by having to pick up a degree from people he holds in contempt, but many of us can identify with having to endure a procedure when all we really want is to hop in the car and leave responsibilities and other people behind. And that's just what Bob and his girl do in this song. (The "locusts" in the song were inspired by the appearance of "Brood X," a hatching of cicadas that occurred at the time.)

Time Passes Slowly
My sweetheart and I
Enjoyed the country life. Now,
We just do our best.

"Time Passes Slowly" is supposed to be one of the happy domesticity songs on this album, along with "New Morning," "If Not for You," "Winterlude," "The Man in Me," "Sign on the Window" and "One More Weekend." I find the song a little too uncertain to be an unequivocal endorsement and reflection on family life.

- Up here in the mountains: time passes slowly, we sit and take walks in paradise, catch fish in the stream and lose ourselves in a dream. This sounds lovely.
- Once, my sweetheart and I sat in her mother's kitchen and gazed at the stars while she was cooking. Time was passing slowly then too on the search for love. Very nice, but this is something that happened and is done.
- No reason to go to town, the fair, up, down, or anywhere. Sounds nice.
- Time still passes slowly. "We stare straight ahead and try so hard to stay right." That to me sounds like an effort to retain the appearance of happiness. This is a key line to the haiku tone, as is the next line, which implies the end of something: "Like the red rose of summer that blooms in the day, time passes slowly and fades away."

Went to See the Gypsy
Bob visits gypsy.
They party with dancing girl.
Girl and gypsy leave.

Some people say it's the story of Dylan meeting Elvis or Jimi Hendrix or someone else. Maybe it's just a story about a gypsy. It is an atmospheric tale, moving through the night as he tells it with suitable music to match, and then the band bursts forth into the dawn. Just as soon as the song starts, it's over. It feels like a song about the discovery of what's possible and what you can do out there in the world, especially as a young person. In other moods, it reminds me of what an adult would feel who has never gone anywhere, upon meeting people who have wandered everywhere and given him a taste of what he could have been. When he makes up his mind to join the gypsy and his pretty dancing girl, he finds them gone, so what else to do but watch the sun rise and prepare for another day at a dull job in a dull town in a dull life? Or a third angle: the gypsy is indeed Elvis. Bob hears the music that will for the first time define his life, thanks to whatever serendipity brought him to a party. He knows his life will change now as he turns away from the "river of tears" and watches the sun rise. Or maybe it won't. There's a nagging line that I always thought was a throwaway, but lately I've begun to think it's pivotal. The singer gets his audience with the gypsy. They make small talk, and the singer goes to the lobby "to make a small call out." It's there that the dancing girl urges him to go back to see the gypsy because of his power to change people – to bring them through the mirror, as she says. You have to wonder what the singer was doing. Telling his wife not to wait up? Telling his boss he would be off tomorrow? Something that could have waited given the life-changing experience that the gypsy could have given him. And he missed his chance, he couldn't "forget about today until tomorrow." Maybe he was calling them to say goodbye, like the man who wanted to keep his hand on the gospel plow, to say goodbye forever and follow the tambourine man.

Winterlude
Man marries his gal
In the middle of winter.
Then they build a fire.

Some clunky rhymes aside, this is a charming waltz. It's all about cuddling up on a cold night with the one you love, just like the song "On a Night Like This" that came out four years later.

Winter interlude dude:

- Tonight no fight. Everything all right.
- Angel tells me love has reason to shine.
- You I adore, you give me more.
- This dude thinks you're fine.
- You: little apple, let's go to chapel, come back and cook.
- Ice skating later, our love bold in cold, please be mine.
- You: little daisy, let's sit by logs in fire.
- Moonlight in window, snowflakes on sand, let's get tight tonight, you are grand.

If Dogs Run Free
If dogs can do it,
We can too. Running free is
Good for harmony.

"If Dogs Run Free" is a singular song in the Bob Dylan catalogue. It is the only jazz arrangement that he's done. The loose tone is accentuated by some inspired (and strange) scat vocalizing from Maeretha Stewart.

- Why can't we run free if dogs can?
- Things will be OK if you just be yourself.
- Que sera sera.
- True love will see you through.

New Morning
Days in the country,
Rabbits, groundhogs, blue skies and
You in the morning.

Most of the songs on this album live in the country, with sunlight pouring out of them, along with rural dirt roads and old cars, running water, blue skies, cool mornings and hot days, and old wooden houses on the farm and rainy nights on Main Street. This one is the epitome of the feeling, an impressionist's painting from the middle of the meadow on a day where you can see forever. The phrase "new morning" must be more than just a literal new morning. I would assume that he's talking about a new chapter in life – wife, family, a dog. But why load meaning into a song that is clear? The music matches the mood. It's just great, and every musician and singer sounds like they're into the vibe.

Sign on the Window
The meaning of life:
Family yes, girlfriend no, go
Fishing, catch some trout.

I've read accounts that say this song is about domestic bliss, and while I think that this is true in part, I sometimes wonder if Dylan is expressing doubt underneath the sentiment. Listen to the phrase that he sings regarding raising kids, being married, having a cabin in Utah and fishing for trout: "That must be what it's all about." It sounds like an insistence in the face of doubt.

- Signs say: Lonely, no company allowed, you don't own me, three's a crowd. If this is about marriage, then I suppose all those might apply to various phases of that domestic arrangement.
- A woman and her boyfriend "change their tune" and go to California. Then Bob's best friend says, "Now, didn't I warn you, Brighton girls are like the moon." I guess that this is some reference to the single life and its discontents.

- The weather report. It's raining tonight on Main Street. Hopefully there won't be sleet.
- Utah, cabin, wife, kids, trout, life.

One More Weekend
Leave the kids at home
And come out for the weekend.
We're gonna have fun.

This is date weekend, courtesy of Dylan. It's a rock n' roll ode to taking the wife out for a few days and leaving the kids home. I don't know why they have to be "slippin' and slidin' like a weasel on the run," but if muskrat love is a thing, then I suppose other mustelids can do it too.

The Man in Me
Bob often will hide
Himself from other people.
You could coax him out.

This is one of my favorite Dylan songs. "The Man in Me" is great by itself, but it fits well into the Coen brothers movie "The Big Lebowski" where it makes a significant appearance. It comes in with a bang, Dylan la-la-la-ing as the backup singers moan sweetly. In its three short minutes, he credits his woman with bringing out his good qualities.

- Ready for any task and for little compensation other than having you around.
- Sometimes it's stormy weather with me. I get fed up. Then I think of you.
- It's great to know you're around.
- "The man in me will hide sometimes to keep from bein' seen. But that's just because he doesn't want to turn into some machine."

Three Angels
Angels blow their horns
While commuters ignore them
And a driver sighs.

"Three Angels" uses a mournful organ backed by the sustained notes of Dylan's backup singers to create a fever dream of belief hiding just beneath the surface of another day in the city. He intones a story over these church-like sounds of three angels sounding their horns and dressed in green robes and protuberant wings, hovering over the city while no one in the busy streets below notices them because each is wrapped in his or her own fog. I imagine the angels come from Revelations 8:13, taken here from the King James Bible: "And I beheld, and heard an angel flying through the midst of heaven, saying with a loud voice, Woe, woe, woe, to the inhabiters of the earth by reason of the other voices of the trumpet of the three angels, which are yet to sound!"

Those three angels, the last of seven to cause calamity and mayhem in this prophecy, do the following things:

- Angel five: star falls to earth, angel opens a bottomless pit, huge mutant locusts come out and torture the unblessed.
- Angel six: releases four angels from the Euphrates river who cause the death of many people.
- Angel seven: tells John to tell everybody that all sorts of bad things will happen to them.

Of course, no one on the ground notices that the apocalypse has come.

Father of Night
Bob lists the blessings
Of God in nature, hitting
Most of the big ones.

"Father of Night" is a short song, with Dylan accompanying himself on piano. The repetitive and short melody is transfixing, but what gives the song its power are the backup singers, moaning like a chorus of ghosts as he sings. It's a chilling song, but lodged in the comfort of faith. I don't know any other song like it. The song reportedly (via Wikipedia) is Dylan's interpretation of the Jewish prayer Amidah. The Amidah is the central prayer of the Jewish liturgy, and contains 19 blessings.

They are:

1. Avot ("Ancestors"): praise of the God of the patriarchs.
2. Gevurot ("Powers"): God is powerful, heals the sick and raises the dead. AKA Tehiyyat ha-Metim. This includes the power to make it rain, spoken in winter. This changes to dew in the summer for some Jews.
3. Kedushat ha-Shem ("The sanctification of the Name"): Praise of God's holiness.
4. Binah ("Understanding"): God grant me wisdom and understanding.
5. Teshuvah ("Return", "repentance"): Help the Jews return to a life of repentance.
6. Selichah: God forgives.
7. Geulah ("Redemption"): God is the rescuer of the Israelites.
8. Refuah ("Healing"): Prayer to heal the sick.
9. Birkat HaShanim ("Blessing for good years"): Bless the crops. Another prayer for rain.
10. Galuyot ("Diasporas"): Bring back the Jewish exiles to Israel.
11. Birkat HaDin ("Justice"): Restore the righteous judges.
12. Birkat HaMinim ("The sectarians, heretics"): Destroy heretics and the slanderers of and informers on Jews.

13. Tzadikim ("Righteous"): Have mercy on those who trust in God. Support the righteous.
14. Bo'ne Yerushalayim ("Builder of Jerusalem"): Rebuild Jerusalem, restore the Kingdom of David.
15. Birkat David ("Blessing of David"): Put David's closest descendant on the throne. He (presumably) becomes the Messiah.
16. Tefillah ("Prayer"): God, accept prayers and have mercy and compassion.
17. Avodah ("Service"): Restore the Temple services and sacrificial services.
18. Hoda'ah ("Thanksgiving"): Thank God for our lives, for our souls, and for daily miracles.
19. Sim Shalom ("Grant peace"): Peace, goodness, blessings, kindness and compassion.

Dylan invokes God 26 times, one for each letter of the alphabet.

1. Night.
2. Day.
3. Takes away darkness.
4. Teaches the bird to fly.
5. Builds rainbows.
6. Loneliness.
7. Pain.
8. Love.
9. Rain.

10. Black.
11. White.
12. Builds mountains.
13. Shapes clouds.
14. Time.
15. Dreams.
16. Rivers and streams.
17. Grain.
18. Wheat.
19. Cold.
20. Heat.
21. Air.
22. Trees.
23. Lives in our hearts and memories.
24. Minutes.
25. Days.
26. Father whom we praise.

Single: **George Jackson**

George Jackson
Prison guards kill George.
They were afraid of his love.
Being black? No help.

The song is a fictionalized account of George Jackson, who was shot dead by guards as he tried to escape from San Quentin State Prison in August 1971. Jackson became a Black Panther after being introduced to Marxism and Maoism through a friend. He was sentenced to one year to life in 1961 for armed robbery ($70 from a gas station), and was 18 when he went to jail. He became a celebrated author, though prison authorities said he was a sociopath who had no interest in revolution. The tale grew darker from there. He died on Aug. 21 after securing a gun and attempting to break out of the prison. He and other inmates took guards hostage, and six guards were killed along with two white prisoners, while several others were shot and stabbed, but survived. Jackson was shot in the prison yard.

Dylan's song does not mention these events, instead indicting a system that dehumanizes people and leads to violent behavior. It contains some facile philosophizing, notably, "Sometimes I think the whole world is one big prison yard. Some of us are prisoners, the rest of us are guards." It also contains the bizarre line about how the prison authorities hated Jackson because they were "scared of his love."

"George Jackson" is one of the few Dylan songs in his catalogue that is nearly impossible to find. He released the song as a single in November 1971, with a band version on the A-side and an acoustic version on the B-side. You can buy the single on vinyl at online shops. The acoustic version also appears on the "Side Tracks" album that accompanies the complete Dylan album reissues series. The "Big Band" version is available on a compilation album called "Masterpieces," released in 1978 in Japan and Australia. It's possible to find copies in the USA, but they're expensive.

Selections from **Bob Dylan's Greatest Hits Vol. II**
Watching the River Flow; Tomorrow Is a Long Time; When I Paint My Masterpiece; I Shall Be Released; You Ain't Goin' Nowhere; Down in the Flood

Watching the River Flow
Read by the river
Until you feel like writing.
It takes flow to flow.

"Watching the River Flow" appeared as a single in 1971, and was included on Dylan's "Greatest Hits Vol. II" album that same year. It's Dylan's description of writer's block, or a dearth of inspiration. He wants to be back in the city with his lover, doing his thing, but until he's able to get the writing to flow, he's going to have to sit like Andrei Tarkovsky and watch the river.

Tomorrow Is a Long Time
Wandering the world
Seems nice until you miss her.
Then you want her near.

So many of Dylan's songs are about being driven to wander despite the affection of the girl back home. "Tomorrow Is a Long Time" takes a different route. In this song, the singer wants nothing more than to be with his lover. What I find so stirring at the end is the rush of the applause, a fine and triumphant end to such an unassuming, direct and melancholy song. It was recorded live in 1963.

When I Paint My Masterpiece
A slog through Europe
Makes Bob think one day he'll quit
And stay home and paint.

"When I Paint My Masterpiece" comes from a time when Dylan wasn't writing much. It's a great song with a simple piano riff that propels it. He's taking a trip in Europe, dealing with the various things a star deals with while trying to find a path to painting his masterpiece.

- Ancient Rome, climbing the Spanish Steps, seeing double on a cold, dark night. Back to the hotel room where he has a date with Botticelli's niece. She said she'd be there when he paints his masterpiece. (The original lyrics said he had a date with a pretty little girl from Greece, which is the version that The Band used on their 1971 album "Cahoots.")
- He's been stuck in the Colosseum, "dodging lions and wasting time." That sounds like a stand-in for life in the music business.
- Traveling around the world in a dirty gondola, wouldn't it be something to be back in the USA - "the land of Coca-Cola."

- FCO –> BRU. It was a bumpy plane ride. Lots of uniformed clergy and young girls pulling muscles. (So say the lyrics, but I would have thought they were pulling mussels given that they're in Brussels.) Lots of people showed up to welcome him, including unruly members of the press. One day, this will all be different.

I Shall Be Released
A man in prison
Awaits release. His friend says
He was wrongly jailed.

Faith, imprisonment, deliverance. "I Shall Be Released" doesn't spell it out, but you get the impression that the singer is a prisoner. The more important theme here is the release from caring about circumstances, which I guess is in some sense a release from caring about life because, after all, it'll be over one day and there won't be any confining walls anymore.

- Everything is replaceable. All distance is far.

Nothing is permanent, nothing is so precious as to be indispensable. Separately, the space that divides me from you, and ourselves from everything else in our minds and in the world, is insurmountable. No one knows what the other person has, thinks or feels. True communication is impossible.

- He remembers everyone who put him in this place.

You don't wind up in a prison, literal or metaphorical, if you're innocent, unless others conspired against you.

- The light shines from the west to the east. One day, he'll be released.

I never thought much about why the light comes from the west to the east unless it means that all he sees is the reflection of the sun against the prison glass, indicating that his world is turned around and everything moves backwards because he's inside the mirror image of a free world. As for "any day now, I shall be released," that could be release from bondage or release from life.

- People say everyone needs protection and that one day, they must fall.

You're nobody until somebody loves you. Or, everyone needs a rabbi. Even then, everybody gets what's coming to them, and everyone must take a fall at one time or another.

- He sees himself reflected high above the walls that surround him.

The reflection of himself as a free man, or perhaps his spirit, considering that it's high above the wall. Like, in heaven.

- In the lonely crowd with a man who says he's been framed.

If you want to get deep about this line, you could say that the other guy is actually the narrator. Maybe this is the man who has been delivered of his earthly cares and concerns looking at the other side of himself, his reflection, who still longs for freedom, even though being on the outside again won't be different than being on the inside. "The Lonely Crowd" was a 1950 sociological analysis by David Riesman, Nathan Glazer and Reuel Denney about the American middle class, a society unable to foster human potential and individual self-knowledge, and falling short of producing a cohesive society because of the striving for esteem and consumer goods rather than the traditions that make up a real culture.

You Ain't Goin' Nowhere
Stay right where you are.
Your bride's coming. Genghis Khan
Has other problems.

- Winter: You're stuck in it with clouds and rain and frozen railings. Might as well think of something more pleasant: "tomorrow's the day my bride's gonna come."

- Morning: It came and went, despite how many letters they sent. And then this contradiction: get your money and pack your tent; you're not going anywhere.
- Shopping list: Flute, gun, tailgates, substitutes. Having done this, "strap yourself to the tree with roots. You ain't goin' nowhere."
- Mongol problems: Genghis Khan's kings need sleep. Khan can't provide it. However difficult that problem, let's wait until we need to deal with it.

Down in the Flood
Bob warns his woman
About a flood and suggests
That they leave, or else.

This is a quirky song based, in part, on the old song "James Alley Blues," particularly the line about "sugar for sugar and salt for salt, if you go down in the flood it's gonna be your fault." That echo aside, it's one of the most creative and original blues songs that Dylan wrote, and is filled with the same kind of concrete-yet-mystical imagery that gives his music from the late 1960s such a rural, spooky air. Generally, it goes like this:

- Floodwaters will overflow the levee. Whatever you do, including rocking the joint and going to Williams Point, won't help much. If you do that, you'll lose your best friend and will have to find a new one.
- If you go into the flood, it's your own fault.
- You need to pack up and leave because this is going to be the meanest flood ever.

Pat Garrett & Billy the Kid

Main Title Theme (Billy); Cantina Theme (Workin' for the Law); Billy 1; Bunkhouse Theme; River Theme; Turkey Chase; Knockin' on Heaven's Door; Final Theme; Billy 4; Billy 7

(Note: The haiku for "Billy" accounts for the tracks "Billy 1," "Billy 4" and "Billy 7" on this album. All contain roughly the same lyrics and tell the same story. Aside from those tracks and "Knockin' on Heaven's Door," the rest of the tracks are instrumentals.)

Billy

Sheriff Pat Garrett
Hunts down bad Billy the Kid.
They used to be friends.

Billy the Kid is on the run from his old friend and fellow outlaw Pat Garrett, who now works for the "law," which is in thrall to the big business interests that want Billy out of their hair.

Knockin' on Heaven's Door

Tough gunfighter dies,
But first he turns back into
An old mama's boy.

The song appears in the original theatrical version when James Coburn, playing Pat Garrett, hops along with old buddies Katy Jurado and Slim Pickens to get some information on the whereabouts of Billy (Kris Kristofferson). The mission doesn't go as planned, and Slim takes a fatal bullet. His gun-toting wife Katy kneels behind him as he dies, and this song plays over the scene, the angry clouds and the glowering, fading sun. It's a strong scene, though Peckinpah's "preview" version that, to me, is the superior cut of the film, leaves out the vocals. Leaving the film aside, it's a request to his mother:

- Take off my badge, it's no use to me. I can't see because I'm dying.
- Bury my guns, I can't use them.

Dylan
Lily of the West; Can't Help Falling in Love; Sarah Jane; The Ballad of Ira Hayes; Mr. Bojangles; Mary Ann; Big Yellow Taxi; A Fool Such As I; Spanish Is the Loving Tongue

Lily of the West
Young Flora trades up.
Her ex kills her new boyfriend.
He goes to prison.

Flora is the so-called "Lily of the West." The song is an old Irish and English ballad. A man falls in love with Flora, a girl in Louisville. She leaves him for another man. He kills the new guy and goes to prison, and pines for Flora. In some versions, he hangs. In others, he escapes prison and goes back to Ireland, or continues to travel through America, seducing maidens, but never forgetting the one who drove him to murder. Barry Taylor on the website contemplation.com says the Reverend S. Baring-Gould collected versions of the song in Devonshire, Yorkshire and elsewhere, and traced the song back to 1837. He also notes that some people trace the song back to western Ireland during the time of Oliver Cromwell.

Can't Help Falling in Love
It might be foolish,
But I love you like the sea
Loves the big river.

This song, set to the tune of "Plaisir d'Amour," was a big hit for Elvis Presley in 1961. This version is shambolic like most of the rest of the songs on this album, but I have affection for it in the way that I would have for an ugly dog. The haiku lines come from the verse of the song that says, "Like a river flows surely to the sea, darling so it goes, some things are meant to be."

Sarah Jane
Dylan's boat is called
The "Big MacMillan." He rides
It with Sarah Jane.

I'm touched that Dylan recorded a song that mentions my last name, but I think he was just looking for the name of a riverboat that would fit the rhythm. "Sarah Jane" is not one of his songs, but an old and obscure slice of Americana that likely comes from Civil War days. One version, performed by Odetta, says, "Yankee built boats for to shoot them rebels. My guns are loaded, and, oh, she's leveled. Oh Saro Jane!" A page on the California State University, Fresno, website says the earliest recorded version is from 1927 and is by Uncle Dave Macon. A note on that site says that the late musician Lyle Lofgren tried and failed to find the name of a riverboat called the Big MacMillan, but that Appalachian folk musician Les Caraher found paperwork for a supply boat that plied the Mississippi River in those days called the Moses McLellan. A search for this boat shows that the Northwestern Union Packet Company sometime in or before the 1860s owned a boat by this name. The Dave Thomson collection on the website steamboats. com features a receipt for "sundries" carried aboard the ship, and notes that it plied the river between LaCrosse, Wisconsin and St. Paul, Minnesota.

Bob's version:

- I have a wife and five children.
- I'm going to take a trip on the Big MacMillan.
- I'm taking Sarah Jane, and plan to rock about her. (You know what that means.)
- Various ills befall the captain and the ship. Gonna have to relax about all that and just rock with Sarah Jane.
- Yankees build boats to shoot at the rebels. Bob's going to hold his own gun steady and level.

The Ballad of Ira Hayes
Indian Marine
Raises Iwo Jima flag.
Goes home, drinks and dies.

The song, which most people know from the Johnny Cash version on "Bitter Tears," is about the death of a Pima tribesman who was among the five U.S. Marines and Navy hospital corpsman who raised the American flag on Mount Suribachi during the Battle of Iwo Jima.

Hayes came home a hero, a status with which he was uncomfortable. He became an alcoholic and eventually froze to death, drunk, in Arizona. Cash's version, written by the late folk singer Peter LaFarge (whose own death at 34, either due to suicide or overdose, was no less tragic than Hayes's), contains the moving line, "He died drunk early one morning, alone in the land he fought to save. Two inches of water in a lonely ditch was a grave for Ira Hayes... Yeah, call him drunken Ira Hayes. But his land is just as dry. And his ghost is lying thirsty in the ditch where Ira died."

Mr. Bojangles
Jailed drunk tells his tale
Of dancing for booze money
And how his dog died.

"Mr. Bojangles" was a hit for Jerry Jeff Walker when he released it in 1968. There are tons of covers out there from all sorts of artists: Garth Brooks, Harry Belafonte, J.J. Cale, Sammy Davis Jr., Neil Diamond, Arlo Guthrie, Whitney Houston, Billy Joel, Elton John, Rod McKuen, Nina Simone, William Shatner, Cat Stevens, Robbie Williams and Dolly Parton. I don't quite understand what makes it irresistible, but it's certainly unforgettable. I don't really like sympathetic songs about chronically stumbling drunks, and the story line is ridiculous, but it forces its nostalgia on me because this was a song that is inseparable from the 1970s when I was growing up. It also makes a naked grab for your emotions, and I hate it when the grab works. Walker said while in jail for public intoxication in 1965, he met a homeless man who called himself "Mr. Bojangles." He had been arrested as part of a police sweep after someone was murdered. They got to talking in the jail cell, and Bojangles told the story about dancing the old soft-shoe and how his dog died. Someone complained that his story was bringing everybody down so Bojangles did a little tap dance to cheer everyone up.

Mary Ann
A man goes sailing.
He promises to return
To sweet Mary Ann.

Mary Ann is a folk variation on the song "The True Lover's Farewell," which likely comes from the 17th or 18th century. Related songs include "A Red, Red Rose" by Robert Burns, as well as "My Dear Mary Ann," "The Turtle Dove" and "Ten Thousand Miles." I love the maritime air of this song, and the backup singers add a soulful tinge over a swirling organ. There are versions to be found from Appalachia to Quebec and the Maritimes and elsewhere.

- Guy leaves Mary Ann. His ship is waiting, the wind is high.
- The trip is 10,000 miles away, 10,000 miles back, but if he doesn't come back, it'll be the end of the world.

- Lobster in the pot, bluefish on the hook. They suffer, but not like he does for you.
- Dream date with Mary Ann: Flask of gin, some sugar cubes, a bowl to mix it all together.

Big Yellow Taxi
They chopped down the trees,
Destroyed the environment.
Nobody noticed.

Joni Mitchell's "Big Yellow Taxi" is, according to most Dylan listeners, one of the man's least impressive attempts to be released. It's inferior to most versions of the song that I've heard, but I'm soft on the kind of music he was recording at the time, so I can't object to it too much. The song documents Mitchell's bemused take on the destruction of the natural world as mankind builds more and more stuff, then fences "nature" off in a museum and charges people to see the trees. She couples it with the big yellow taxi that comes to take away her lover because he's had enough. It's famous for the line, "Don't it always seem to go, you don't know what you've got till it's gone, they paved paradise and put up a parking lot."

A Fool Such As I
Sometimes you find fools
Who let their hearts get broken.
I am such a fool.

There are two commercially released recordings of Dylan's performance of this delightful song, first popularized by country singer and Nova Scotian Hank Snow. The first to be released was on "Dylan." Dylan's other recording of the song comes from the 1967 Basement Tapes sessions.

- A fool like me comes along but once in a while. You can recognize me because I'm sentimental in breakups. When you leave me, you can expect me to cry, and I'll dream about you after you're gone.
- You taught me how to love and then you taught me what getting a broken heart is like. I plan to remain in love with you forever, by the way.

Spanish Is the Loving Tongue
Gambler loves a girl,
Flees Mexico after fight,
Leaves girl heartbroken.

This song comes from a poem from 1907 by Charles Badger Clark. It's about a man who falls in love with a Spanish girl down in Sonora. He's not a terribly upstanding guy. He gets into a fight while gambling and must flee across the border to America for his liberty. She begs him not to go, but he goes anyway. He says he misses her, but in such a nonchalant "yeah I sort of think about her" way that he sounds like a cad. But I suspect that he was lying to himself. This version was recorded with a full band, complete with kitschy cowboy/loping-horse chord accompaniment and a bunch of backup singers singing a loud Spanish "la-la-la" over the fade. There also is a beautiful version of him performing it on solo piano. That version was released in 1971 as the flip side to the "Watching the River Flow" single.

Planet Waves

On a Night Like This; Going Going Gone; Tough Mama; Hazel; Something There Is About You; Forever Young; Forever Young; Dirge; You Angel You; Never Say Goodbye; Wedding Song

On a Night Like This

It's snowing outside.
This is the kind of night made
For loving and bliss.

"On a Night Like This" is a woodsy, wintery, swinging love song capturing the jubilation of being with your sweetheart in an old cabin on a snowy night. I've read that the line about throwing a log on the fire and letting it "burn, burn burn burn" is a Jack Kerouac reference.

Going Going Gone

The end of the tale
Is good if your love is strong.
If not, stop reading.

"Planet Waves" matches its straightforward love songs with more abstract, obscure and challenging lyrics. After the direct declaration of love and romance on "On a Night Like This" come the more difficult charms of "Going Going Gone." Claims that this is a song about suicide don't work for me. I know that no subject is closed to a writer willing to explore it, but it seems like a case of people looking for something that isn't there. If anything, it sounds like the moral of the tale is to bail out before you fail out. I should note that this is what an auctioneer would say just before declaring an item sold, a point that Philippe Margotin and Jean-Michel Guesdon make in their book "Bob Dylan: All the Songs: The Story Behind Every Track."

- He just got to the place where the willow won't bend. There are no words left, it's the end. Gone.
- Time to stop reading. Close the book. It's not the end, but who cares what happens next.
- He's been hanging on threads and telling the truth, but it's time to go before it gets late.
- His grandmother said he should follow his heart, and that all would be well. Not everything that is gold shines, and by the way, he should stick with his lover.
- He's living on the edge, but is going before he gets to the ledge.

There is a minor argument to be made in favor of this being a song about getting tired and going to sleep, but I'm sure that it's not as simple as that.

Tough Mama
I love you, mama,
I'm enlightened, not hungry.
Meet me when you're free.

"Tough Mama" is a gritty rock n' roll number that lurches around in the beat, giving the song a rough-edged sound that feels like he and the Band were right at home together. It takes place out on the roads and the plains, not explicitly, but in feeling. It has grit on it.

Names for his lady:

- Tough Mama: meat's shaking on her bones.
- Dark Beauty: time for her to move over and make some room because he's going to bring her down to where the flowers bloom. She came through the ashes and dust, flying all night to him. He wants to meet her at the border at night.
- Sweet Goddess: born of bright light and changing wind. She shouldn't be modest about it.
- Silver Angel: She's a refugee of the road. He wants to give her a wedding ring.

Other characters:

- Papa: he's in prison, his working days are through.
- Jack the Cowboy: up north, buried in the past.
- Lone Wolf: "he went out drinking, that was over pretty fast."

Hazel
She has what he wants,
But she makes him wait around.
Hazel, don't, he says.

I haven't looked around, but I'm willing to bet that there aren't many pop songs out there about gals named Hazel. It's one of his more earnest love songs – though I wonder who thought that he might not want to be seen with her, given his comment that "I wouldn't be ashamed to be seen with you anywhere."

A little more about Hazel:
She has dirty-blonde hair. She has something he wants plenty of – love. She also has stardust in her eyes, and he would give her the sky in return for some of her love. His love for her is making him blind, and he sure doesn't need anyone to remind him of how he feels. Most significantly, he's on a hill and she's not there with him. That's too bad because she was the one who called him there, and he doesn't like waiting. (I note with some curiosity Dylan's repeated references to having trouble on hills. He worries about dying on top of one in "It Takes a Lot to Laugh, It Takes a Train to Cry," and his hero "Lucky" in the song "Minstrel Boy" is stuck on a hill with a bunch of girls, but he still feels alone.)

Something There Is About You
Dylan's youth, Duluth...
Something about you baby,
Takes him back in time.

Dylan takes a journey through the past. His gal reminds him of a long-forgotten truth, his old pals Danny Lopez and Ruth, and walking the hills of old Duluth. (Hills again!)

Forever Young
Anti-aging tricks:
Be strong, good and courageous.
Stay busy, stay swift.

There are few sweeter songs in the Dylan catalogue than "Forever Young." It is the last song on side one of "Planet Waves"... and also the first song on side two. The first is solemn and sweet. It's the "make you cry" version. The second is a different take that chugs along on railroad track furnished by the Band. It's the "divorced from sentimentality" version, and feels completely different.

You can stay forever young by following these simple steps:

God willing: bless and keep, fulfill wishes, help people and be helped, reach the stars, be right and true and aware of the goodness of the universe, be strong and brave, be busy and fleet footed, be a rock when the earthquake strikes, be happy, be known. And of course, be young at heart, if you should survive to a hundred and five.

Dirge
She sings freedom songs
And he hates the slavery
Of needing her love.

"In this age of fiberglass, I'm searching for a gem." Whoever the gem is, you won't find him or her in this song. This was a quickie, recorded with Bob on piano and Robbie Robertson on a prickly acoustic guitar. Its original title is "Dirge for Martha." Self loathing starts and ends the song, with Dylan singing, "I hate myself for loving you and the weakness that it showed," and ends with "I hate myself for loving you, but I'll soon get over that." The repeated up-and-down minor-key melody of the piano and Robertson's angry-Spaniard licks on the guitar are brilliant. The song sometimes feels like a collection of great phrases, any one of which would make an acrid cross-stitch homily to hang on any room in the house where you want people to feel alienated.

You Angel You
You're quite an angel.
If that's love you're bringing me,
I will buy in bulk.

Here's another lovey-dovey song.

She:

- Has him under her wing.
- Has a way of walking and talking.
- Is fine as anything's fine.
- Is fine as can be.
- Smiles like a baby child.

He:

- Could almost sing.
- Lets her play on his mind.
- Can't sleep at night for trying.
- Never felt like this before.
- Gets up at night and paces.
- Wants more and more and more and more.
- Lets her love fall all over him.

Never Say Goodbye
Snow and frozen lake
At dusk make setting for me
To say I love you.

"Never Say Goodbye" is one of those unadulterated love songs that Dylan wrote so few of that he leaves you wondering what could have happened if he'd spent more time producing them. He might be the master of the abstract and the symbolic, not to mention the bitter and sour, but he knew how to write a simple love note like few others. The only unusual item is the line about how his dreams "are made of iron and steel." I've always assumed that this is a personal reference to his metal sculptures.

Wedding Song
He loves you enough
To forsake everything else.
You should marry him.

Though it's not my job to connect real-life events to these songs, it's impossible to not associate the timing of this song with the coming split between Dylan and his wife, and see this more as an entreaty to keep things together than a literal wedding song. Leaving all that aside, these are lovely, profound words. There's also a quick reference to how Dylan never intended to "remake the world at large" or "sound a battle charge." This is of a piece with his desire to live a quiet family life, something he said he was often unable to do given how famous he became as the popularly elected but misnamed spokesman for a generation.

Blood on the Tracks

Tangled Up in Blue; Simple Twist of Fate; You're a Big Girl Now; Idiot Wind; You're Gonna Make Me Lonesome When You Go; Meet Me in the Morning; Lily, Rosemary and the Jack of Hearts; If You See Her, Say Hello; Shelter From the Storm; Buckets of Rain

Tangled Up in Blue

A couple breaks up.
He sorts of meets her later,
But he keeps drifting.

"Tangled Up in Blue" is an only slightly detached account of a relationship and two (or more) lives and how their connection fell apart without ever really being severed. You could argue that the song is far too personal and, in its way, self pitying, to resonate with such a wide audience, but I think that people who love the song identify with the sad drifters/lost lovers – or maybe people just like stories of star-crossed lovers. It's also noteworthy for its changing narrative perspectives and its apparent disregard of linear time. There's also another way to look at it that I've read about online: the song is actually about one woman and several men who tell their tales about her.

How tangled?

- He's lying in bed wondering what she's like nowadays. He should have known it wouldn't work out. Her parents said as much. They thought his parents were too poor for her (mama's homemade dress, daddy's bank account). Now he's standing on the road in the rain, hoping to hitchhike to the East Coast.

- She was married when they met, but she got divorced – with his help. They had a long run, but broke up in the darkness of the night. She says they'll meet again.

- He gets a job in Minnesota's North Woods, working as a cook. He then gets a job on a fishing boat in Louisiana. The past keeps catching up with him. He keeps thinking about his ex.

- He meets a woman working in a strip club. She says, "don't I know your name?"

- She prepares a pipe for him at her place, then shares with him some poems from an Italian poet in the 13th century, whom I would take to be Dante Aligheri. He realizes that there's something between him and her, the more he listens to her read these magic words that pour into his soul like fire.

- Another shift: "he" is living with "them" in a basement apartment on Montague Street. There's music and revolution, but once "he" starts dealing with slaves, he's no longer the man he used to be. She suffers because of his work, which he calls dealing with slaves. Like a slave trader, or does the line indicate something more personal, like, say, dealing with the music business. They break up, and "he" keeps moving on.

- He's going to look for her and to try to win her back. Everyone they knew has changed into someone else, usually not for the better, but this one remains a traveler. (And then there are the women who became "carpenters' wives," which practically begs for some evocation of a domesticated Jesus, no longer the big man that he used to be after taking the easy way out and moving to New Jersey to raise the kids.) And then he ends with that famous, cryptic line about how they always felt the same but saw things from a different point of view.

Simple Twist of Fate
Love affair hinges
On unexpected plot twists,
And it has to end.

A short story about a love affair, "Simple Twist of Fate" is widely seen as a tragic tale of Bob and Sara. They meet, go to a hotel on a hot summer evening. She leaves. He tries not to care and then spends his time hunting for her by the docks among the sailors shipping in and out. A talking parrot makes an appearance.

You're a Big Girl Now
He's sighing, crying,
And learning to love too late –
She's already gone.

"You're a Big Girl Now" must be the saddest breakup song that I've ever heard. It's nearly too much to take. It's a great song, but I can understand where Dylan was coming from when he said in his cranky way to an interviewer that he doesn't understand how people can consider the projection of such pain "entertainment."

Idiot Wind
We had some good times,
But I'd much rather focus
On hating you now.

"Idiot Wind" is nearly eight minutes of anger, rage, betrayal, scorn and an acknowledgment that the singer is just as much of an "idiot" as the person or people at whom the song is directed. The intensity of the lyrics and Dylan's vocal delivery don't make for a light listen. "Idiot Wind" goes beyond the breakup into a world of disgust at the state of humanity and a despairing cry by Dylan at being misunderstood after 12 years of singing his heart out.

- Press paranoia: reporters are writing lies about him. One is that he shot a man and took his wife to Italy, and inherited her money when she died. He's just lucky, not calculating.

- People lose their shit when they're around him. Big ideas, images, distorted facts. Someone asks Bob "where's it at?" Seriously? As he sang in "Ballad of a Thin Man," "You know something is happening here, but you don't know what it is."
- Fortune teller: lightning might strike you. He can't remember peace and quiet. Then we get into the symbols: Lone soldier on the cross, smoke pouring out of a train door. Soldier loses every battle, wins war.
- Bob dreams by the roadside: visions of her horse hurt his head. Then there's you who hurts the ones he loves best and lies. One day you will be in the ditch with flies around your eyes and blood on your saddle.
- Gravity and destiny destroy them. She tames "the lion in his cage," but that didn't move his heart. Everything's upside down – good/bad/bad/good. Top/bottom/bottom/top.
- You're blinded by corruption and ritual. He can't face you. More symbols: priest in black on Sunday, no emotion as building burns. He waits for you near cypress trees, all summer long.
- He can't be near her. He can't even touch her books. He wishes he were someone else. She's full of glory, he can't escape her memory.

- Free after much double crossing. He complains about how she'll never understand his pain. He admits that he could have done better trying to understand hers.

You're Gonna Make Me Lonesome When You Go

He loves you so much,
He'll be lonely when you go.
Maybe change your plans.

You could see it as a breakup song or maybe even a song about death. Appearing amidst the carnage of broken love that's splattered all over this album, it carries at its heart hope, as if love's only doom is death, and even then love will outlast the end of the lovers.

- Love this time: close, easy, slow.
- Until now he was "shooting in the dark too long" and all was wrong.
- Before: careless love. Now: correct, on target, direct.
- Beautiful colors of the clover, Queen Anne's Lace and your red hair. You could make him cry. Before: can't remember what he was thinking about. Your love spoils him.
- Flowers and crickets and the lazy blue river. "I could stay with you forever and never realize the time."

- Before: bad relationships, sad relationships, relationships like that of Verlaine and Rimbaud. Now: this is much better.
- Why would he ever be without you? He should sit right down and write himself a letter.
- Where you might be: Honolulu, San Francisco, Ashtabula. Now you're gone, but I'll see you in the sky, the grass and my loved ones.

Meet Me in the Morning
I crawl through barbed wire
To love you, and you know what?
It doesn't feel good.

I've never heard a song that sounds like "Meet Me in the Morning." It's not the form, which is blues, and it's not the lyrics, which are harrowing though conventional. There's something eerie about the easygoing country sound of the guitars combined with the tale of the singer who is only too willing to go through many trials to be with his love – and when he gets what he wants, he gets the sinking feeling that it's not all that good for him. The song moves into some strange, spooky territory with the music. I don't know what kind of drums they're using on the song or how it was recorded. They thump along in some muffled away along with creative hi-hat use and are accompanied at one point at the end of the song by a fuzzy guitar solo and some other guitar sounds that take the song into a whole new territory of beauty.

Lily, Rosemary and the Jack of Hearts

Jack robs bank. Lily
Cuckolds Rosemary with Jim.
Rose kills him, then hangs.

This epic robbery, lust and revenge story feels to me like it could have contained a few more verses to explain what on earth is going on. But continuity isn't the point; it's atmosphere.

In short:

- The Jack of Hearts and his boys are robbing the bank safe located two doors down from the gambling hall/saloon in an old western town. They're not even bothering to hide the noise they're making. Everybody has something else on their minds. Most people are getting ready for the show that's going to happen in the saloon that night.
- Lily's hanging out with the girls backstage, playing cards. She came from a broken home and had plenty of affairs with plenty of men, but nobody like the Jack of Hearts.
- Big Jim owns the diamond mine and is a richie-rich about town. He's having an affair with Lily. He's also concerned about this Jack of Hearts, but he's not sure why.

- The stage manager knows that something strange is happening, but he can't rouse the hanging judge because the hanging judge is drunk. He runs into the lead actor, dressed as a monk.
- Big Jim's wife Rosemary wants out of her marriage. She's depressed and has contemplated suicide and done other bad things. She's looking to do one good deed before dying. She's also a drunk.
- The hanging judge: he's not drunk after the burglary ends and Jack flees town. Ultimately, he solves everybody's problems. Jack busts out at gunpoint, Rosemary drops Jim with her knife, the judge sobers up in time to send Rosemary to the gallows, and Lily is left alone with her thoughts.

If You See Her, Say Hello
He pretends he's fine,
But it's not true. He's in love
Despite their breakup.

"If You See Her, Say Hello" is a beautiful song, but boy is it dreary. Maybe the less judgmental way to say it is: the music fits the mood. It captures the essence of why they say breaking up is hard to do. Though Burt and Hal suggested that you "Make It Easy on Yourself," Dylan chooses the opposite path to work through his pain.

What she did and what she's doing:

- Might be in Tangier.
- Left me early last spring.
- Might think I've forgotten her. (Wrong.)
- Lives inside of me.

What happened:

- A falling out.
- She busted out and got free.

What I'm up to:

- Dealing with the bitter taste.
- Going here and there, seeing people, hearing people mention her name.
- Not getting used to things.
- Being too sensitive, getting soft.
- Replaying the past.

What you should do:

- Say hello.
- Tell her things get slow, but I'm OK.
- Tell her I'm thinking of her.
- Kiss her for me.
- Tell her that I want what's best for her.
- Tell her that I'd love to see her if she's in town.

Shelter From the Storm
A helpful woman
Offer shelter to a man
In need of plenty.

"Shelter From the Storm" is loaded with symbolism that I'm sure many people have tried to interpret. The basic story: a woman offers shelter to a man. The storm is not the literal meteorological phenomenon.

- He enters the world, void of form, coming from the wilderness. He gets shelter.
- He'll always do her a solid if he comes back again.
- Their relationship was left unresolved, but he would love to get shelter again.
- He was burned out, buried in hail, poisoned and "blown out on the trail." He also was hunted and ravaged. She offers shelter.
- She's a beautiful vision. Even better, she removes crowns of thorns from self-styled martyrs.
- Something went wrong in their relationship.
- There's a deputy and there's a preacher. Deputy's on nails and the preacher is on horseback. Doom is all that counts. There's also a one-eyed undertaker with a horn.
- Crying infants, lovelorn old men.
- He was beset by philistines in a village. They gambled for his clothes. He bargained for salvation and got poison instead. He offered his

innocence and was scorned. A scene from the crucifixion.

- Now he's living over the border, though he'll come back. "Beauty walks the razor's edge, someday I'll make it mine." He wishes he could turn back time to when she gave him shelter from the storm. This is almost certainly a reference to the novel by W. Somerset Maugham, who wrote "The sharp edge of a razor is difficult to pass over; thus the wise say the path to Salvation is hard." Nobody knows that more than Bob. This phrase is from the Katha-Upanishad, which in part tells the story of the hard road to liberation of the soul. Maugham used these lines after visiting India and meeting Ramana Maharishi at an ashram in Tamil Nadu.

Buckets of Rain
Everything she does
He adores, but she brings him
Buckets of sadness.

After the epic tears of "Blood on the Tracks," we get this straight-faced, dry-eyed epilogue. Everything about this woman makes him happy. There's the cool way she looks at him. There's her smile and her fingertips, the way she "loves me strong and slow." He even says "I'm taking you with me, honey baby, when I go." But there's always the shadow of love in love: he says baldly, "Everything about you is bringing me misery."

Selections from **The Basement Tapes**

Odds and Ends; Million Dollar Bash; Goin' to Acapulco; Lo and Behold!; Clothes Line Saga; Apple Suckling Tree; Please, Mrs. Henry; Tears of Rage; Too Much of Nothing; Yea! Heavy and a Bottle of Bread; Tiny Montgomery; Nothing Was Delivered; Open the Door, Homer; This Wheel's on Fire

(Note: These songs were first released on this album from 1975. They come from informal recording sessions with Dylan and the Band in Saugerties, New York, in 1967. The complete recordings from those sessions were released in 2014. These songs appear in this section while the complete recordings arrive later in this book.)

Odds and Ends
Baby, I don't love you.
You don't love me. You just pour
Some juice on my head.

"Odds and Ends" sounds like nonsense, but contains a horse-sense homily straight from the woods and fields and the Farmer's Almanac.

- You break your promise "all over the place." The promise was love, but instead you just spill juice on me.
- "Odds and ends, odds and ends, lost time is not found again."

- You take file, bend my head, I forget all that you said. You don't really love me, as your juice spilling suggests.
- My box: clean. You: know what I'm saying and what I mean. You'd better find another guy and keep your juice for yourself.

Million Dollar Bash

It's nearly bash time.
The boys mash their potatoes
And head on over.

Million Dollar Bash is about some people getting ready to go to a party, and how much they're looking forward to it. Well, it's about more than that too, but I'm not sure that any of it makes any sense. It's a fun song, though.

Events on the day of the bash:

- Big Dumb Blonde and Turtle plan to show up at the bash. She has a wheel in the gorge, while Turtle's checks are forged. He also has cheeks in a chunk and cheese in the cash.
- Everybody here and there has the same law of physics that they must observe: the bigger they come, the harder they crack. Meanwhile, Bob invites Sweet Cream to flash as they plan to meet at the bash.

- Bob takes his lawyer to the barn where Silly Nelly tells him a story. Jones shows up and takes out the trash, and then they go to the bash.
- At night, he's "hitting it too hard" and his "stones won't take." He sleeps late, and then he and whoever he wakes up with do a hello-goodbye-push-then-crash routine. Then they go to the bash.
- Bob looks at watch, looks at wrist, punches self in face with fist. Then he goes to get his potatoes mashed, then goes to the bash.

Goin' to Acapulco
Rose Marie awaits
In Mexico. I see her,
Have fun and go home.

My suspicion is that she's a sometime-girlfriend who doesn't mind performing some for-profit body work on Bob when he needs his annual inspection. Either that or she's a madam down in Mexico. I would imagine that this is the case because she:

- Never does him wrong.
- Puts it to him plain.
- Gives it to him for a song.
- Offers him quick eats.
- Lets him blow his plum (not sure what that's about) and drink his rum.

As for the singer, he's your typical guy:

- Wicked life, but everyone has to eat.
- He's like everyone else, scratching for his meat.
- He tries to tell the truth and not listen to jokes or engage in pranks.
- He just wants to have fun.

Lo and Behold!
Bob goes to Pittsburgh
Which he calls Chicken Town, and
Buys a herd of moose.

"Lo and Behold!" is epic silliness. The music rumbles along like an old car or train, calling as little attention to itself as possible.

- Bob boards a train, pulling out for San Antonio. He's feeling good, he plans to meet his woman there. The coachman "hit me for my hook," then asks Bob his name. Bob gives it to him, but he's ashamed.
- Bob arrives in Pittsburgh. It's 6:30. He finds himself a seat, puts down his hat, and asks Molly what's the matter with her "mound." She replies: "What's it to ya, Moby Dick? This is chicken town!"
- He buys his girlfriend a herd of moose, but they fly away. She looks for them. Bob thinks he'll go

to Tennessee and buy a truck, but he also thinks he might save his money and rip it up.

- He arrives at his next destination on a Ferris wheel, all slick and coming in like a ton of bricks, and all while laying down some tricks. He goes back to Pittsburgh, counts to 30, rounds the horn and rides a herd, though we don't know whether they're the moose from earlier in the song or whether they're cattle.

Clothes Line Saga
Neighbor tells family
The vice president's gone mad.
They keep doing chores.

"Clothes Line Saga" might be the craziest of the Basement Tapes songs, and it is certainly the most evocative of that summer of '67, with its politicians and hippies calling on one another to drop out. Dylan tells the story of a family doing chores on a cold day in late January. There's some light, slightly irritated banter between family members, the kind of low-level hum of annoyance that families get when winter cabin fever sets in.

Day 1:

- They bring the clothes in.
- Mama picks up a book, Papa asks what it is, Mama says "What do you care?"

- The clothes must be wet still, so they hang them back on the line.

Day 2:

- Everyone's chief concern upon waking is seeing if the clothes have dried.
- Dogs bark. Neighbor passes.
- Neighbor is grinning. He tells mama that the vice president went mad downtown the night before.
- Mama says, well, that's just the way it goes. The neighbor says, we'll have to forget.
- Mama asks Bob if the clothes are wet.
- Bob touches his shirt, but the neighbor interrupts his mission. The neighbor wants to know if some of the clothes are Bob's and if he helps out with the chores. Bob tells him "some of them, not all of them" and "sometime, not all the time."
- Papa tells Bob that Mama wants him to come in and bring the clothes.
- Bob meets Mama inside and they shut all the doors.

I can't say whether there's supposed to be some deeper meaning. The laconic pace and the deadpan, delivery of the words indicate to me that the song is about nothing more than it claims to be, though people have suggested anti-war statements regarding Vietnam and the White

House, as well as some kind of answer to the song "Ode to Billy Joe." (Dylan initially called the song "Answer to Ode.") The refusal of the family to engage with the neighbor reminds me of people who don't get much out of the awareness of current events, and prefer to focus on home rather than wondering about the crazy world. I like it more as an absurd, Luis Buñuel-style short film that's about clothes, neighbors and a family. It fits right in with the strange picture of Ruritania that so much of the rest of the Basement Tapes delivers in that weird, spooky way that it does.

Apple Suckling Tree
We're under a tree.
An old man is in a boat,
And my wife's with me.

Lots of fun in this sing-along, but I'm pretty sure that the lyrics aren't supposed to mean anything. The one thing to which he returns is that there's just gonna be you and me under that apple suckling tree, "oh yeah."

Please, Mrs. Henry
He's looking for sex,
But he's too drunk and he's broke.
Mrs. Henry knows.

My suspicion is that the singer is looking for some paid company with a lady of the night named Mrs.

Henry, but he doesn't have any money so he would like a freebie. Complicating matters: he's drunk. It's undetermined whether he's able to perform despite his boasting.

A confession to Mrs. Henry:

- I've had two beers, and a broom could sweep me up right about now.
- Will you take me to my room?
- I'm a good boy, but I've had too many eggs and kegs and I've done too much socializing.
- I'm on my knees and I don't have a dime.
- I'm groaning in the hallway and I'm going mad.
- Maybe you should take me to your dad.
- I can: drink life a fish, crawl like a snake, bite like a turkey and slam like a drake.
- I'm a sweet bourbon daddy, but if you crowd me, I'll fill up your shoe. (By peeing in it, one might surmise.)
- I'm starting to drain, and my "crane" might leak.
- Perhaps you might look my way and "pump me a few."

Tears of Rage
Family grieves about
A daughter whom they raised right,
But turns out wrong instead.

This is a three-verse dirge for a wayward daughter – or maybe a wayward country – that has resisted or ignored all attempts to give her a good upbringing. Some see in this song a scolding of the United States, brought up on high ideals and a dream, ripping itself apart over a useless war, betraying its ideals, and obsessing over the enrichment of wealth.

- They carried her in their arms on Independence Day, but now she throws them aside. What kind of daughter would do that to her doting parents and family?
- They gave her instructions and wrote her name in the sand (like the shifting sands of time), but she saw it as only a convenient place for her to stand. When she discovered that there were no true people, no true ideals, they stood around and watched and thought she was just acting like a child.
- It didn't hurt, they didn't notice, when she filled her head with false instruction. And though they're full of love for her, this love for her just spoils.

Too Much of Nothing
Too much of nothing
Makes a man make bad choices
Like lying and such.

If you dig around the Internet enough, you'll see that this is one of several Dylan songs that some people say is rooted in "King Lear" by William Shakespeare, with its fear of the void, the resentment a parent feels for children who turned out bad and its futile railing against nothingness. I suppose that this is possible. I see more of the kind of backwoods moralizing of the Farmer's Almanac. The reference to T.S. Eliot and his wives, in which he says to say hello to Valerie and Vivian, and to send them his salary on the waters of oblivion supports the idea that Dylan was singing about madness and loss in this song. Consider Eliot's wife Vivienne, whom Eliot divorced (and whose brother later committed her to a mental asylum where she died). Eliot then married Valerie, who was 38 years younger than he.

The effects of too much nothing:

- A man can feel ill at ease.
- One man's temper rises. Another's freezes.
- No one has control.
- Too much nothing makes people boastful, even to the point of abusing the king.
- But they don't know a thing.
- This all has been written in the book, but "when there's too much of nothing, nobody should look."
- Turns men to liars. Some sleep on nails, others eat fire.
- Makes a fella mean.

Yea! Heavy and a Bottle of Bread
Catch the bus with Bob.
Pack the bread and the meat and
Go fishing for trout.

The bottle of bread means "bottle of beer."

Story:

- Comic book and I get on a bus. The chauffeur stays home with a nose full of pus. YEA! Heavy and a bottle of bread!
- This is a brown one-track town. Let's pack up the meat, sweet. We're off to Wichita to catch a trout.
- See that drummer behind the bottle? Pull him out. Gonna shake my pipe, then slap the drummer with a smelly pie. Then let's go to California.

Tiny Montgomery
Better grease that pig
Because the king of the drunks
Is coming to party.

The nickname "Tiny" usually is applied to someone who is large (think Little John), so I'm assuming that Tiny is a big drunkard who's coming to town and one of his friends is announcing to a bunch of people in San Francisco (or maybe Frisco, Texas?) that Tiny's arriving to shake things up and have a good time. I've always imagined him as a huge man from the first years of the 20th century, wearing a black-and-gold striped waistcoat, an old-timey suit, a bowler hat and that stern, dignified look of men who wore waxed moustaches at this time. A low-rent William H. Taft, maybe. The lyrics on this song, like many of the Basement Tapes songs, veer toward silliness and comedy. The names, especially, evoke images of long-ago bars and bruisers and knuckleheads:

Tiny's coming to Frisco.

- He's gonna "shake that thing" when he gets there, which will give every boy and girl a bang.
- Skinny Moo and Half-Track Frank are about to get out of the joint.
- There's a buzzard and crow in here too. Tell them Tiny says hello.
- He squeezes too. "Watch out, Lester, take it, Lou."
- Tell the monks and the CIO that Tiny says hello. I'm assuming that this means the Congress of Industrial Organizations.
- Tell the three-legged man and the hot-lipped ho that Tiny says hello.
- Other things to do: Scratch your dad, suck a pig and bring it home, pick drip, bake dough, grease pig, sing praise, gas dog, trick in, honk stink, take it down and watch it grow, play it low, pick it up, take it in.

Nothing Was Delivered
Either deliver
Or refund everyone's cash,
And stop telling lies.

- Nothing was delivered. I hope you don't mind, but you owe us. The less you argue, the sooner you can go.
- I can't sympathize with you over your fate because you are a liar. What were you thinking when you made us pay?

Some people seem to think that it's a warning to a drug dealer to deliver the drugs for which the buyers paid. I think that when you get a bunch of people who are into country rock/hippie rock, they will interpret song lyrics according to their preoccupations, one of which is the drug deal. But the enduring quality of songs from the Basement Tapes is their woodsy, homespun, old homily-and-proverb nature. These songs, however nonsensical some of the lyrics be, are about old saws, maxims and fireside truths, all touched with the shadow and weight of dead ancestors in what Greil Marcus called "the old, weird America." Narrowing a song with such general admonishments as this to a frustrated attempt to buy drugs injures the song. What are they singing about? I think there's a basic morality tale that says that you must right the scales to balance what you give with what you take, whether that's an item, advice, a lesson or anything. A good deed unreciprocated by a good deed of its own is an offense to universal equilibrium.

Open the Door, Homer
Bob's proverb service:
Remember your memories
And forgive the sick.

"Open the Door, Richard" (as it should be called) is listed on the album as "Open the Door, Homer." It is a variation on an old Vaudeville number. What elevates this song above other material from those recordings in Saugerties that summer are its mysterious admonitions about living a moral life, combined with the apparently nonsensical "Open the door, Richard" chorus. There are a ton of versions of this song going back nearly a century, and "Open the Door Richard" apparently became a catchphrase for some time, appearing on TV shows, films, cartoons and so on.

- The lesson he learned from Jim: You have to swim in a certain way if you want to live off the fat of the land.
- The lesson he learned from Mouse, the man who always blushes: flush your house or else house flushes.
- The lesson he learned from Mick: Preserve your memories. You can't relive them.

- The other lesson he learned from Mick: you must forgive the sick when trying to heal them.

The original song, which was a black Vaudeville song, is about a drunk guy who leaves the bar to go home. It's raining, and his roommate Richard won't let him in. This became the basis for a lot of ad libbing, including complaints about racism from the cops and all sorts of other issues, though the basic tone of the song is comic.

This Wheel's on Fire
We will meet again.
You asked me for favors. Well,
I tried, but no luck.

I find this a mysterious, complicated song, warning of some kind of doom just around the bend. It also feels tentative and somehow incomplete, but that's just a personal view.

- I'm going to sit and wait for you because you know we were fated to meet again. There's a fiery wheel rolling down the road, and it may explode while I'm near it. Better tell my next of kin now.
- If you remember, my plan was to take your lace and wrap it in a sailor's knot and hide it in your case. But I don't know if it's really yours.
- You were the one who wanted me to do things for you. And that's all there is to it. That and the fact that we are fated to meet again.

Desire

Hurricane; Isis; Mozambique; One More Cup of Coffee; Oh, Sister; Joey; Romance in Durango; Black Diamond Bay; Sara

Hurricane

Police frame boxer
For murder while the bad guys
Get away with it.

The story of the wrongful imprisonment of middleweight boxer Rubin "Hurricane" Carter is well known to many younger people because of the Norman Jewison film starring Denzel Washington as Carter. Dylan's version remains well known long after the events took place. Carter was charged with a triple murder at a bar in Paterson, New Jersey in 1966 and sent to jail. A second trial produced a guilty verdict and a sentence of two consecutive life terms. In 1985, a judge ruled that Carter did not receive a fair trial, and that racism was to blame. The prosecution in 1988 declined to seek a third trial, and a Superior Court judge dropped the charges. If you dig into the background of this song, you'll hear detractors say that Dylan got a number of the facts wrong. OK – it's not quite journalism in the traditional sense.

Isis

Man leaves a woman,
Tomb-raids icy pyramid,
Comes back to woman.

"Forget about it, Jake, it's Egypttown."

"Isis," which gave audiences a completely different mystery to ponder after "Hurricane," is one of the most curious stories that he has ever produced. I get an overwhelming sense that Dylan narrates the tale in reverse chronological order, except for the journey to the icy pyramids and the part where he discovers who's meant to be buried in them.

- Guy marries Isis on May 5, i.e., Cinco de Mayo.
- He loses Isis pretty quickly, cuts off his hair (mourning?), rides off to the wild country in search of opportunity.
- Arrives at high place. Darkness/light. Town divided down the middle – is this the boundary between two mirror worlds? Guy hitches his pony on the right side, and takes his clothes to the laundry.
- Stranger asks for a match. Guy finds him strange. Stranger asks the singer if he's looking for some easy work. Guy says he has no money. Stranger says, it's cool.
- They head north. Guy lends stranger a blanket, guy lends the singer his promise. He says they'll be back by the fourth, which is one day before our singer married Isis.
- Singer thinks about jewels and gold. They ride through freezing canyons and he thinks about Isis.

- She once told him that they could try again and things would be different, but she needs his patience. She said more and better, but he can't remember what.
- The men arrive at pyramids embedded in ice. The stranger says he needs to rob a corpse from them so he can make a lot of money.
- Wind and snow. They chop through the ice. Stranger dies. Singer keeps going.
- No body. Damn.
- Singer puts the stranger's body in the pyramid, the second instance in this song of time running either backward or in a circular motion.
- Singer returns to Isis. The sun's in his eyes and he's coming in from the East, so it must be evening, or else it's morning in a world where time runs backward.
- She asks where he's been. He hems and haws. She asks if he'll stay. He says, OK, but only if you want me to.
- Good lyric alert: "What drives me to you is what drives me insane." Singer reminisces about the rainy day when he married Isis.

Mozambique
Summer holidays
In Mozambique sound like fun.
Watch out for landmines.

"Mozambique" is one of the stranger songs in Dylan's catalogue. Like most of the songs on the album, he wrote it with psychoanalyst, English professor and "Oh! Calcutta!" musical director Jacques Levy. It's a short song about a romantic getaway to the sunny beaches and tropical paradise of Mozambique. At that time, the southeastern African nation and former Portuguese colony was just getting over a 10-year insurgency against its former colonizer, and was mined to the gills.

One More Cup of Coffee
Man leaves woman.
She's mysterious and wild.
She gives him coffee.

A man falls in love with an uneducated, sexy gypsy woman. Her father seems to have been a big deal once, but now the old man is weak and tired.

Oh, Sister
You are my sister,
And Dad will be angry if
You don't sleep with me.

It's not a song about incest. It refers to his spiritual sister, and the father is God. Still, this song makes putting out a religious duty rather than George Michael's more straightforward, "I Want Your Sex." Michael says it's natural; Dylan says it's scriptural. And if anything, he seems insistent, kind of like a religious Elvis Presley saying, "It's now or never, my love won't wait."

Essence of verse 1:
Why do you not want to have sex with me? God would be unhappy. That's dangerous. Have sex with me.

Essence of verse 2:
I deserve to have sex with you. We were put on this earth to have sex. It's what God wants. Have sex with me.

Essence of verse 3:
We had sex in a previous life. I can't explain it, but I think we should have sex in this life too.

Essence of verse 4:
We should have sex. If you don't, you'll make me sad. You'll make God sad. I can tolerate this for only so long. Otherwise, I might find someone else to have sex with.

Joey
Mobster Joe Gallo
Shoots up the town, goes to jail,
Gets out, gets murdered.

I'm not a "Joey" fan, though not because it's historically inaccurate. Nobody asked Dylan to write a musical documentary of Crazy Joe Gallo. I just can't accept the elegiac tone that Dylan and Levy apply to the story. I like mob movies and I'm a fan of "The Sopranos," and I can understand how killers, drug dealers, loan sharks and other such people have emotions, feelings, families and so on just like we do, and that bad things happen to them too. But to devote an 11-minute elegy to someone like Gallo and make him seem like a martyr of innocence seems like a stretch.

Romance in Durango
Lovers on the lam
In Mexico can't avoid
Their persecutors.

"No llores, mi querida, Dios nos vigila, soon the horse will take us to Durango. Agarrame, mi vida, soon the desert will be gone..."

"Romance in Durango," delivered in an odd time signature, feels like it came straight from the Sam Peckinpah songbook. Like some combination of "The Getaway," "The Wild Bunch," "Pat Garrett & Billy the Kid" and "Bring Me the Head of Alfredo Garcia," this song is about two lovers and one guitar and a horse, on the run from some unidentified bad guys. They're wandering through Mexico with the chilies drying in the sun. He sells his guitar to the baker's boy for some food and a hiding place. Don't worry, Magdalena, he says, we'll go to Durango and leave the desert behind and dance the fandango. They travel past the Aztec ruins, and dream of church bells and the moon. He remembers his crime, but vaguely: did he shoot that guy in the cantina? No matter, it happened, and we can't change the past. They plan to watch a bullfight and drink tequila in the old village of their ancestors, who rode with Pancho Villa into Torreón. They'll get married in the little church, and get dressed up, and then they'll have a reception watched over by God "with his serpent eyes of obsidian." But calamity strikes. His pursuers find him and shoot him from a distance. Wounded, he gives his gun to his sweetheart and bids her to aim well because they might not survive the night.

Black Diamond Bay

Earthquake kills the guests
At tropical resort. Bob
Couldn't care at all.

Dylan brings a cinematic scope to "Black Diamond Bay." A bunch of preoccupied, neurotic international types whom you would expect to find in a Graham Greene novel get up to various intrigues before a volcano erupts and an earthquake visits destruction on this tropical resort island. The whole place vanishes from the earth, leaving a Panama hat worn by the woman we meet in the first verse, and a pair of old Greek shoes, presumably worn by the Greek man we meet in verse two (who's mistaken by the woman for the Soviet ambassador), who showed up at the front desk to ask for rope (suicide) and a pen (note). There's a gambler, a desk clerk, a dwarf, a soldier... a cast of characters extensive enough to rival that of Robert Altman's "Nashville."

Sara
Bob wants his wife back.
She was a sad-eyed lady,
Now she's just plain sad.

"Sara" is the natural bookend to "Sad Eyed Lady of the Lowlands" from 10 years earlier. If that song was the wedding song, this one is the divorce song. It's an urgent, heartfelt plea to Sara to remember the good times that they had doing this and that and going here and there.

Single: **Rita May**

Rita May
Bob doesn't get her.
There's something about Rita:
She has a strong mind.

"Rita May" was recorded in 1975 and released in 1976 on the B-side of a single whose other side was a live version of "Stuck Inside of Mobile With the Memphis Blues Again" from the live album "Hard Rain." The song doesn't say it for sure, but it sounds like a paean to author Rita Mae Brown. It is available on the "Masterpieces" compilation from 1978.

- Rita May got her body in the way. She's nonchalant, but Dylan wants her body. What's he going to do? Make a lesbian reconsider her options? She makes him huff and puff.
- How did she get this way? Doesn't she ever see the light, or does she ever get scared when she doesn't see it? Either way, she has Bob burning and turning. He must be learning something.
- His friends say he'll go blind if he keeps hanging around with her. But when she holds him, there must be something deep that she's thinking of.
- Rita's lying in a stack of hay. What's she doing there? "I'm gonna have to go to college 'cause you are the book of knowledge, Rita May."

Street-Legal
Changing of the Guards; New Pony; No Time to Think; Baby, Stop Crying; Is Your Love in Vain?; Señor (Tales of Yankee Power); True Love Tends to Forget; We Better Talk This Over; Where Are You Tonight? (Journey Through Dark Heat)

Changing of the Guards
Bob makes some changes
Sixteen years into his job.
He might have found God.

"Changing of the Guards" is an anthem full of willful obscurity, best heard from a distance. Musically it sounds fine, but my experience always has been that I listen to the words more as sounds and focus on the music, or else I start asking myself too many questions about "what it all means." I concluded that in 1978, 16 years after his commercial debut, Dylan was announcing a number of changes in his moral, spiritual and musical path. Why 16? Because the song begins with the words, "Sixteen years, sixteen banners united over the field where the good shepherd grieves." I assume that the shepherd is our host, grieving over the state of his life, but making those assumptions is always dangerous with Dylan. Then there's divorce and opposition and departure: "Desperate men, desperate women divided, Spreading their wings 'neath the falling leaves."

Other "clues":

- Entrance upon the professional stage: "Fortune calls, I stepped from the shadows to the marketplace."
- His historical problem with hangers-on and managers.
- What to make of the captain sending loving thoughts to a woman beyond communication, with an "ebony face," and who eventually has her head shaved and is torn between Jupiter and Apollo? No idea. He follows her past a fountain, but it sounds like he loses her.
- Then there's the heart-shaped tattoo with stitches still mending, dog soldiers reflected in a palace of mirrors, lovemaking with a blonde, long-haired guy and gal amid mountain laurel, another rejection of the music business: He shined their shoes, marked their cards and moved their mountains.
- And finally, peace comes, but it's represented by false idols – perhaps an early reference to the more explicitly stated idea on the "Infidels" album that "sometimes Satan comes as a man of peace." And then there's a thoroughly obscure reference to death surrendering, and the death of death retreating between two tarot cards.

New Pony
Bob's new pony is
Sexier than the last one.
He's gonna ride her.

Dylan here is all about "naked" intent. He's singing about lust and sexual confusion, and the dirty, grinding blues of the song underlines his intent. It's one of his most raw songs, and I think it's effective. The blues guitar solo in the middle is rude, and is exceeded only by the nasty saxophone on the fade-out. The backup singers, sometimes off the beat, bellow, "How much longer?" in a terrifying way as Dylan growls through the verses, including his vocal fills, like "well-lllllll" and so on. I love this song.

No Time to Think
You go through troubles,
All meaning is doubled, and
Thinking is rubbled.

"No Time to Think" could have been subtitled "Dylan in the Bunker." The song spreads 18 verses over more than eight minutes. Each describes his travails in the midst of danger, fear, paranoia, alcohol, depression and anger, while a few contain strings of words with similar endings and rhymes. Ultimately, it's a pity party, brimming with self indulgence, suspicion of others and shaded portraits of self martyrdom. I confess that I tune out the words when I listen to this song because they're so dreary. I don't know what the "concept noun" rhymes are doing here other than to overstuff this already stuffed narrative. Here they are, along with the other parts of this airplane engine of a song, which I have taken apart piece by piece and presented here, though I left out any summary of each verse because they don't reflect much unless they're put together. I also left out some remark about the "Federal City," likely Washington. It pops up in the song, never to return.

Strings of unrelated nouns:

- Loneliness/tenderness.
- High society/notoriety.
- Memory/ecstasy/tyranny/hypocrisy.
- China doll/alcohol.
- Duality/morality.
- Paradise/sacrifice.
- Mortality/reality.
- Equality/liberty/humility/simplicity.
- Gravity/nobility/humility.
- Socialism/hypnotism/patriotism/materialism.
- Loyalty/unity/epitome/rigidity.

Words in the song that rhyme with "think," as in "No time to think":

- Sink.
- Link.
- Wink.
- Ink.
- Drink.
- Brink.
- Clink.
- Pink.
- Blink.

Characters in the song:

- You.
- Child.
- Wife.
- Empress.
- Judges.
- Country priestess.
- China doll.
- Destiny.
- Tyrant.
- Lion.
- Lamb.
- Traitor.
- Magician.
- Madmen.
- Warlords of sorrow.
- Queens of tomorrow.
- Her.

- Lovers.
- Fools.
- Babylon girl with rose in hair.
- Camille.
- Death.

What you are:

- Soldier of mercy.

Things you do or are done to you:

- Face life while in death.
- Fight for the throne.
- Travel alone.
- You're unknown as you sink.
- You're cold and you curse.
- Been blown and shown pity for pieces of change. (Judas.)
- Attracted by empress.
- Distracted by oppression.
- Feel violent and strange.
- Betrayed by a kiss. (Jesus.)
- Haunted by judge.
- Wanted by country priestess.
- See decoys.
- Feel depressed.
- Betrayed by your conscience.

- Waylaid by tyrant.
- Can't find salvation.
- Have no expectations.
- Murder your vanity.
- Bury your sanity.
- Resist something for pleasure.
- Lovers obey you.
- You aren't swayed by lovers.
- Lovers aren't sure you exist.
- Released upon seeing starlight in the east.
- Harmed by bullets.
- Disarmed by death.
- Deceived by no one.
- Stripped of virtue.
- Crawl in the dirt.
- Give.
- Not receive.
- Choose, lose, say goodbye, prepare for the victim, suffer, blink, think.

Baby, Stop Crying
Some asshole hurt you,
I'll avenge you and love you,
But please be quiet.

Bloated, bilious, but enjoyable, just like Dylan himself at the time, judging by the sound of the album. The singer is angry because this woman's former lover treated her meanly enough that he's ready to shoot him. He then asks her to stop crying, and follows it up with an invitation to take advantage of his services as a friend, and most likely something more than that.

Is Your Love in Vain?
I don't trust your love.
You should give me alone time.
Would you be my maid?

The milk of human kindness, soured. That's "Is Your Love in Vain?" which seems to capture the spirit that Dylan found himself in while recording the album.

- Do you love me or is that just good will?
- This isn't the first time I've been hurt, and I won't complain if you give me an answer that I don't want to hear, but look, I need to know, is your love in vain?
- Don't you know that I need alone time? Why do you bother me then? Do you know anything about me? Can't you let me be myself?
- I've been high and low, I've eaten with kings, and I've never been too impressed by that jazz.
- OK, fine, I'll be your lover. I'll even give you more time than I know that I can give. Meanwhile, can you cook and sew and keep a garden? While doing that, can you understand my pain?

Señor (Tales of Yankee Power)
Where are we going?
What are we doing? Bob asks.
Senor doesn't say.

"Señor (Tales of Yankee Power)" has long been a fan fa-
vorite. It captures a kind of weary post-Vietnam malaise
and disillusionment with America – at least in the title.
The rest of the song is more mysterious and obscure.
What's going on? I don't know.

- Are we going to Lincoln County Road or
  Armageddon? Either way, I think I've been here
  before. Could this be true, señor?
- Where is she? How long is our trip going to
  take? How long must I watch the door? (I guess
  the high school literature class key would say
  that this is a reference to love and death and how
  long do we have in this world.)
- What's going on and where: Upper deck: wick-
  ed wind blowing. Her neck: iron cross hanging.
  Vacant lot: marching band. Also in the vacant
  lot: her telling me, "forget me not."
- I see a painted wagon (pioneers?) and smell a
  dragon's tail (heroin?). I'm getting impatient.
  I need someone to contact in this strange
  place.
- I had to strip and kneel. Before that happened, I
  saw a bunch of fools on a train. They were beset

by magnetic force. I also saw a gypsy with a bro-
ken flag and a flashing ring, and he was telling
me that I wasn't dreaming.

- Some unidentified party's heart is as hard as
leather. Meanwhile, I need to get it together.
Give me a minute, here, señor.

- This whole damned place makes no sense. I'm
going to overturn the tables and disconnect the
cables. What are we waiting for? (Is this a state-
ment of suicidal intent?)

True Love Tends to Forget
Marital discord
Can't last if you love your spouse
Because love forgets.

"True Love Tends to Forget" is the moment in the
breakup at which one of the parties says "whatever" to
the most callous insults and transgressions because they
seem preferable to losing someone entirely. Hence the
recitation of various grievances, along with the assur-
ance that he can deal with all this.

We Better Talk This Over
Breakup suggestion:
Let's go our separate ways and
Act like we're OK.

For all the words that Dylan has devoted to missing lovers, you would think that a song like "We Better Talk This Over" would never appear. But people are complicated. If you assume that the unnamed departed woman of the yearning songs of the past few years is his ex-wife, then you get the other side here.

Where Are You Tonight? (Journey Through Dark Heat)

Woman and friends gone,
Parties and despair remain.
Can he persevere?

Sometimes it's hard to be a woman, spurning all the love of just one man. "Where Are You Tonight? (Journey Through Dark Heat)" reads like a bunch of neuroses pureed in a blender, with the results left out in the sun on an old paper plate with an empty bottle of cheap gin and half a pack of menthols.

- Train in rain, tears on letter, miss woman/want touch. She's drifting like satellite.
- Green smoky haze. She bathes in heat.
- Cherokee father says relationship not gonna last. (Echoes of "Tangled Up in Blue" here.)
- Angry woman got baby. Stripper on stage with clock and page of unwritten book. Where you

at tonight? (More echoes of "Tangled Up in Blue" here.)

- Truth: obscure, profound, pure. Can't live with it without risk of explosion. You and me agree sacrifice is the road.

- Marcel, St. John and I: strong dudes full of doubt. Couldn't share thoughts with my woman. She finds them out all the same.

- She puts flowers on shelf. I climb her hair. She feels my despair.

- Lion? In road. Demon? Escaped. Million dreams? Gone. Landscape? Being raped. Her beauty? Faded.

- Fight with my twin. We both lose. My maladies: horseplay and disease. Law doesn't notice.

- Your partners in crime want my money. Your new boyfriend is an addict. I kick him in the face. Didn't want to, but he leaves me no choice.

- Bite into root of forbidden fruit. Juice runs down my leg. (Hint: it's not juice.) I see your boss who doesn't know loss, too proud to beg.

- Dark room, diamond gloom. Path to the stars. You think this life is fun? Not so. Check these scars.

- Dawn. I arrive. I survive. Can't believe I alive. All good, but no you makes it not right. Where you at tonight?

Single: **Trouble in Mind**

Trouble in Mind
Your life is all wrong.
Satan's got your number, but
God has your answer.

"Trouble in Mind" is a "get thee behind me, Satan" song that was slated for inclusion on the 1979 album "Slow Train Coming." From what I understand, it's the first song that Dylan worked on for the album, but it didn't hold together well in the studio. In the end, it was released as the B-side to "Gotta Serve Somebody," the first song on the album, when it came out as a single. That's the only place it's ever appeared, so if you want a hard copy of it, you must buy the 45-rpm vinyl.

Temptation and sin, in six chapters:

- I need some self control. I could die from my behavior. Satan whispers, "Well, I don't want to bore ya, but when ya get tired of the Miss So-and-So, I got another woman for ya."
- Meaningless deeds might as well not have happened. It's what's on the inside that counts. You can't hide and be alone, God's always there. Ask Lot about that when his wife comes up in conversation.

- Satan is prince of the air. He'll "make you a law unto yourself" and he'll build a bird's nest in your hair. He'll let you focus on your own ambition and creations until you're no better than a servant to people in foreign lands.

- Got caught cheating, eh? You say, "Baby, everybody's doing it so I guess it can't be wrong." How does it feel to be a liar and trying to defend what you know you can't justify?

- Many men want to be the chiefs of their destinies. They can't relate to the idea of the kingdom of heaven on earth. They hurt themselves out of misery, value themselves based on their goods, their jobs and their wives.

- Life is short, but suffering is long. How much longer for me? "Satan will give you a little taste, then he'll move in with rapid speed. Lord, keep my blind side covered and see that I don't bleed."

Slow Train Coming

Gotta Serve Somebody; Precious Angel; I Believe in You; Slow Train; Gonna Change My Way of Thinking; Do Right to Me Baby (Do Unto Others); When You Gonna Wake Up; Man Gave Names to All the Animals; When He Returns

Gotta Serve Somebody

Whatever your job,
You can choose one manager:
The Devil or God.

"Gotta Serve Somebody" makes clear that whatever you choose to do in your life, you're serving one master or the other, and if it's not God or the Devil, it's someone else. The argument cuts across class, race and every other way we slice up humanity. Dylan won a Grammy Award for best male rock vocal performance for this song.

Things you could be, while still having to serve somebody:

- Ambassador to England.
- Ambassador to France.
- Gambler.
- Dancer.
- World heavyweight champion.
- Socialite with pearls.
- Rock 'n' roll addict.
- Drug dealer.

- User of women.
- Businessman.
- Thief.
- Doctor.
- Chief.
- State trooper.
- Young Turk.
- TV network executive.
- Rich.
- Poor.
- Blind.
- Lame.
- Expatriate or émigré.
- Incognito.
- Construction worker.
- Mansion inhabitant.
- Dome inhabitant.
- Gun runner.
- Tank seller.
- Landlord.
- Banker.
- Preacher.
- City councilman taking bribes.
- Barber.
- Mistress.
- Heir.
- Wearer of cotton.
- Wearer of silk.
- Drinker of whiskey.

- Drinker of milk.
- Eater of caviar.
- Eater of bread.
- Someone sleeping on the floor.
- Someone sleeping in a bed.

Precious Angel
Angel helps Bob see
The lie his life was before.
Bob asks for more light.

"Precious Angel" is the story of how a woman led him to spiritual salvation. It just so happens that he's attracted to her.

I Believe in You
Bob's credit in God
Debits him big-time on earth,
But he doesn't care.

"I Believe in You" is Christian slow-dance music. The song is Dylan's prayer to Jesus or God, a reminder that he doesn't mind if everyone thinks he's cracked because he became a Christian.

- Is his love real? They frown. They don't want him in town.
- They kick him out, say don't come back. He walks all alone.

- He believes in you through tears, laughter, separation, close to dawn and all the time.
- Keep him close by, don't let him drift. He's in your debt and doesn't mind though it costs him.
- He believes in you through different seasons and colors and despite being unpopular, and even if his friends leave him.
- He asks you to make sure he keeps feeling this way and aloof from the madding crowd. He's fine with the pain and rain as he will sustain.

Slow Train

Fools practice folly,
The country's going to hell.
Bob predicts trouble.

"Slow Train" begins with Dylan's exclamation that he feels low-down and disgusted, and he can't help but wonder what has happened to his friends. Are they lost or found? Soon they will have to understand that they'll have to leave behind everything that they hold dear because Judgment Day is on the way... or the apocalypse or some kind of reckoning, symbolized by a slow train that's just around the bend.

Gonna Change My Way of Thinking

There's a new playbook:
Do what God says, get yourself
A Christian woman.

"Gonna Change My Way of Thinking" is the Bob Dylan contender for best use of cowbell in a pop song. In fact, the band is on fire, just as it is for much of the album, Dylan's first of three born-again Christian-themed offerings. The song might not make you see the light, but it will make you feel the music. This song is a hard-edged blues with a great horn section and fine lead guitar playing from Mark Knopfler of Dire Straits.

Basic themes:

- Change way of thinking. Make new set of rules. Best foot forward. No more fools.
- Too much oppression. Sons marrying their mothers. Fathers turning daughters into whores.
- You're covered in stripes, stabbed by swords and blood flows everywhere.
- Sinner 1: does his own thing. Sinner 2: Tries to be cool. Both sinners: remember brass ring, forget golden rule.
- You can mislead people, but the only real authority is God.
- I have a Christian girlfriend. She fears God and she doesn't cost me too much money.
- Jesus said "Be ready, for you know not the hour in which I come." (Matthew 24:44, Matthew 25:13, Luke 12:40.) My favorite line of the song is here: "He said, he who is not for me is against me, just so you know where he's coming from."

- Heaven: no pain of birth. As Bob says, "The Lord created it, mister, about the same time he made the earth."

Do Right to Me Baby (Do Unto Others)
It's the Golden Rule.
Use it, don't lose it.
And don't touch me.

The song emphasizes adherence to the so-called Golden Rule, and comes with a list of things that Bob doesn't want to do, indicating that he believes in the Golden Rule too.

Things Bob doesn't want to do:

- Judge/Be judged.
- Touch/Be touched.
- Hurt/Be hurt.
- Treat people like dirt.
- Shoot/be shot.
- Buy/Be bought.
- Bury/Be buried.
- Marry/Be married.
- Burn/Be burned.
- Learn/Stuff that must be unlearned.
- Cheat/Be cheated.

- Defeat/Be defeated.
- Wink/Be winked at.
- Be used for a doormat.
- Confuse/Be confused.
- Amuse/Be amused.
- Betray/Be betrayed.
- Play/Be waylaid.
- Miss/Be missed.
- Put faith in people.

When You Gonna Wake Up
Wake up already.
God is not your errand boy.
You are his servant.

Here's some groovy religion. "When You Gonna Wake Up" is a variation on the old preacher question of when are you going to get right with God? Before it's too late?

Man Gave Names to All the Animals
Man names some creatures.
He's doing all right until
He discovers snakes.

Man scratches his head and cups his chin and looks at the beasts in the fields. Things go wrong at the end when he discovers the reptile of temptation.

Here are the rest:

- Bear: Growl, howl, furry paws, furry hair.
- Cow: Hill, grass filled, how now?
- Bull: Snort, horns not too short. Nothing he can't pull.
- Pig: muddy trail, curly tail, neither small nor big.
- Sheep: something man did meet, wool on back, hooves on feet. Eating on a mountainside steep.

When He Returns
God is coming soon
So throw out your day planner
And prepare for him.

"When He Returns" is a gorgeous piano song that closes the album. When I was younger, I cringed at the naked profession of faith in Jesus returning for Judgment Day, etc. Now I appreciate the intelligence that went into it, even if I can't profess the same faith.

- Iron hand (power of nations, for example) = no match for iron rod. Walls fall before God.
- "Truth is an arrow and the gate is narrow that it passes through." (A variation on a comment in the Gospel of Matthew in the Bible.) When can

he stop listening to lies and statements of fear? When, the end to loyalty and pride?

- Jesus knows what you're up to and what you want before you ask. The song ends on the old adage: man plans, God laughs.

Saved

A Satisfied Mind; Saved; Covenant Woman; What Can I Do for You? Solid Rock; Pressing On; In the Garden; Saving Grace; Are You Ready

A Satisfied Mind

I was a rich man.
Money I lost, faith I gained,
Now my mind's at ease.

This song by Joe "Red" Hays and Jack Rhodes is a rousing, if short introduction to the gospel barn burner and title track of the album, and it starts slowly, but the back-up singers add great tent-show color and tambourines. It's another one of those Christian songs that I don't mind listening to one bit.

Saved

Bob was almost gone,
But God's love and sacrifice
Saved him from hellfire.

"Saved" is one of Dylan's most electrifying born-again Christian songs. It comes in rumbling and stuttering along to a savage gospel beat. The album cut is forceful enough, but if you really want to get this song full throttle, it's worth searching online for his performance at Massey Hall in Toronto in April 1980. The band is out of this world.

Covenant Woman
Man with covenant
Seeks single woman with same.
Christians only, please.

"Covenant Woman" takes to new levels the idea that "the Lord will provide." Instead of sending three boats to save the man on the roof from the rising flood waters, God gets the credit for sending Bob a woman who's operating under the same theological principles that he does.

- She has a contract with God. She has a big reward coming in heaven and she shines like the morning star.
- He's going to stick with her, especially for praying to God on Bob's behalf.
- God's going to rebuild Bob, the broken cup, and he knows that this will happen because of the evidence that he produces saying that God sent him the covenant woman. If he did that, surely he will perform some heavier bodywork soon.
- Isn't she lucky to be stuck to Bob on this fitful and passing journey through life? Coincidence of coincidences: he has a covenant just like she does.

What Can I Do for You?
God, since you've saved Bob,
He wants to give something back.
What can he get you?

"What Can I Do for You?" is a recitation of favors that Jesus has done for him, so Dylan would like to know what he can do in return.

Solid Rock

This world is chaos.
Bob hangs on like a limpet
To faith's foundation.

"Solid Rock" uses the metaphor of the rock of salvation in contrast to the shifting ground and loyalties of living without God in your life. Dylan goes full-tilt gospel rock, which keeps the song from sliding into sentimental territory.

Pressing On

Predestination:
It's back in fashion again.
Bob is wearing it.

Predestination is a more complicated topic as it relates to Christian belief than what Dylan is aiming at. That being said, St. Augustine suggested that the desire for salvation hinges somewhat on God's awareness of it, and affects God's determination to "save" some people for heaven and damn others to hell. Dylan also refers to belief coming from within. What kind of sign do the people need, Dylan asks, "When what's lost has been found, what's to come has already been?"

- He's pressing on, pressing on, pressing on to the higher calling of God.
- Obstacles: People try to stop him, and say he should prove that God exists. What kind of sign would satisfy them, he wonders, if belief is on the inside and fate has been determined?
- Transcendence: Wipe the dust off your feet, don't look back. You lack for nothing. You might be tempted, and that's hard. Adam queered the entire situation for the rest of us when he messed around with Eve and the apple and the snake in the garden.

In the Garden
Despite evidence,
People failed to recognize
Jesus as special.

"In the Garden" is one of the more earnest songs on "Saved." It builds and builds in intensity, one plodding step at a time. The song is a series of rhetorical questions that tell you all about the losers who failed to believe that Jesus was the messiah. Songs like this are what gave Dylan a bad reputation among people who couldn't understand why he turned into such a sourpuss over Jesus.

Saving Grace
Being good is rough.
Bob finds it too tough sometimes.
But he has his faith.

What's better than one song on an album called "Saved" with the word "save" in it? Two songs. "Saving Grace" is another thank-you note to God and Jesus for showing him the error of his ways and setting him on the blessed – though difficult – path toward righteousness and salvation.

Witness!

- I should apologize to you for saving me.
- I've had my nine lives and by rights I should be dead. It's my faith that keeps me alive, and I must admit that I weep real tears for your saving grace.
- First death, then resurrection. Either way, I'm welcome wherever you will have me. For that, I place my confidence in the protection of God.
- Now, don't get me wrong. The devil's light shines bright, and that's easy to see, and searching for love is searching for vanity. I'll take saving grace instead.
- You can't fake peace. Take note of this, wicked people. The real road to salvation is the road to Calvary. It's not a happy or easy road, but that's the one you gotta take.

Are You Ready
Are you ready for
Jesus? Are you sure that he
Is ready for you?

I like "Are You Ready" because it's a grinding blues number. It has a good beat, the backup singers are great, but the "you have to choose, it's either heaven or hell for you" lyrics along with the implication that the singer knows the right answer to his question can make for tough going if you have a problem with religious music.

Shot of Love

Shot of Love; Heart of Mine; Property of Jesus; Lenny Bruce; Watered-Down Love; The Groom's Still Waiting at the Altar; Dead Man, Dead Man; In the Summertime; Trouble; Every Grain of Sand

Shot of Love

The world's against him.
Love's the drug he's thinking of.
Inoculate him.

"Shot of Love" is a good, solid rocker, and shows the beginnings of a move away from the overtly Christian themes of his previous two albums. What remains strong in this song as with some of his other Christian albums is an irritation with the persecution that he feels other people are visiting on him because of his beliefs.

Pains, prescriptions and proscriptions:

- What I don't need: heroin, turpentine, codeine and whiskey. What I do need: a shot of love.
- I'm disgusted with the kingdoms of the world. I need a Medicaid plan to deal with this. My disease won't hurt me, but it will kill me, just like the disciples who ran into trouble when the Romans decided that they had enough of Jesus.
- I don't need alibis for spending time with you (Him). I don't need books or movies.

- Why would I hate you? All you did was murder my father and rape his wife, abuse my babies, mock my god and humiliate my buddies.
- I don't want to be with any woman tonight. My enemy is threatening me, so what do you think I'm going to do? Just wait for him to show up?
- Why is the wind blowing so strongly tonight? I want to stay home. I called my home town and found out everybody moved away. And my conscience is bothering me.

Heart of Mine
Keep your love hidden
Or else that girl will hurt you.
Help me out here, heart.

He seems to be aware that the heart does what it wants, and doesn't usually listen to the rest of him.

Property of Jesus
Tease the Jesus freak.
Go ahead, but keep in mind:
His name is Dylan.

"Property of Jesus" is among the more sour-toned songs that the seemingly eternally persecuted Dylan wrote about his faith. That said, the song rocks, and the lyrics are sharp and smart.

Lenny Bruce

Lenny was the best.
He was funny and truthful,
And better than you.

This eulogy to comedian "Lenny Bruce" arrived 15 years after Bruce died. It's a ham-fisted ode that serves mostly to chide listeners over their inability to be as real and as human as Bruce.

Watered-Down Love

Bob knows what love is.
He also knows that you don't.
Don't dilute your love.

"Watered-Down Love" has one flaw, at least to me: it hectors some subject, unnamed. In that absence, it feels like he's hectoring the listener.

The right kind of love:

- Hopes and believes all things.
- Doesn't pull strings.
- Doesn't sneak into your room.
- Doesn't make false claims.
- Helps you instead of blaming you.
- Won't deceive or lead you to sin.
- Won't demand false confessions.
- Won't lead you astray.

- Won't hold you back or screw up your day.
- Won't pervert or corrupt you.
- Won't make you envious or suspicious.
- It's always on time and content, burning quietly forever.
- It's not proud or yearning.

The love that you want, though, is impure, drowned and watered down.

The Groom's Still Waiting at the Altar

Jesus kept waiting
At the altar while Claudette
Played runaway bride.

There are times when you can't help but love Bob Dylan's mind and appreciate the mystery of how it works:

"What can I say about Claudette?
Ain't seen her since January,
She could be respectably married or running a whorehouse in Buenos Aires."

That he manages to make the line fit in the verse is a testament to his quicksilver tongue. The song is one of Dylan's best attempts to merge pop music with the evening news. The timing was good too. This song came out as the newswires were swelling with reports of terrorism, dirty and less organized wars and the sophisticated coldness of the 1980s, when rock and roll singers started wearing suits and shades, and discovering that in the gleaming corridors of the 51st floor, the money can be made if you really want some more.

- We find him praying in the ghetto with his face in cement. There's a dying boxer, the massacre of innocents. A woman walking down the halls (away, presumably) as the walls fall apart.
- Pure at heart = arrest for robbery. Shyness = aloofness. Silence = snobbery. How people twist your motives/interpret your behavior. How mad it is to become what you never were meant to become?
- Claudette? Whatever I say can and will be used against me. I had to leave her as soon as she began to want me. God have mercy, I would have done anything for her if she weren't expecting it already.
- Do I have a fever, baby? If you want something, take it. You might not be able to keep it.
- Cities on fire, phones aren't working, fighting on the border, nuns and soldiers getting killed. Claudette could be up to one thing or the other.

Dead Man, Dead Man
Dead man (false prophet?)
Tempts a righteous Christian man
Who's not having it.

In "Dead Man, Dead Man," Dylan spends a few minutes pouring invective on someone whom he feels is plying him with false information and wants to take him to hell. Or is he talking to himself?

- Words from a reprobate mind, dying on the vine, can't separate the good from the bad. He can't stand it. Dead man has cobwebs in his mind and dust on his eyes.
- Satan has the bad man by the heel, the man has a bird's nest in his hair, he might not have love or faith. His head hurts, he curses God with every move.
- Glamour, lights and politics of sin. Bad man builds a ghetto, but ends up living in it himself. He pretends to be smart.
- He tries to overpower Bob with the doctrine or the gun. He wants to take Bob to hell, all the while wearing a tuxedo with a flower in the lapel.

In the Summertime
They went through bad times,
But teamwork proved to be a
Good investment plan.

- He was in her presence for a short time. They're not together now or else he would have not used the past tense.

- The sun never set, the trees were low, there was a nice, shining sea.
- Bob asks if she respects him for what he did do, didn't do, or trying to keep his mind hidden. Then he asks if he lost his mind when he tried to get rid of everything she sees.
- He has heart, she has blood. They can cut through anything.
- Then there's the warning before the flood "that set everybody free."
- Fools make mockery of sin, they want Bob's and his gal's loyalty. She's closer than everyone else, including his next of kin.
- Evil strangers meddled in his affairs. But no matter, things will be better.

Trouble
No embellishments.
Chorus says it all: Trouble,
Nothing but trouble.

"Trouble" is another one from the "grouchy Bob Dylan" files. Here's the kind of trouble he's talking about:

- In the city, on the farm.
- It resists the rabbit's foot and your good-luck charm.
- It's here and there and everywhere.
- Revolution won't stop it.

- "Drought and starvation, packaging of the soul. Persecution, execution, governments out of control."
- It's been here since the beginning of time, and if you take a peek at infinity, you'll see more of it.

Every Grain of Sand
Every so often,
I get a feeling that I'm
Part of a big plan.

Whatever universal mind is out there opened up the gates to Dylan's head, and out came the words. People have made all kinds of comparisons to William Blake, and have noted how this song isn't a "Dylan vs. the world" song like many of his other Christian songs. Instead, he sees himself (as we would ourselves) in the web of the universe, eternity and so on. He casts this realization of everything/everyone being numbered, therefore known to a creator and accounted for and classified, against the chaos of hurt feelings, broken people and various temptations that would lead someone without a sense of place in the universe to a bitter end.

- Time of confession, deepest need, pool of tears flooding every seed, dying voice, danger and the morals of despair.
- No dwelling on mistakes. Break a chain of events. Then the first of the great lyrics in the song: "In

the fury of the moment, I can see the Master's hand, in every leaf that trembles, in every grain of sand." I've asked before, just like many people, How does he *do* this?

- Flowers of indulgence, criminals, the sun beats on the steps of time, gives light, eases the pain of idleness, memory of decay.

- The doorway of temptation's angry flame. Every hair is numbered.

- Sorrow of the night, rags to riches, summer's dream, winter chill, loneliness fading, the broken mirror of innocence on forgotten faces.

- The last lines speak for themselves, and must be quoted in full. It's an amazing passage: "I am hanging in the balance of the reality of man. Like every sparrow falling, like every grain of sand."

Single: **<u>Angel Flying Too Close to the Ground</u>**

Angel Flying Too Close to the Ground
Touched by angel:
She makes a guy fall in love,
Then she flies away.

Willie Nelson wrote this. Dylan performed it during the sessions for the 1983 album "Infidels," then released it as the B-side to "Jokerman" and, I think, one or two other songs from that album, but only in international editions. I have a 45-rpm single of this that comes from Brazil. Angel falls to the ground, guy heals her, she flies away again because she is an angel. He provides the gentlest of guilt trips.

Infidels

Jokerman; Sweetheart Like You; Neighborhood Bully; License to Kill; Man of Peace; Union Sundown; I and I; Don't Fall Apart on Me Tonight

Jokerman

Man of influence
And power doesn't know how
To fix the world.

There's no way to say for sure what this song is about, though I hear a battle for the soul of humanity, waged between God and Satan. Unlike other Dylan songs along these lines, the dividing line between good and evil is harder to discern. It's better to sit back and enjoy the lush, beautiful music that this amazing band produced. The clues are there for anyone to work with:

- You: casting bread on the water in front of an iron-headed idol with glowing eyes. You were born with snakes in your hands in a hurricane. Freedom is close, but truth is far.
- You're the Jokerman, dancing to the tune of a nightingale in the moonlight.
- You're slippery, one step ahead of fate. You twist dreams and manipulate the people. A friend to martyrs and whores, you gaze on the rich man in the fires of hell.

- You were taught by the Old Testament, the law of the jungle and the law of the sea. Beautiful and classical.
- Assassins and priests seek the souls of the weak and the crippled. Street riots, protests, Molotov cocktails, stone throwing. Corrupt judges harming themselves. The sun's going down on goodness. (Plenty of references here to the Israel-Palestinian conflict.)
- "It's a shadowy world, skies are slippery gray." Moral compasses are thrown off by magnetic people. A woman gave birth to a prince. He'll dress in red, own the priests, save the orphans and make them children to a whore.

Sweetheart Like You
Sweetheart in a dump
Should be at home with her man
Instead of with Bob.

I've never quite understood what's going on in this song. I like the music, the band is hot, and the atmosphere works, but who is the singer to tell a woman where she should be rather than where she is? (Refrain: "What's a sweetheart like you doing in a dump like this?") If it's such a dump, what's he doing there? It reminds me of the great moment in Mel Brooks's 1968 movie "The Producers" when the great con man/ladies' man and faded Broadway producer Max Bialystock tries to lighten up the uptight accountant

Leo Bloom. Max takes Leo out for a day in Manhattan, and they end up in the boat pond in Central Park, sitting on a rowboat with their pant legs rolled up and dangling their feet in the water. Leo is nervous, and says something like, "What if someone from the office should see me?" Max replies: "And they'd see you. And you'd see them. And what are they not doing in the office?"

"Got to be an important person to be in here, honey, got to have done some evil deed." That line plays on the theme of reincarnation. I was going to say that perhaps the sweetheart in question was Jesus, and that Dylan was singing to a savior with flaws, but I think this sweetheart is some more ethereal figure who is supposed to remain deliberately obscure.

Unrelated to anything, I love the working title of this song when they were rehearsing in the studio: "By the Way, That's a Cute Hat."

Neighborhood Bully
They call Israel
A neighborhood bully, but
It's not the bad guy.

After his time spent making Christian music, it was interesting to see him embrace, to some extent, his Jewish origins, particularly with this song about Israel's attempts to defend itself against hostile neighbors while being labeled the bad guy. The shot of Dylan in Jerusalem on the album's inner sleeve reinforces the notion that Dylan was looking elsewhere besides the cross for inspiration.

License to Kill
Mankind hurts the earth.
Space travel, lies and deceit
Will destroy us all.

Dylan inveighs against the space race, the mistreatment of well-meaning people, world destruction, lies and the usual things that were on his mind at the time.

Man of Peace
Want to spot Satan?
Look for the best guy around.
It's probably him.

Attributes and avatars of Satan:

- The Führer.
- Local priest.
- Man of peace.
- Gift of gab.
- Harmonious tongue.
- Knows all the love songs.
- Hands full of grease. (Greasing palms.)

- First he's in the background, then he's in the front.
- He always looks like he's on a rabbit hunt.
- The chief of police can't see through him.
- He always shows up when you're looking for sunlight and a solution to your troubles.
- You'd never suspect it was Satan standing next to you in a crowd.
- Fascinating.
- Dull.
- Rides down Niagara Falls in a barrel made of your skull.
- He's a cook.
- He's a humanitarian.
- He's a philanthropist.
- He knows how to touch you and kiss you.
- He has the tender touch of the beast.
- He howls like a wolf and crawls like a snake.
- He uproots old trees.
- He specializes in coming after single people, so you had better get married.

Union Sundown
Capitalism
Kills jobs here and makes slaves there.
So much for unions.

Capitalism kills American jobs, and the unions aren't helping. That's the message. Where Bob's stuff comes from now that globalization is happening:

Flashlight: Singapore.
Tablecloth: Malaysia.
Belt buckle: the Amazon.
Shirt: the Philippines.
Chevrolet: Argentina.
Silk dress: Hong Kong.
Pearls: Japan.
Dog collar: India.
Flower pot: Pakistan.
Furniture: Brazil.

I and I
Bob leaves girl sleeping,
Doesn't want talk, takes a walk,
Ponders truth, justice.

"I and I" features reggae and dub masters Sly & Robbie on drum and bass. The term is Rastafarian, referring to the oneness of God and humans, and how each is in the other. Here's a look at how Dylan deploys this in his song:

- Bob finally gets a new woman to spend the night with him. It's been a while. She's pretty cool, and must have been married to a king in her previous life. Maybe a Biblical king.
- He goes for a walk and leaves her sleeping because she'll just want to talk and he feels like being quiet.

- Once Bob took a path less traveled, where the slow win. It's path for people who know the truth. He needed a stranger to show this to him, as well as how to look at the Hammurabi code of "eye for an eye and tooth for a tooth" that is inherent to the concept of justice.
- Two men sit on a train platform. He walks by them. He remembers the woman sleeping in his bed. He thinks the world could end right now.
- The next day: He's still walking, this time through a particularly dark stretch of road. He notes that someone else is speaking with his mouth while he listens to his heart, and that "I've made shoes for everyone, even you, while I still go barefoot."

Don't Fall Apart on Me Tonight

"Don't leave me," he says.
"We can work things out. Just keep
Your shit together."

The song comes from that time in the 80s when Dylan was finding new ways to lecture women instead of the old way of ruing their departure and pouring scorn on them. The band is first-rate: Mark Knopfler and Alan Clark from Dire Straits, Sly & Robbie, and Mick Taylor from the Rolling Stones.

Empire Burlesque

Tight Connection to My Heart (Has Anybody Seen My Love); Seeing the Real You at Last; I'll Remember You; Clean Cut Kid; Never Gonna Be the Same Again; Trust Yourself; Emotionally Yours; When the Night Comes Falling From the Sky; Something's Burning, Baby; Dark Eyes

Tight Connection to My Heart (Has Anybody Seen My Love)

Looking for my love,
I stumble on a film noir
And try to escape.

This is one of my Dylan soft spots. It's a strange song about strange goings-on surrounding a woman with whom the singer is no longer involved. It's a reworking of a 1983 song that he recorded called "Someone's Got a Hold of My Heart," and as essayist Jonathan Lethem points, out, "Tight Connection" replaces a number of the more heartfelt lines that appeared in the earlier version with hardboiled lines from Humphrey Bogart movies as well as some other films, including one featuring Gary Cooper. I don't know why he did it, and many people say that it doesn't work. I think it does. It works even better when you watch the MTV video for the song. It takes place in Tokyo, where Dylan is facing trouble with the police over a possible murder. Two mysterious women who might be murderers vie for him, three Japanese girls sing karaoke in a bar with Dylan's voice emanating from their mouths, an American woman sings in a different bar, and a fight between some folks on a Japan street breaks out. It makes no sense that I can see, but it's fun. Director Paul Schrader (the writer of "Taxi Driver" and director of "Autofocus") hated the experience so much that he said he would never make another music video.

Seeing the Real You at Last

Bob has had enough.
A little trouble is fine
But you were too much.

If there's one thing we know about the time that Dylan wrote the songs for "Empire Burlesque," he seems to have spent plenty of it watching movies. "Seeing the Real You at Last," which is the second song on the album, is made up of a whole bunch of movie lines. I suppose that it could be about a woman, but it could just as easily be about God and religion.

- I risked everything for you and rose above some unfortunate circumstances too.
- I went through long and sleepless nights for you, but only now am I seeing who you really are.

I'll Remember You

He'll remember her
Even though she left because
He did things his way.

Song fit for a high-school slow dance.

- You're the best so I'll remember you and only you.
- I'll remember you when the roses and I die.
- We shared intimate moments, like that time you and I wept together while we were getting rained on.
- I'll remember you when the wind blows through the pine trees.

Clean Cut Kid
Vietnam victim
Leaves the service. Once sweetheart,
He's now a killer.

This up-tempo song is one of Dylan's attempts at social commentary on the scars of war that veterans suffer and how some Vietnam veterans in particular couldn't cope with life after they came home. From being raised in the Eisenhower-era security blanket of American supremacy and, in its way, post-war innocence, then to the jungle, then back into society without much more than a thank you, and so on and so on, "Clean Cut Kid" is part of the narrative of films and art at the time that blamed the U.S. government and society for failing to support its troops. I'm thinking of movies like "The Deer Hunter," "Coming Home" and later, "Born on the Fourth of July." The trouble with this song is that the lyrics are goofy, and the production of the song hovers in a void of big 80's rock, doot-doot-style vocal group backup singing and outrage that doesn't sound all that outraged. Burger King? Peter O'Toole? Rolls-Royce in a swimming pool? Tennis star? Boxing gloves? The trouble with tragedy is that it can turn into comedy.

Never Gonna Be the Same Again
Woman changes man,
And he stays changed even when
She breaks up with him.

"Never Gonna Be the Same Again" is an unfairly ignored song. The backup singers add punch, particularly at the fade as they and Dylan improvise on the vocals – "You're too hot, darlin'," "Come on, darlin'" etc. It fairly swings as it makes it exit.

Trust Yourself
Don't trust me, trust you.
Don't trust beauty or "the truth."
Don't trust. Period.

After three years of lectures about getting right with God and Jesus to avoid eternal damnation, Dylan used "Empire Burlesque" to tell people two things:

- Trust yourself.
- Don't trust anyone, including me.

Emotionally Yours
I'm unraveling
While traveling, but am yours
Emotionally.

- Find me remind me. (My origins.)
- Show me you know me. (Tell me you're the one, regardless of the truth.)
- I'm learning you're yearning. (See behind closed doors, emotionally yours.)
- Rock me lock me. (In your heart's shadows.)
- Teach me reach me. (Start playing the music.)
- I might be making this up. (This thing about living for you.)
- You wiped my entire hard drive when we met. You re-imaged my computer.
- This might be crazy.
- Shake me take me. (That's all I need.)
- Hold me help me. (I have arms, they're wide open.)
- Unraveling traveling. (Even when traveling overseas.)

When the Night Comes Falling From the Sky
You'll need him at dusk.
Until then, you'll be mostly
Wasting all your time.

Some people mock this song for its dance-club style mix thanks to producer Arthur Baker. It's true that the style doesn't fit the song, and it's generally true that the style doesn't fit Dylan at all. But even in an alternate arrangement released on the Bootleg Series, I find this song a little too diffuse to enjoy. It's a variation on the theme of Dylan addressing a former lover for whom he still has feelings, but he's been burned enough to know better that the person he's missing has made him feel bad too. He meanwhile predicts that all sorts of things will happen when the night comes, most of them involving her coming around to him in some way, whether he's willing to give or not.

- He's returning. You have smoke in your eye because you've been burning his letters.
- He might love you or you might love him. Doesn't matter.
- You're hurting, but you managed to escape disaster.
- He doesn't have all the answers. He wouldn't lie to you and say he did.
- He thinks you've been seeing somebody, though you've not said so.
- Some people have been victims of darkness and the lust for money. Not us.
- He sees his reflection in your tears. He doesn't want to be starving for affection, nor does he want to drown in someone else's wine.
- He'll always remember "that icy wind that's howling in your eye." You might find him in the wasteland of your mind.

- He wrote you a letter as you were "gambling" for support. It was cold that day so you burned the letter. He has a better memory these days so he'll remember this about you.
- He asks for freedom and you'll give it. If not, he'll take it anyway.

Something's Burning, Baby
I suspect we're through.
Having said that, I'm still here
If you should want me.

"Something's Burning, Baby" slipped out of view shortly after it appeared. It's not bad.

What's burning:

- Something's burning, could it be smoke in her hair? Is she still his friend? Or is the love she has for him turning blind?
- He's looking for her missing file. He wants to know what's going on with her. Why is the love light no longer in her eyes?
- Is he no longer part of her plan? What happened? Something clearly has changed.
- He thinks another guy is on her mind.
- This stage of their relationship: charity is supposed to cover up sins. But where is she? And why does she just stare into the distance?

- She can't live by bread alone or roll back the stone from the tomb all by herself.
- She shouldn't just fade away without comment.
- She's giving him the Mexico City blues.
- When she's ready to reconsider, if she's ready to reconsider, she should call him. "I believe in the impossible, you know that I do."

Dark Eyes
Life goes on outside
While Bob thinks about the dead
And distressed people.

"Dark Eyes" is one of the most perplexing songs that Dylan has written, one that I find as resistant to analysis and scrutiny as a carbon cube or some kind of diamond. You can see through it from one side to the other, but it yields nothing. It's all the more interesting for being the only "unproduced" song on the album. A short closer to an album full of synthesizers, drums, overdubs and big '80s-style-sounding rock bands, "Dark Eyes" is spare and flat, just Dylan with his guitar and harmonica. He has told stories about being inspired to write the song by seeing a strung-out young woman in a hotel hallway in the middle of the night, and I suppose that's as good a starting point as any, but the song in four short verses spins through a universe of its own.

- Gentlemen talking, moon on the riverside. They're drinking, but it's time for him to leave. He lives in a world where life and death are memorized, the earth is strung with lover's pearls and he sees dark eyes.
- Cock crows, soldier prays at dawn, mother misses a child gone wandering, while "nature's beast" fears the rise of the dead who march to a drumbeat.
- He hears that revenge is sweet, and maybe that's true, but he doesn't believe it because their game means "beauty goes unrecognized."
- French girl in paradise, drunkard at the wheel. Hunger pays a heavy price to falling gods of speed and steel. Time short, days sweet, passion rules the arrow that flies. (Where did he get such a great line?)

Selections from **Biograph**

I'll Keep It With Mine; Percy's Song; Jet Pilot; Lay Down Your Weary Tune; Abandoned Love; Caribbean Wind; Up to Me; Baby, I'm in the Mood for You; I Wanna Be Your Lover

(Note: This is a collection of greatest hits, alternate versions and unreleased songs. Only the latter category is included here.)

I'll Keep It With Mine

You have many fans
Eager to earn your favors.
Ignore them, choose me.

"I'll Keep It With Mine" saw its first release on a Judy Collins single in 1965, and then on Nico's 1967 debut album. Dylan wrote the song in 1964 as a demo for the M. Witmark & Sons publishing company. You can find that version on the ninth volume of the Bootleg Series. He also tried recording it for the 1965 album "Bringing It All Back Home," but left it off. That version is available on this album. A version for the "Blonde on Blonde" album in 1966 appeared on volume 1 of the Bootleg series in 1991. There are other versions too.

As for the song, Bob is lecturing a woman on what's good for her:

- She searches for what's not lost.

- He notes people will help her and be kind, but he might be able to save her some time by being her main man.
- He might seem odd to you because he loves you for what you're not.
- Again, people *might* try to help you, but he's a better bet for the job.
- Separately, there's a train leaving at 10:30, but it will be back tomorrow.

Percy's Song
Bob implores the judge
Who sentenced his guilty friend.
The judge says, "Tough shit."

"Percy's Song" is about a friend of the singer involved in a fatal car crash who is sentenced to 99 years in prison. Dylan asks the judge to reconsider what he considers an overly harsh sentence. The judge is having none of it, and leaves the singer to muse about the cruel rain and the wind.

The song was recorded in 1963.

Jet Pilot
Jet pilot got the
Attention of the boys, but
She's really a man.

Forty-nine seconds of silly from sessions in 1965.

Lay Down Your Weary Tune
Though your song be good,
Nature can do it better,
Be quiet... listen...

"Lay Down Your Weary Tune" was recorded in 1963 for the album "The Times They Are a-Changin'," but was left off the final cut. Rather than striving for the surreal, he pursues a sound of natural beauty, to use Neil Young's term from the "Harvest Moon" album, which he tries to convey with guitar and voice. I hear the sound of waterfalls and wind in the trees, waves on the beach and the rhythms of the universe, especially in Dylan's use of alliteration and the pairing of words that don't necessarily go together – the "strength of strings," for example. It makes me think a little of William Wordsworth, or even Henry Wadsworth Longfellow conjuring up Hiawatha on the Gitche Gumee.

Abandoned Love
We are breaking up.
Not sure who's responsible.
Let's have sex again.

This song, say the Dylan scholars, relates to his breakup with his wife Sara. Regardless of whether that's true, let's leave aside the biographical particulars and concentrate on the lyrics. The singer is ready to leave, though it might be possible that it's the woman who's doing the leaving. One thing is certain: he wants a little more loving before he departs into the chasm of melancholy.

Caribbean Wind
Tropical leftist
Embarks on doomed romance with
Bob, preaching gospel.

This 1981 song didn't make the final cut of "Shot of Love." "Caribbean Wind" is another one of those Dylan songs that is heavy on the imagery and symbolism, sometimes at the cost of clarity and plot. Where do I get that the woman was a leftist? I don't know. I concluded that it was unlikely that she and her brothers would be getting shot at in the jungle by gunmen on an embassy roof in the late 1970's if they weren't leftists, particularly if the back story takes place in Brazil, as the lyrics suggest. In brief:

- She's the rose of Sharon from paradise lost, from a seven-hilled city near a cross. (Rio de Janeiro? Rome?) He's playing a concert and preaching about Jesus in Miami in a theater of "divine comedy." She tells him her brothers were killed in a jungle by a guy dancing on the roof of an embassy.
- Did she use him? It's possible.
- Chorus: Caribbean winds blow from Nassau to Mexico, fanning flames in the furnace of desire.

Ships of liberty on iron waves are bold and free, but apparently are bringing everything that's close to Bob close to the fire.

- She says a mutual friend has their best interests in mind, but it seems that however well connected he is, she has him in a trap because he's in her debt for some reason.

- They meet in a church on a hot day. She tells him he can't do something about whatever he's thinking.

- Bob's in Atlantic City. It's cold out. He hears someone calling him "daddy," but there's no one there. The news reports are full of stories about famines and earthquakes.

- He wonders whether he should have married her.

Up to Me
Why I'm single now:
True to me or true to you?
I made a hard choice.

"Up to Me" is undoubtedly an achievement, but Dylan left it off the 1975 album "Blood on the Tracks," an album that underwent significant revision at Dylan's behest just before its release. Given the themes of abandonment and divorce, and the broken hearts beating at the center, it's not surprising that Dylan's brother, after hearing some of the stark songs that he recorded in New York City, suggested that he lighten up the tone if he wanted to sell some records. "Up to Me" didn't make it at all. While it's a significant, lovely piece of work, it's full of words. I know that this should be a good thing, and on a song like "Idiot Wind," the words are on fire and they move the story along. On this one, they are more static. There are events unspoken, but you get the impression that this event has set everybody on a solo course. Bad things happen to good people, love fades, the singer is forced to accept responsibility that he seems to feel is more than his share.

- Bad to worse. Death on the trail. Someone has to say what they want in this thing of ours. Guess it's gonna be me.
- I would have died if I'd lived my life the way other people wanted me to live it.
- I smiled once in 14 months and it was an accident. Train's leaving as the orchids bloom. My one good shirt smells like perfume. I'm looking for you.
- You betrayed me with your touch. I unlocked your heart.
- I watched you go hang out with a bunch of men all night long.
- When I worked in the Post Office, I took your picture down from the wall near my cage to protect your identity. (Sounds like a general judgment on his career and ability to manage family life until that time.)
- It's amazing how much in love you can fall with someone. You must resist it.

- The Sermon on the Mount sure is complicated. So is biting off more than you can chew.
- Side story: Dupree comes to the Thunderbird Cafe, pimping. Crystal wants to talk to him. I can't bear it.
- I left a note for Estelle. You thought there was something going on there, but there wasn't.
- Life's a stage and a dream. Boys, that woman I'm with, I'm not really with. Try your luck.
- We might be through, but remember that song I played for you? Only I could play it.

Baby, I'm in the Mood for You
I want you so bad
Sometimes. Other times I want
To do other things.

This is a song from 1962 that was left off "The Freewheelin' Bob Dylan." The situation is pretty simple: There are a number of things that Bob finds himself in the mood for, but then again, as he says, sometimes he's in the mood for you.

Here is the unexpurgated list of things for which Bob is in the mood at one time or another:

- Leave lonesome home.
- Hear milk cow moan.
- Hit highway road.

- You.
- Overflowin' fill.
- Final will.
- Walkin' hill.
- You.
- Lay down, die.
- Climb up to sky.
- Laugh until cry.
- You.
- Sleep in pony's stall.
- Nothin' at all.
- Fly like cannonball.
- You.
- Back up against wall.
- Run till have to crawl.
- Nothin' at all.
- You.
- Change house around.
- Change this here town.
- Change world around.
- You.

I Wanna Be Your Lover
Rasputin and friends
Get up to no good. Not Bob,
He wants your loving.

Very little of this 1965 song matters. The key is the chorus:

"I wanna be your lover, baby
I don't wanna be hers, I wanna be yours."

It's a riff on the Beatles song "I Wanna Be Your Man."

The rest is fake symbolism:

- Rainman/magic wand.
- Judge: "Mona can't have no bond." (She cries, Rainman leaves as Wolfman.)
- Undertaker/midnight suit addresses masked man: "Ain't you cute?"
- Masked man feels the same way about the undertaker.
- Jumpin' Judy reaches maximum altitude.
- Rasputin touches her head and dies.
- Phaedra has a looking glass. She faints on the grass because she's obvious (and you are not).

Knocked Out Loaded

You Wanna Ramble; They Killed Him; Driftin' Too Far From Shore; Precious Memories; Maybe Someday; Brownsville Girl; Got My Mind Made Up; Under Your Spell

You Wanna Ramble

Leave me. It's your life.
Oh, if you need someone killed,
I know what it costs.

"You Wanna Ramble" starts off well, but team Dylan sacrificed that momentum on the next song, "They Killed Him." This song, based on Little Junior Parker's "I Wanna Ramble," is short and cryptic:

- Baby, I know where you have been and who you are. You want to ramble.
- The night is quiet and still. Did you know that it costs only $1,500 to have anyone killed?
- Whatever happens to you next is up to you, not to me.

They Killed Him

Every time someone
Tries to make the world better,
Somebody kills them.

This cover of Kris Kristofferson's song is hard to love. I don't mind the trite melody line played out on a tinny keyboard, nor do I fault the effort of the musicians. It's the high-fructose corn syrup of the children's choir singing this song of praise to history's martyrs that does it in.

Driftin' Too Far From Shore
She left by surprise.
Bob writes her off as a loss,
But this still grieves him.

"No gentleman likes making love to a servant, especially when he's in his father's house." The Dylan forensics team down at the station might spend years working on that line. The song is a super-charged '80s rocker – big drums, small drum machines, artificial synthesizers, big backup vocals, a bit of stadium delivery in Dylan's voice as he dismisses another lover who wasn't up to his standards, even though he misses her.

Precious Memories
Youthful memories
Overcome an older man.
They make him happy.

It's easy to be cynical about granddaddy religious songs such as these, but I admit that "Precious Memories" is an affecting tune. I'm just not at all sure that it's affecting when listening to Dylan's version, which he converted to reggae and subjected to the '80s production process. The song is a hymn of sorts, written by Tennessean J.B.F.

Wright in 1925. It's also been covered by, among others, Rosetta Tharpe, Johnny Cash, Jim Reeves and J.J. Cale.

Maybe Someday

Someday you'll know I
Was the man for you, but I'm
Not holding my breath.

This song is conventional enough, but it sounds like the producer mixed Dylan's vocal track, that of the backup singers and those of all the instruments from different sessions. It's another bitter goodbye to a woman who failed to take their relationship seriously. Dylan proposes that maybe someday she'll know why she was wrong and why he was so good. He salts the song with religion too, but not enough to offend the casual listener. I like the "uh-huh-uh" of the backup singers at the end. The throwaway line about how he was in San Francisco for a party once gets stuck in my head.

Brownsville Girl

Gregory Peck films
Haunt man who yearns for a girl
And dates another.

Everything about this song suggests that the end product should be ridiculous, but it isn't. "Brownsville Girl," co-written with actor/playwright Sam Shepard, is an absurd tale that is nearly impossible to relate. It's over the top, and clocks in at 11 minutes. The plot jumps all over the place. The verses emphasize talking over singing. The backup girls sound like they just came from a Pink Floyd concert. There are more references to Gregory Peck than any song should have. And it's a masterpiece. Here is the blow-by-blow of this wacky, if melancholy tale of love, loss and confused memories in the dusty old Southwest:

- Guy remembers going to see "The Gunfighter," a western with Gregory Peck. A young man shoots the old gunfighter, and the town wants to hang him.
- The marshal beats the kid, but Peck says let him go because, in words that chill to the bone, "I want him to feel what it's like to every moment face his death."
- Bob reminisces about the movie as he misses his gal.
- She showed up on the painted desert in platform heels and driving a beaten-up Ford.
- They drive to San Antonio. They sleep together. She goes to Mexico and never comes back. He doesn't chase her because he fears having his head blown off.
- Now he's in a car with another woman, but the first woman's soul is with them and she haunts them.
- They cross the Texas panhandle for Amarillo. They arrive at Henry Porter's wrecking yard

where his wife Ruby says Henry's not in, but they can hang around for a while. She's washing clothes.

- Times are tough and she's thinking of leaving. In the classic ridiculous line of the song, she says, "Even the swap meets around here are getting pretty corrupt."

- Ruby asks where Bob and his gal are going. They say they're going anywhere until the car falls apart. Ruby says some babies never learn.

- Bob thinks about the Gregory Peck movie again, and discovers that he's in the film.

- Either in real life or in the film, Bob is crossing the street when armed men looking for someone in a pompadour take shots at him. In another classically ridiculous line, he says, "I didn't know whether to duck or run so I ran," which I think is a quote from a film, but I don't remember which. He hears that they have the man cornered in a churchyard. Is he the man?

- The second woman sees Bob's picture in the Corpus Christi newspaper with the words "man with no alibi" written in the caption. She lies to the judge to get him off, whatever crime it is that he's supposed to have committed.

- Bob's never been the kind of guy who likes to trespass, but sometimes he can't help it. He needs an original thought. He feels OK, but that's not saying much.

- He's in line to see a Gregory Peck film. Not "The Gunfighter," but a new one. He doesn't know the name, but he'd watch Peck in anything so he stands in line.
- Things don't turn out as planned. We learn that Henry Porter's name wasn't Henry Porter. Bob remembers being with the first woman, or maybe the second one, in the French Quarter in New Orleans.
- He ruminates on how people who suffer together have more in common than people who are most content, most likely taking a page from Leo Tolstoy's opening lines of "Anna Karenina."

He remembers, again, seeing "The Gunfighter" with Gregory Peck, and concludes with the goose-bump line, "Seems like a long time ago, long before the stars were torn down."

Got My Mind Made Up
You used me all up.
I'm off to Libya, or
Wherever you aren't.

The obscure song "Got My Mind Made Up" brings great attitude courtesy of Tom Petty and the Heartbreakers, but the song curdles milk. Bob complains about a woman whom he helped and who in turn used him and quite probably abandoned him. Now he's done with her and off to Libya to meet a man who's been living in an oil refinery for three years. We're not clear on Bob's plans.

Under Your Spell
Incompatible:
They seem to miss each other,
But remain apart.

They're playing our song! I never expected a song to be written by Dylan with soft ballad lyricist Carole Bayer Sager, but one exists. It's one of the first of the "later-phase" Dylan songs dealing with unrequited love for a woman long gone. You know what Carole says: Nobody Does It Better.

- He was knocked out loaded when he noticed you. What a story!
- You know what he's like, and you know where to find him.
- "I'll call you tomorrow if there's phones where I am, baby, caught between heaven and hell."
- You'll never get rid of him.
- It's 4 a.m. and he's looking at your picture and thinking of things that you said.
- Wherever you go, you break someone's heart. You're too hot to handle.
- He's not leaving without a kiss goodbye.
- He might die two feet from your well.

Down in the Groove

Let's Stick Together; When Did You Leave Heaven?; Sally Sue Brown; Death Is Not the End; Had a Dream About You, Baby; Ugliest Girl in the World; Silvio; Ninety Miles an Hour (Down a Dead End Street); Shenandoah; Rank Strangers to Me

Let's Stick Together

We should not split up.
We made a promise, and we
Have a little child.

Wilbert Harrison failed to chart with this single when he released it in 1962. He changed it to "Let's Work Together," issued it again in 1969 and it became a hit. It's not hard to see why. It's simple, it moves and it's fun. Bryan Ferry scored his highest-charting single with this song in 1976 on the album of the same name, and featured an incredibly strange vocal interlude from Jerry Hall. Dylan's version offers a ramshackle good time.

- Marriage is a sacred rite. Why reverse it? We made a vow.
- You never miss your water until your well runs dry. I'm the water.
- Stay with me, if not for my sake, then at least for the sake of our child.

When Did You Leave Heaven?
That you left heaven
At all is a big surprise.
Kiss me, you angel.

"When Did You Leave Heaven?" is a song by Richard Whiting and Walter Bullock that appeared in the 1936 movie "Sing, Baby, Sing." It became something of a standard, and was nominated for an Academy Award. (Whiting, incidentally, wrote the standards "Hooray for Hollywood" – which you can hear at the end of Robert Altman's movie "The Long Goodbye" – as well as "Ain't We Got Fun?" and "On the Good Ship Lollipop.") You can find versions of this song by Big Bill Broonzy, Nancy Wilson, Louis Armstrong, Jimmy Scott and others.

Sally Sue Brown
Sally's dangerous.
She's too hot for all you guys.
Let me handle her.

Here's the rundown on Brown:

- She's back in town, so boys, run for cover or else you will be broken-hearted lovers.
- She looks hot in her tight skirt and with her big bright eyes, but watch out, she tells lies.

- I don't care what she's been up to, I'm "goin' south" and doing it all again. I'd prefer to have my heart broken than pass up a chance to get with Sally Sue Brown.
- I'm going to be a fool for that girl and lay at the foot of her bed like a dog.

Death Is Not the End
Things might suck now, but
Don't worry; they'll suck much more
After you are dead.

I stole the idea for this haiku from Nick Cave. He and the Bad Seeds covered the song on their 1996 album "Murder Ballads," a smorgasbord of violence, death and gore. Cave at one time suggested that the song, which sounds like a reassurance of deliverance after life in a painful world, could be read to suggest that the vale of tears is infinite because, as Dylan tells us in each verse after describing something awful, "Death is not the end." I had to laugh when I heard that, and the more I thought about it, I'm not sure that Dylan didn't mean it that way when he released it.

Here are the things that should reassure or horrify you when you discover that death is not the end:

- Sadness, loneliness, no friends, everything sacred broken and can't be mended.

- Crossroads you can't comprehend, dreams vanished, unknown surprises around the bend.
- Storm clouds, heavy rains, no one to comfort you, no one to lend a hand.
- Cities on fire with the burning flesh of men, a lack of law-abiding citizens.

Had a Dream About You, Baby
Bob dreams of a girl
He picks up. They go dancing,
Then they get coffee.

As far as dreams go, "Had a Dream About You, Baby" sounds like a good one.

- She has a strange rhythm when she walks. She makes him nervous when she talks.
- She says to take her to the nearest town.
- They go dancing. The joint, as expected, is "jumpin'."
- Later, she kisses him in the coffee shop. He gets nervous.
- She's wearing a rag on her head and is wearing a dress of fire-engine red.

Ugliest Girl in the World
Bob likes 'em ugly,
As the song's title attests.
They like him as well.

The music's pretty good, but the song "Ugliest Girl in the World" surely represents some kind of low point for Dylan. Main points: she's superlatively ugly, and "I'm in love with the ugliest girl in the world." The lyrics, I think, are by Robert Hunter of Grateful Dead fame.

Qualities:

- Hook in her nose.
- Unibrow.
- Old clothes.
- Stutters.
- Hops.
- Flat feet.
- Knock knees.
- Knuckles crack.
- Snores in bed.
- Five-inch smile.
- Sweet breath.
- Prizefighter nose.
- Cauliflower ears.
- Run in her hose.

Why she's a catch:

- She has a way of calling his name that drives him crazy.
- Weird sense of humor that's all her own.
- She cheers him up.

Silvio
Power and pleasure
Are tempered by pain and loss.
Take them as they come.

I don't know why this one doesn't work for me, but along with "Ugliest Girl in the World," it lowers the quality of a shaky album. Still, it became a big fan favorite, in no small part, I suspect, because of the inclusion of members of the Grateful Dead on backup vocals. I'm not saying that this song, which Dylan wrote with Hunter, is bad. It has a nice groove and chugs along, but I can't stand those doo-doo-doo Dead backup vocals. I also find the lyrics muddy in meaning, particularly the pot-fueled back-porch joint-rolling existentialism which you hear from time to time in Dead land.

The smoke-rings of their minds:

- Stake future on a hell of a past. Tomorrow could be the last day. I'm not complaining about what I have. Everybody's seen better times, so who am I to whine?
- FYI Silvio: you can't buy back your joie de vivre with silver and gold. The narrator says he has to leave and go find something "only dead men know."
- Don't throw me any bones. I'm just an old weevil looking for a home. And as the old Irish drinking

song goes, "If you don't like it, you can leave me alone."

- I can summon rain and make it go away with the snap of my fingers. I can make you feel good too. I even can charm the whistle of a train.
- I give and take as much as I want. I want you, but when you want to leave, nobody will stop you.
- "You give something up for everything you gain. Since every pleasure's got an edge of pain, pay for your ticket and don't complain." The philosophical spice of life that comes along with doo-rags, dime-bags and freshman orientation name-tags.
- I'm going to the valley and I will sing my song. I'll let the echo decide if it sucks or not.

Ninety Miles an Hour (Down a Dead End Street)
They're with others, but
Hook up after a party.
They go past first base.

This is about a crash of the heart, not a literal crash. Country singer Hank Snow wrote this song with country pianist Don Robertson.

- They leave a party, they kiss for fun, but things get hot and they move to more passionate activities.

- They're both with other people, so what they're doing is crazy, like riding a motorcycle with the devil and going 90 miles an hour down a dead-end street.
- It's too late to heed the warnings.
- She can never be his, but they're going for it anyway.
- Disaster is coming.

Shenandoah
Wandering trader
Falls for an Indian girl.
Then he wanders off.

"Shenandoah" is a lovely, minimal precursor to the kind of modern roots country and Americana music that NPR listeners like, and Dylan adds to that kind of woodsy groove the backup singers who give the song a nice push. The song apparently comes from the early 19th century. It's about the Indian chief Shenandoah, or Oskanondonha, as well as his beautiful daughter, whom a trader in a canoe wants to marry, but ends up leaving.

Rank Strangers to Me
Man goes home again.
Everyone he knows has gone.
The rest are strangers.

Drawing on the same spirit that Thomas Wolfe chan-
neled into his novels "Look Homeward Angel," "Of
Time and the River," "The Web and the Rock" and
"You Can't Go Home Again," Albert Brumley wrote this
song about finding out what happens when you return to
your home town and discover that you don't know any-
body anymore. I'm assuming that Dylan heard it from
Ralph Stanley and the Clinch Mountain Boys, though I
don't know if that's true. Brumley was from Oklahoma,
but this song about a vanished home in the mountains
plays right into the Piedmont and Shenandoah home
turf of Stanley and Wolfe.

Selections from **The Traveling Wilburys Vol. 1**
*Handle With Care; Dirty World; Congratulations; Tweeter
and the Monkey Man; Like a Ship*

*(Note: The songs that I chose from this album are the ones
that contain an identifiable vocal from Dylan. "Like a
Ship" is a bonus track on a later compilation of Wilburys
material.)*

Handle With Care
Old rock n' rollers
Need TLC from young girls.
Won't you help them out?

Nowhere in the lyrics of this lovely song do the Wilburys
say or imply that the "baby" who's the subject of the song
is a younger woman. Nevertheless, old rock 'n rollers
have a history of hooking up with women who, as they
say, "stay the same age."

Things that have happened to our old men:

- Beaten up, battered around, sent up, shot down,
  fobbed off, fooled, robbed, ridiculed, stuck in
  airports, terrorized, sent to meetings, hypno-
  tized, overexposed, commercialized, been made
  to feel uptight, been a mess.

Locations of abuse:

- Daycare centers, night schools, airports.

Instructions for proper use:

- Handle me with care, show that you care, put your body next to mine, dream on.

The proper candidate:

- Be the best thing I've ever found.
- Be adorable.
- Be able to receive some love.
- Careful.
- Be open to being leaned upon.

Dirty World
She's like a fast car,
She's unsafe at any speed,
But sexy in gear.

"Dirty World" offers a lighter tone than some of the classic rock nostalgia that gives other parts of the album its bittersweet autumn guitar feeling.

What he loves about you:

- Sexy body, dirty mind.
- Grabbing him from behind.
- The thought of introducing her to the other members of his gang.
- How you make his legs quiver and his mind bend.
- Your sense of humor and your disposition.

He also wants to change your oil for free, but knows you don't need a wax job because you're already smooth enough. He offers to drive your pickup truck and park it where the sun doesn't shine. Of course, she goes to the airport in the end and he goes home to cry. Then Bob, George, Roy, Jeff and Tom tell you other things that they like about you:

- Electric dumplings.
- Red bell peppers.
- Fuel injection.
- Service charge.
- Five-speed gearbox.
- Long endurance.
- Quest for junk food.
- Big refrigerator.
- Tremblin' Wilbury.
- Marble earrings.
- Purple curtains.

- Power steering.
- Bottled water.
- Parts and service.

Congratulations
Good job, heartbreaker.
You weren't happy until
You walked out on me.

I remember the summer when this came out because I had my first job, as a busboy and dishwasher at the Village Cheese Shop in Haddonfield, New Jersey. I worked with an allegedly cocaine-addled, hostile cook/country-western songwriter, rear to rear in a tiny kitchen, with the radio tuned to 94.1 FM, WYSP Philadelphia, the classic rock station. The debut of the Traveling Wilburys was a hot event for rock n' roll fans. I can't remember if we first heard these songs on 94.1 or 93.3 WMMR, but I do remember that this and all the other songs on this album were on all summer. To prevent illegal taping and distribution, the DJs would speak at times during the song, sullying the delivery and frustrating bootleggers. I fell in love with the album, and have always come back to it. "Congratulations" isn't one of the tracks that the record company and radio stations pumped as heavily as others, but it's a great song.

Here are the things for which Bob wishes his former lover congratulations:

- Breaking my heart.
- Tearing it all apart.
- Leaving me in need.
- Bringing me down.
- Leaving me sorrow bound.
- Getting a good deal.
- How good you must feel.
- Making me wait.
- Making it too late.
- Coming out on top.
- Never knowing when to stop.

Tweeter and the Monkey Man
Cop chases dealers.
His sister loves one of them.
Welcome to Jersey.

This is one of those guys-on-the-lam stories involving some of the shadier and weirder members of the blue-collar professions, and perhaps in another universe could have belonged to Tom Waits or Barry Adamson. It also owes a bit to Bruce Springsteen (Highway 99 as in "Johnny 99," "Thunder Road," the New Jersey setting, etc.), who I imagine could have done this Nebraska-style if he wanted to. Someone told me it was a Springsteen send-up, but I don't know if that's true.

Characters:

- Tweeter.
- Monkey Man.
- Undercover cop.
- Jan, his sister.
- Bill.
- State trooper.

The plot:

- Tweeter and the Monkey man are selling cocaine and hash because they need money.
- They're selling it to an undercover cop, whose sister Jan loves the Monkey Man.
- Tweeter was a boy scout, then a Vietnam vet. Life's been cold to him.
- Tweeter and Monkey steal a car and take Highway 99 across the Jersey line. (Bruce!)
- The cop hates the Monkey Man and wants to put him away.
- Jan married a racketeer named Bill at 14 and called the Monkey Man secretly from her mansion.

- Tweeter and the Monkey Man are on Thunder Road (Bruce!) and they run in to the undercover cop, who demands that they surrender.

- Ambulance and a state trooper arrive. Tweeter relieves him of his gun and "messes up his mind."

- They tie the undercover cop to a tree near an abandoned factory and a souvenir stand.

- The cop is pissed off, and now it's personal. He remembers Jan telling him, "It was you to me who taught: In Jersey anything's legal as long as you don't get caught."

- Tweeter and the Monkey Man run out of gas near Rahway Prison.

- Jan, at home, has a telepathic urge. She tells Bill, "'There's someplace I gotta go'. She took a gun out of the drawer and said, 'It's best if you don't know.'"

- The cop turns up dead, face down in a field. The police are closing in on Tweeter and the Monkey Man meanwhile. Monkey's on the bridge, using Tweeter as a shield.

- Presumably, they go down shooting.

- Bob's sitting in a bar called the Lion's Den in Jersey City, thinking it's time to beat it for Florida.

Like a Ship
I wish she'd leave, as
Her love is a ship, and I'm
Gonna be keel-hauled.

A Traveling Wilburys single. The song was released as
a bonus track on the 2007 reissue of the first Traveling
Wilburys album. The album first came out in 1988.

"Like a ship on the sea, her love rose over me
Go 'way, go 'way, let me be..."

Oh Mercy

Political World; Where Teardrops Fall; Everything Is Broken; Ring Them Bells; Man in the Long Black Coat; Most of the Time; What Good Am I?; Disease of Conceit; What Was It You Wanted; Shooting Star

Political World

Political world:
Crime, death, fear, compromise: yes.
Love, mercy, God: no.

"Political World" is a general list of grievances about the state of the world, a table of contents of woe.

- Love has no place.
- People commit crimes.
- Crime has no face.
- Icicles.
- People get married.
- Clouds cover the ground.
- Wisdom is incarcerated, and placed safely out of the public's reach.
- Mercy walks the plank.
- Life is only a reflection of reality.
- Death lives in banks.
- Courage is obsolete.
- Houses haunted.
- Children unwanted.
- Every day could be your last.

- Even though we know nothing is real, everything seems real.
- The deck is stacked.
- Cities are lonely and frightening.
- Nobody knows the meaning of life.
- We're under the microscope.
- You can go anywhere and do what you want, and there's always enough rope lying around to hang yourself with if you want.
- We're trained to take the easy way out.
- Peace is unwelcome and we often bully it.
- Everything belongs to someone.
- People are attention seekers.
- Televangelists shout God's name on air without knowing what they're talking about.

Where Teardrops Fall
I know where you are.
I follow a teardrop trail
And you're at the end.

It sounds like we're dealing with a broken-up couple. She's sad about it, he's sorry about it, and he's proposing a reconciliation.

- You're hanging out where the teardrops fall. They're likely yours. Soft winds, far away.
- It's past the stormy night and the wall. You're there in flickering light.

- "We banged the drum slowly, And played the fife lowly, You know the song in my heart." This refers to the song "Streets of Laredo," about a cowboy who's dying of a gunshot wound and requests that his chums play a funeral dirge as they carry him to his coffin. It's based on an older Scottish song about a young man dying because of mistreatment by a maiden – quite possibly a case of fatal syphilis. But that's another story. Dylan, meanwhile, suggests that his gal might show him "a new place to start."

- "I've torn my clothes and I've drained the cup, strippin' away at it all." I assume that the cup refers to the Last Supper. The clothes tearing is an old Jewish tradition to express grief, a broken heart and other unhappy emotions. It also expresses a devotion to God. Note that when Herod and the Romans mocked Jesus before nailing him to the tree, they made him wear expensive robes as an ironic expression of his status as "king of the Jews." The garments were seamless, so when the Roman soldiers divided his possessions for themselves, they ended up not being able to rend the garment as that would have made it useless. Anyway...

- If we met, we could toast the cutting of fences.

- "I just might have to come see you where teardrops fall."

Everything Is Broken
If you can name it,
You probably can break it.
You think I'm jokin'?

"Everything Is Broken" is like swinging at the most depressing bar in the bayou.

Here's the boulevard of broken things:

Lines, strings, threads, springs, idols, heads, beds, bottles, plates, switches, gates, dishes, parts, hearts, words, cutters, saws, buckles, laws, bodies, bones, voices, phones, hands, ploughs, treaties, vows, pipes, tools, rules.

What people are doing:
Sleeping (improbably), jiving (don't bother), joking (there's no point), speaking (futile), hitting the ground (every time you turn around), breathing (but you're choking), bending rules (they're broken anyway).

Ring Them Bells
The saints ring their bells
For the world's lost and found
In moral decay.

This song sounds like a plea to the saints and to wise men and women to ring the bells of truth and goodness in a world that doesn't want to hear them. These bells are the small, clear voices that suggest a path to redemption, righteousness and paradise in a wounded world where there is little demand for that path. The even, soft tone of the song indicates that patience, not fury at the oncoming apocalypse, is the right way to react to a world out of balance.

- Ring the bells, heathens, in the city of dreams and across valleys and streams. Do it because the waters are dark and deep and the world is off kilter.
- St. Peter, ring the bells with a steady hand. "Oh it's rush hour now, on the wheel and the plow, and the sun is going down upon the sacred cow." To me, that says people are rushing and speeding to keep their hand on the gospel plow, as the old spiritual says, the straight path to the Lord and to redemption, but there are no shortcuts to salvation. Same goes for the sacred cow, upon which the sun is setting. This is the idol that the Israelites worshipped when they turned their backs on God during their 40 years between the bondage of Pharaoh and the establishment of a proper state.
- Martha, perhaps of Mary and Martha in the New Testament, the women who gave shelter to Jesus, should ring the bells for the poor. Only the chosen people will hear them. They will know that God is one, even though they wander lost through the mountains like sheep.

- Ring the bells for the people who are chosen and who are damned, and for the people who are too blind and deaf to know which ones they are. Judgment Day is coming, and someone needs to provide mercy and love for the child who "cries when innocence dies."

Man in the Long Black Coat
The man in the coat
Takes the woman away. She
Left without remorse.

"Day of the Locusts" on the 1970 album "New Morning" begins with the sound of locusts. And "Man in the Long Black Coat" begins with the lyric, "Crickets are chirpin', the water is high..." and indeed, you can hear the chirping of crickets as the song begins. The crickets don't do much more than set the scene here, which is an empty house where a woman once lived and doesn't live anymore.

People who know their music say that she's the woman from the song "House Carpenter," which Dylan sang on earlier recordings. If you don't know the song, she's the woman who married a house carpenter and had a kid before her old lover returned and said, "come away with me and leave these people." She does so, but discovers only too late, once they're sailing on the sea, that he's come to take her to hell because he's actually a demon.

Notes on sin:

- The preacher says the conscience of men is vile and depraved, and you can't depend on it for guidance, and you must guide it in turn.

Notes on life:

- Some say there are no mistakes in life. You can look it that way... if you want.
- Some people drift through life instead of living or dying.

Most of the Time
You're not on his mind,
And you haven't been for years,
But sometimes you are.

"Most of the Time" is a great set of lyrics and music. Over its five minutes and five seconds, it proves itself to be worth a full box of tissue because it's a weeper. Dylan sings about how he doesn't miss a woman anymore, except every once in a while.

Most of the time:
Focused, grounded, clear, on the right road, handling what goes wrong, not noticing she gone, not inclined to change the past, holding one's own, surviving, enduring, not thinking about her, above hate, rational, rejecting

illusions, immune to confusion, not remembering what it feels like to kiss her, not remembering what she looks like, halfway content, clear on why the relationship ended, not cheating on oneself, in plain sight, denying real feelings, uncompromising, realistic.

What Good Am I?
I'm not much good
If I just let you founder.
But my hands are tied.

Praise of compassion from someone who evidently has not been able to display any.

Disease of Conceit
Universal ill:
Everyone is conceited.
You can die from it.

"Disease of Conceit" is a Diagnostic and Statistical Manual of Mental Disorders entry for the seven deadly sins. This one, I suppose, falls under pride, or maybe the old sin of "vainglory," which "pride" bought out in a private equity deal led by Pope Gregory and a group of cardinals. Dylan reportedly has said that the disgraced televangelist Jimmy Swaggart might have been the inspiration for the song, but who knows.

- Many people suffer from the disease. It's not sweet, it's conceit.
- It breaks and shakes hearts. It eats your soul and robs you of control of your senses. It's not discreet, it's conceit.
- People die and cry from conceit. It turns you into meat, it's conceit.
- There's no cure, but plenty of research, and yet no one's sure.
- People are in trouble with delusions of grandeur. Once you think you're too good to die, you get buried – from your head to your feet, because it's conceit.

What Was It You Wanted
Did you want something?
Am I supposed to get it?
Why should it be me?

"What Was It You Wanted" comes from the land of bad moods. Dylan hectors the subject of his song from the beginning, a subject who seems to be having trouble getting the right words out. This is a song about someone who he thinks has done him wrong, and he has the advantage so he's going to use it, not to get the outcome he wants, but to make sure that whoever is winning pays for it by feeling bad.

Shooting Star

You gotta let go
Of some folks to survive, but
You still will miss them.

"Shooting Star" is a fantastic, bittersweet ending song. I suppose that you could read it on any level that you want, but the two most common ones seem to be:

- Elegy for the one true love that got away, cast against the blanket of a starry night.
- A vision of the end of the world, in which, as the Blind Boys of Alabama said, "this may be the last time we ever pray together. It may be the last time, I don't know."

What better than a quiet night lost in the stars and in the throes of gentle regret, years after a failure to connect with someone, thinking about what you could have done differently? On a different level, I always considered the shooting star as a symbol for someone who was too high, wild and fast to catch, and who would occasionally land in your yard – but would prove impossible to keep. And even more than that, I always considered the shooting star to symbolize someone who was not just all these things, but who was too bright to survive in this dull world, and streaked across the sky until they burned out, maybe at the cost of their life.

Under the Red Sky

Wiggle Wiggle; Under the Red Sky; Unbelievable; Born in Time; T.V. Talkin' Song; 10,000 Men; 2 X 2; God Knows; Handy Dandy; Cat's in the Well

Wiggle Wiggle

Wiggle like a snake.
Wiggle like silk or like milk.
Wiggle till you're high.

What can I say about "Wiggle Wiggle?" It's Dylan's dumbest song, but come on, what's not to like about wiggling?

Wiggle wiggle instructions:
Dress in green, like a gypsy queen, let the blue moon see you, wear boots or shoes, have nothing to lose, do it like a swarm of bees on your hands and knees, move fore, move aft, do it till it shuts and cuts, do it like a bowl of soup or a hoop, a ton of lead or in a way that will raise the dead, get so high you vomit fire, hum, come, be like satin and silk or a bucket of milk. Finally, rattle and shake and wiggle like a big fat snake.

Under the Red Sky

Moon man, boy and girl
Live under red sky. The kids
Get baked in a pie.

Some songs are sad even as they sound wild and free. "Under the Red Sky" is one of them. George Harrison's lead guitar adds the right melancholic note.

- The wind blew low, then the wind blew high. The boy and girl were baked in a pie.
- The man in the moon went home and the river went dry.
- Little girl, here's something to look forward to: one day everything will be new. You'll get a diamond as big as your shoe. These are the keys to the kingdom and this is the town and this is the blind horse that leads you around.

Unbelievable
All kinds of bad things
Happen every day despite
How odd they might seem.

"Unbelievable" is righteous indignation.

- It's unbelievable that it would get this far. (It's strange and true and could happen to you.)
- It's indescribable. They said we were in the land of milk and honey, but we're in the land of money. Look how rich you can get and how quick.
- With me, every urge is satisfied. Gold, silver, sweethearts...

There is an interesting music video for this song featuring Dylan, a hot Molly Ringwald and a handsome fella. Partly shot in New Jersey, apparently.

Born in Time

She's a dream lover,
But he can't be with her now.
They weren't born in time.

In "Born in Time," Dylan tells a woman that her vision is coming to his mind in the middle of the night, that whatever relationship they had failed, and somehow she remains on his mind. He makes repeated references to how they were "born in time," but whether that means they were born on schedule, born in some more general temporal measure or whatever else he might have been thinking, the meaning goes slipping by.

T.V. Talkin' Song

TV's bad for you.
Bob knows it, but still gets trapped
In channel surfing.

Bob takes a walk in Hyde Park and he comes to the Speakers' Corner. He listens to some people talk to the crowd as one does in Hyde Park. There's a religious man telling everyone that they shouldn't watch TV. The god of TV causes pain with its bright light. Better to have never seen one. Another guy starts arguing with TV preacher. The preacher's words cause a riot with lots of pushing and shoving as the angry crowd tries to attack the man. A TV news crew gets footage of the melee. Bob goes home and watches it on TV.

10,000 Men
10,000 men work.
10,000 women like Bob.
His gal brings him tea.

- 10,000 men on a hill. Some gonna be killed.
- 10,000 men dressed in Oxford blue. They're drumming in the morning, and coming for you later.
- 10,000 men on the move. And then this riddle of a line: "None of them doing nothin' that your mama wouldn't disapprove." Think about that for a second. The opposite would be: All of them doing something that your mother would approve of. Or, are none of them doing something that she would approve of? Or maybe it's a combination: none of them are doing anything that your mother would disapprove of.
- 10,000 men digging for silver and gold. They're all clean shaven.
- Who's your lover? "Let me eat off his head so you can really see."

- 10,000 women dressed in white.
- 10,000 men looking weak. Each has seven wives who just got out of jail.
- 10,000 women sweeping my room. They spill his buttermilk and sweep it up with a broom. (You know what he's talking about.)
- My favorite line: "Ooh, baby, thank you for my tea! Baby, thank you for my tea! It's so sweet of you to be so nice to me."

2 X 2

Various people
Seem to have a good time, but
They're actually not.

I don't mind listening to this song with my mind turned off. But when I try to climb into it, I find that I can't. All I can see is that this Noah's Ark procession of people seems to start off OK, and winds up in less fortunate circumstances than those in which it started.

The 1x2 2x2 3x3 sequence, as ordered in the song:

1. They follow the sun until there are none.
2. They fly to their lovers in the dew.
3. They dance on the sea.
4. The dance on the shore.
5. They try to survive.

6. They play with tricks.
7. They go to heaven.
8. They get to the gate.
9. They drink the wine.
10. They drink it again.
2. They step in the ark.
3. They turn the key.
4. They turn it more.
2. They follow the sun to another rendezvous.

How many/much:

- Paths did they try and fail?
- Of their siblings are in jail?
- Poison did they inhale?
- Black cats did they encounter?
- Tomorrows have they given away?
- Tomorrows without reward?
- More tomorrows can they afford?

God Knows
God's got your number.
He'll see you through even if
You don't know the way.

What God knows:

- You ain't pretty. (It's true.)
- There's nobody who can take your place.

- It's a struggle.
- It's a crime.
- No more water next time, just fire.
- It's fragile.
- Everything.
- Everything could snap right now like scissors on a string.
- It's terrifying.
- Everything that unfolds.
- When you see it, you cry.
- The secrets of your heart.
- There's a river.
- How to make that river flow.
- You won't take anything with you when you go.
- There's a purpose.
- There's a chance.
- You can rise above the worst of anything.
- There's a heaven.
- It's invisible.
- We can get there from here even if we have to walk a million miles with only a candle.

Handy Dandy
Handy's been around.
He likes a drink, gets things done.
What keeps him going?

Handy Dandy is a hard portrait to get in focus because he seems to be made of many people, somewhere between artist and bullshit artist. Medicine show sales-man, crazy uncles who whirl into town from time to time and amuse the kids, things like that – but they always have some private weakness or hurt that they've papered over with boasts, words and a desire to please everyone by doing what they can, even though they might be cons:

- Controversy surrounds this world traveler, and something in the moonlight hounds him.
- He's just like sugar and candy.
- He could take a beating and would never admit that he had all his bones broken.
- He has an all-girl orchestra.
- Dialogue: You say: "what are you made of?" He: "Can you repeat that?" You: "What are you afraid of?" Him: "Nothing!"
- He has a stick and money.
- When he asks a lady how much time he has, she says he can have it all.
- He has a crystal fountain, soft skin and a fortress on a mountain.
- He says: Need a gun? She says, are you crazy?
- He likes his brandy.

The last verse of the song is one I like to repeat because it's among my favorite Dylan lines:

"Handy Dandy, he got a basket of flowers and a bag full of sorrow
He finishes his drink, he gets up from the table, he says
'Okay, boys, I'll see you tomorrow'."

Cat's in the Well

While you slept, the wolf
Trapped the cat inside the well.
Hope God has mercy.

- Cat's in the well, wolf looks down. He has a bushy tail dragging on the ground.
- Cat's still in the well. Lady is asleep. She can't hear anything.
- Cat's still in the well, upset. World is being slaughtered, it's a disgrace.
- Cat remains in the well, horse goes bumpety-bump. Back-Alley Sally does the American Jump.
- Cat persists in the well, balding papa is reading the news while his daughters need shoes.
- Cat languishes in the well, barn is full of bull, table is full.
- Cat's in the well, as ever. Servant's at the door, drinks are ready, dogs are going to war.
- That damned cat is still in the well, it's autumn, "God have mercy on us all."

Selections from **Traveling Wilburys Vol. 3**

She's My Baby; Inside Out; If You Belonged to Me; The Devil's Been Busy; 7 Deadly Sins; Where Were You Last Night?; New Blue Moon; Wilbury Twist; Nobody's Child; Runaway

(Note: I chose songs from this album that contained an identifiable vocal from Dylan. "Nobody's Child," a song that initially appeared on a charity album for Romanian orphans, was later included on a Wilburys compilation. So was the song "Runaway," which first appeared as a single.)

She's My Baby

My girlfriend makes
Pudding, builds boats, and can stick
Her tongue in my throat.

This is a silly song. See what I'm talking about:

- She has good pudding in the oven. She'd better not go to Hollywood, or I won't have such good pudding ever again.
- My baby drives a truck, a train and an airplane. She's good to look at in the rain.
- She's a stumbling drunk. She goes to far-off places.
- Body: for business. Head: for sin. She knocks me over like a bowling pin.

- She can build a boat, play guitar and stick her tongue right down my throat. She's my baby.

Inside Out
Yellow grass and sky
Suggest environmental
Problems lie ahead.

The Traveling Wilburys investigate the following settings and discover that not all is as it should be:

- Outside window: grass is yellow. See what they mean?
- Up the chimney: sky is yellow. You know it.
- Down the drainpipe: it's yellow. You can't fool me.
- Into the future via crystal ball: it's yellow if it's there.

The problem:

- You can't figure it all out.
- Outside's in.
- Downside's up.
- Upside's right.
- You want to twist and shout.

PS:

- There's something funny in the air. Watch your breathing.

If You Belonged to Me
If you were with me
Instead of that jerk, you would
Know what "happy" means.

I think that the song is by George Harrison, but Dylan takes pilot duty. It's the usual compare-and-save-on-boyfriends pitch: she's in dire straits, not least because her boyfriend is a loser. The singer offers a chance to switch to a new fella at 0% APR for an extended period.

- You're dancing in someone else's clothes. You come out of things smelling like a rose, as usual.
- You wouldn't be full of misery if you belonged to me.
- You have no sympathy. You want to go to the rodeo just to see the cowboy fall.
- You say you're free, but you'd be happier if you belonged to me.
- You're hard to get to.
- You say you're washed up.
- You would be happy with me like a baby on daddy's knee.
- You have a ruthless pimp for a boyfriend. He spends the money you give him on cocaine.

- You have another option: me.

The Devil's Been Busy
People are wrapped up
In their own troubles, while the
World goes to hell.

This is one of those collaborative "sound of 1,000 acoustic guitars strumming" Traveling Wilburys efforts. "The Devil's Been Busy" starts off with two verses about the suffering environment. Tom Petty sings about poison sprayed on the golf course, with members of the county club too busy sinking birdies and keeping scorecards to care. Then there are the lines about trucks of toxic waste driving down the highway, with no place to stash it, barring outer space. From there, Dylan takes over, and the lyrics grow more abstract. He delivers a verse about your second cousin and how he was wasted in a fight, then acting in a western, and then a pitch for the crowd who say ignorance is bliss. Jeff Lynne rounds it all up with some reference to unnamed people coming down Piccadilly, "dripping at the dash" and "Wasting Sticky Willy, covering him with their cash." They're beating Willy, whoever he is, just like Bob's second cousin earlier in the song. The only reference I can find anywhere else to "sticky willy" says that it's an it, not a he. It's a weed, otherwise known as galium aparine, clivers, goosegrass, catchweed, stickyweed, sticky willow, velcro weed and grip grass. It causes contact dermatitis, but you can make a tea from it and it is edible if cooked before its fruits appear.

7 Deadly Sins
Seven deadly sins
Are seven sins too few with
A woman like this.

A 1950's-style doo-wop-type breakup song. Here's the breakdown:

7 deadly sins are:

- How the world begins.
- Something to watch out for.
- Where the fun begins.
- Never ending once they start.
- Something to watch out for around the bend.

The song lists three of the sins, leaving the rest up to you to fill in:

- You left me.
- You said goodbye.
- You lied to me.

Where Were You Last Night?
Where were you last night?
In fact, where were you last year?
Who's my substitute?

"Where Were You Last Night?" is a line with a long history in blues music. It contains the suspicious questions that blues singers often present to unnamed lovers who have been less than present in their relationships.

- Where were you last night? What did you do, whom did you see?
- "Were you with someone who reminded you of me?"
- What about last week? Up a creek? I stayed up all night pacing and wondering.
- Where were you last year?

New Blue Moon

Waiting for this girl
Is like waiting for blue moons.
Sightings are quite rare.

"New Blue Moon" nearly didn't make it into this collection as it feels much more like a George Harrison song. Still, Bob gets a decent slice of the minimal lyrics to himself, the verse that begins with "So many moons have come and gone." Most of them were not blue.

Wilbury Twist

The underwear dance:
Hop, ball and spin like a screw.
Now you get the gist.

Here are the instructions, as printed in the album notes:

"To dance the Wilbury Twist, you must have some idea of the basic steps and hand motions. Grace is the key to successful dancing. Fluid, co-ordinated movements are what make a dancer outstanding. Good dancers do not wiggle their hips, but move them naturally in rhythm with the steps and music. Briefly, there are three things to remember: 1. Feet keep time. 2. Swaying-hips is a natural movement that accentuates rhythm. 3. Hands and facial expressions interpret the meaning of the dance."

- Hand on head, foot in air, hop around room in underwear.
- Lift other foot up, fall on ass, get up, put teeth in glass.
- Roll up rug, dust broom, ball jack, howl at moon.
- Turn lights low, put on blindfold, wonder where your friends have gone.
- Wait for years to be missed.
- Spin body like screw.
- Don't forget twist on shopping list.
- Get gist.

Suck it, Nijinsky.

Nobody's Child
Crying orphan boy
Says nobody wants him, and
He's one of many.

This was first released on the compilation "Nobody's Child: Romanian Angel Appeal," a benefit album for Romanian orphans, many of them HIV-positive. The song later was included on a 2007 box set collecting the two Traveling Wilburys albums and some singles miscellany. The song was written by Cy Coben and Mel Foree, and performed by Hank Snow in 1949. It's about orphans.

"No mama's arms to hold me, no daddy's smile
Nobody wants me, I'm nobody's child."

Runaway
She left him, it rains.
He wah-wah-wah-wah-wonders
Why she ran away.

Del Shannon's classic rock-and-roll song, done Wilburys-style. First released on a single, it was later included on the box set compilation of their work in 2007.

Selections from **The Bootleg Series Volumes 1-3
(Rare & Unreleased) 1961-1991**

*Hard Times in New York Town; He Was a Friend of
Mine; Man on the Street; No More Auction Block; House
Carpenter; Talkin' Bear Mountain Picnic Massacre Blues;
Let Me Die in My Footsteps; Rambling, Gambling Willie;
Talkin' Hava Negeilah Blues; Quit Your Low Down Ways;
Worried Blues; Kingsport Town; Walkin' Down the Line;
Walls of Red Wing; Paths of Victory; Talkin' John Birch
Paranoid Blues; Who Killed Davey Moore?; Only a Hobo;
Moonshiner; Last Thoughts on Woody Guthrie; Seven
Curses; Eternal Circle; Mama, You Been on My Mind;
Farewell, Angelina; Sitting on a Barbed Wire Fence; She's
Your Lover Now; Santa-Fe; Wallflower; Nobody 'Cept You;
Call Letter Blues; Golden Loom; Catfish; Seven Days; Ye
Shall Be Changed; You Changed My Life; Need a Woman;
Angelina; Someone's Got a Hold of My Heart; Tell Me; Lord
Protect My Child; Foot of Pride; Blind Willie McTell; Series
of Dreams*

Hard Times in New York Town
Poor folks in New York.
Bob wants to live there, but he
Loves to hate the place.

"If you got a lot o' money you can make yourself mer-
ry. If you only got a nickel, it's the Staten Island Ferry."
"Hard Times in New York Town" is one of Dylan's earli-
est songs, recorded in 1961. It's a Woody Guthrie-style

ode to New York City, giving the listener both sides of town depending on how much or little money they have.

He Was a Friend of Mine

Bob's friend up and dies
And Bob can't keep from crying.
Understandable.

The song's earliest known version is an Alan Lomax recording of a prisoner named Smith Casey performing it in Texas in 1939. The premise: This guy who died out on the road and never had much money was a friend of mine, and when I think about him dying, I cry. I know how he felt. He did nothing wrong except to be stranded a thousand miles from home.

Man on the Street

Man dies in the street.
A cop kicks his corpse one time.
Tough city, New York.

The melody comes from a song called "Young Man Who Wouldn't Hoe Corn." The song was recorded during the 1961 sessions for the "Bob Dylan" album.

- Man never did wrong, but he was a bum. They found him dead on the street one day.
- They looked at him on the sidewalk, then continued walking.

- A cop tells the dead body to get up or go to jail, not knowing he's dead. He jabs him with his billy club.
- He realizes that the man is dead. The wagon takes him away.

No More Auction Block

No more auctioning,
No more whips or slavery.
We've had too many.

This is a spiritual sung by slaves in the 19th century who escaped to Canada and won their freedom. Dylan's version was recorded in concert in 1962.

House Carpenter

Woman leaves family,
Misses kids. Demon lover
Takes her straight to hell.

"House Carpenter" isn't so different from a million other spooky songs from the British Isles, but I've always thought this one was pretty frightening. The original title of this Scottish ballad is "The Daemon Lover," and is also known as "James Harris" or "James Herries."

It is a cautionary tale for married women who might be reviewing their options. As the original title page went from the 17th-century edition of the song, "A Warning for Married Women, being an example of Mrs. Jane Reynolds (a West-country woman), born near Plymouth, who, having plighted her troth to a Seaman, was afterwards married to a Carpenter, and at last carried away by a Spirit, the manner how shall be presently recited. To a West-country Tune, calld [sic], The fair Maid of Bristol: or, John True, etc."

The story: A man returns to his former lover. She's married to a carpenter and has three babies. He convinces her to run off with him to Italy. They board a ship and sail out to sea. She misses her children and regrets her action. Then she spies two coasts. One is bright and beautiful. The other is dark and frightening. She asks which coasts they are and her lover tells her. He lets her know that they're bound for the worse of the two options. At that point, she discovers that he is a demon or the devil or some other malevolent supernatural force. He destroys the ship and she dies, sunk at the bottom of the sea. This version is from 1961 from the sessions for "Bob Dylan." Another version from nearly a decade later during his sessions for the "Self Portrait" album appears on volume 10 of the Bootleg Series.

Talkin' Bear Mountain Picnic Massacre Blues
A family picnic
Turns into a big fracas.
They should have stayed home.

Hudson River Father's Day cruise to Bear Mountain goes wrong when someone sells counterfeit tickets and too many people show up. Dylan took this one from a newspaper article and turned it into a talking-blues song. It's from the sessions for "The Freewheelin' Bob Dylan."

Let Me Die in My Footsteps

Bob says, if there's war,
Let him die outside, not in
A fallout shelter.

Better to die standing up than on your knees, more or less. "Let Me Die in My Footsteps" is Dylan's reaction to fallout shelters and the threat of nuclear war. Dylan suggests that it's better to enjoy the world and its natural wonders, and if you must die, you die among them rather than cooped in a living grave. The song was intended for the 1963 album "The Freewheelin' Bob Dylan," but was replaced by "A Hard Rain's a-Gonna Fall."

Rambling, Gambling Willie

Willie won at cards,
Shared his money and his dick.
Then someone killed him.

"Rambling, Gambling Willie" is an affectionate portrait of a coarse male gambler and slut named Will O'Conley who was good to all the women by whom he got his 27 children. O'Conley had one job, as they say, and he did it well, and then one day a guy blamed him for a bad poker hand and shot him in the head, and that was that for ol' Willie. This is an outtake from the 1962 sessions for "The Freewheelin' Bob Dylan."

Talkin' Hava Negeilah Blues
Hava Negeilah:
First you say it slowly, then
You yodel loudly.

This is a silly song from the 1962 "Freewheelin'" sessions. Dylan refers to a "foreign song" that he learned in Utah and it goes something like this etc...

"Ha va
Ha va na
Hava Na...
Ge, Ha va na gei
Lah, Ha va na gei lah."

And it ends in a yodel: o-de-ley-e-e-oo!

Quit Your Low Down Ways
God and the White House
Won't put you on the right track.
That's a job for me.

This is a vague song about a woman who's doing things that apparently are "low down." Once she realizes that she will be punished for her behavior, she embarks on a variety of acts to atone for them, but the singer knows that none of those things will do the trick. He suggests that he might be the answer that she is looking for. The song was recorded in 1962 during the "Freewheelin' Bob Dylan" sessions.

Things that won't absolve you of your low-down ways:

- Reading the Bible.
- Praying.
- Going to the White House.
- Looking at the Capitol.
- Asking the president for a pardon.
- Rolling around in the hot desert sand.
- Swearing in a court of law.
- Hitchhiking.

What might help absolve you of your low-down ways:

- Me.

Worried Blues
Don't leave me, baby.
I need to go where it's warm.
I've never been there.

"Worried Blues" is another "Freewheelin'" outtake. It's an old folk song that riffs off the line in "Going Down the Road Feeling Bad" about going somewhere warm, as in, "I'm going where the climate suits my clothes." That's the line that Fred Neil used and Harry Nilsson sang in "Everybody's Talkin'," the theme song to "Midnight Cowboy."

- Got worried blues. Need to go somewhere new where chilly winds don't blow and where the climate suits my clothes.
- Don't leave me. I have trouble on my mind.
- Listening to the cold train whistle.

Kingsport Town

Cops chase man from town.
He messed around with a girl.
He thinks she'll miss him.

"Kingsport Town" is a 1962 song from the sessions for "The Freewheelin' Bob Dylan."

- It's winter, a man is on the run, and cold. He's thinking of a girl.
- Does she remember him? She's the reason he had to leave Kingsport and the reason that the police are chasing him.
- Who's going to stroke her black hair and sandy skin and kiss her "Memphis lips?"
- Who's going to walk by her side and reassure her? Who's going to be her man and look her in the eye and hold her "bad-luck hand?"
- Damn, it's cold out.

Walkin' Down the Line
Time for walking shoes.
Troubled man, troubled woman.
She's sick, he's walkin'.

This is a short folk song about wandering, women and money from 1963. Dylan wrote it and performed it in a demo form for the Witmark publishing company.

- He's walking, feet flying, mind troubled.
- Gal: heavy-headed. Not feeling well. Feeling better? Time will tell.
- Money: comes/goes. Holes/pockets/clothes.
- Sunrise: I saw it. Didn't sleep all night.
- Shoes: the walking variety. Can't lose with these shoes, though I got the blues.

Walls of Red Wing
Life in reform school
Isn't so pleasant if the
School is Red Wing.

The Red Wing, Minnesota juvie hall that Dylan describes here sounds like it would have been a paradise playground for Jean Genet, all full of boys aged 12-17, every one of them treated miserably, like bandits and criminals. But this is fiction. Dylan writes a portrait of a teenage lockdown as if it were designed by the team that brought you ADX Florence. It was recorded during the "Freewheelin'" sessions.

Paths of Victory

Walking a tough road
Of battles and troubles leads
You to victory.

If you're looking for a roadmap to success, you could probably do with "Paths of Victory." The chorus is like an orientation guide for those of you looking to reorient yourselves once in a while as the paths toward social justice, harmony and victory grow hard to follow, given the various travails that people suffer while engaged in cumbersome tasks. The song was recorded in 1963 for the album "The Times They Are a-Changin'," though it didn't make the cut. The song was based on a gospel song by the Rev. John B. Matthias in 1836. It's also known as "Deliverance Will Come" and "The Way-worn Traveler."

Talkin' John Birch Paranoid Blues

Spotting communists
Is hard when there aren't any.
Best to keep checking.

This is an interesting song that was slated for performance on the Ed Sullivan show until CBS corporate executives demanded that he not play it to avoid risking a libel lawsuit from the John Birch Society, a group of ridiculous sentinels who were trying to guard America against the infiltration of Communists. Dylan walked off the set rather than consider the demands. Sullivan backed Dylan on this, but the performance didn't happen. CBS also forced Dylan to remove the song from the lineup for his second album "The Freewheelin' Bob Dylan." This recording is from a Carnegie Hall performance.

- Communists everywhere. Woe betide, etc.
- He joins the John Birch Society.
- John Birchers think Hitler was OK despite the Holocaust because he was an anti-Communist. He looks for Communists under his bed, in the sink, behind the door and in the glove compartment of his car. He finds none.
- He looks in the sink and underneath the chair and in the chimney and in the toilet bowl. They must have escaped.
- They might be in the TV set. He checks, get an electric shock. Communists must have done it.
- He quits his job, changes his name to Sherlock Holmes, discovers the color red in the American flag. Clearly Betsy Ross was a Communist.
- He reads all the books in the library and determines that most of them have Communist

leanings and must be burned. The other 2% are John Birch Society books.

- Eisenhower = Russian spy. Lincoln, Jefferson, Roosevelt = Russian spies. The only real American is American Nazi Party leader George Lincoln Rockwell. You know because he picketed "Exodus."
- He runs out of things to investigate so he investigates himself.

Who Killed Davey Moore?

Boxer dies in ring.
The boxing business is shocked,
Says, "It's not our fault."

Here's a song that Dylan wrote in 1963 about the death of boxer Davey Moore, who suffered irreversible brain damage after a fight and never recovered. It's one of Dylan's journalism songs. It's done in the style of "Who Killed Cock Robin?" This recording is from a Carnegie Hall concert.

Alibis for suspects in the murder of Davey Moore:

- Referee: I'm obligated to give the crowd the fight that it wants.
- Crowd: We didn't show up for lethal action. We came to see a bit of sweat, which is legal.
- Manager: He should have said something if he didn't feel well.

- Gambler: I just bet on the fight. I didn't hit him myself.
- Journalist: Boxing isn't the only dangerous sport, you know. And I can't make boxing go away so I'm going to write about it.
- The other boxer: I'm paid to box. This isn't murder, it's God's will.

Only a Hobo
Bum dies on the street.
He might not mean much to you,
But he's human too.

A social conscience song from 1963. "Only a Hobo" doesn't specifically say that the guy died, but "His face was all grounded in the cold sidewalk floor" and "Only a hobo, but one more is gone" suggest to me that he did. It was intended for the album "The Times They Are a-Changin'."

Moonshiner
Drinking will kill me,
Women good, drinking better.
I'll drink till I die.

This is Dylan's take on an old Irish or American folk song. He recorded it in 1963 during the sessions for "The Times They Are a-Changin'."

- He's been a moonshiner for 17 years. He spent the proceeds on whiskey and beer. He hangs out at his still and figures that if the whiskey doesn't kill him, something else will.
- He drinks at the bar with his guy friends because women can't go there. Still, he wishes he could have those women because of their sweet, dewy breath.
- Old Irish bar song: "Let me eat when I am hungry, Let me drink when I am dry, A dollar when I am hard up, Religion when I die."
- Philosopher: "The whole world's a bottle, And life's but a dram, When the bottle gets empty, It sure ain't worth a damn."

Last Thoughts on Woody Guthrie

Want to fix your blues?
Woody Guthrie has the tool
Inside his songbag.

Dylan recited "Last Thoughts on Woody Guthrie" at the end of a concert on April 12, 1963 at Town Hall in New York City. It's a long complaint or lament about the impossibility of modern life, followed by a short cadenza urging you to seek the real meaning of what it's all about at the Grand Canyon at sunset. It's a recitation, not a song.

Seven Curses
Woman sleeps with judge
To spare dad from death. Judge lies,
And lets Papa hang.

Here's a creepy tale of the daughter of Old Reilly. He stole a stallion and got caught. They put him in chains and locked him in jail and sentenced him to death by hanging. Old Reilly's daughter hears about this and asks the judge for mercy. She's willing to pay him off, and she's been riding all night with gold and silver. The old man judge takes one look at Reilly's daughter, and has a different idea: he'll intercede if she has sex with him. Reilly doesn't like the idea, saying he'd rather be dead than know the judge has been all over his daughter. She says death is certain if she doesn't do it, so she needs to take the chance. She goes to bed with the judge, and discovers that he lied. They hanged her father despite her gambit. She wishes curses on the judge.

The song was recorded in 1963 in the "Times They Are a-Changin'" sessions.

Eternal Circle
Bob spies a woman
While on stage. She leaves before
He can hit on her.

This song from late 1963, recorded during the sessions for "The Times They Are a-Changin'," is a glimpse into the life of a hard-working folk singer who has needs like any man. He sings his song and notices that a woman is making eyes at him. He keeps singing his song – a long one – only to find that she doesn't stick around until the end. It must have been the song, not the singer.

Mama, You Been on My Mind
Is it the weather?
Or is it that I miss you?
Whatever it is...

Dylan recorded this song in 1964 for the album "Another Side of Bob Dylan," though it didn't make the final cut. Plenty of other people covered it in the meantime, including Judy Collins, Ricky Nelson, Johnny Cash, Dion and the Belmonts, Linda Ronstadt and Rod Stewart.

Why might he be thinking of you?

- Maybe the color of the sun.
- Maybe the weather.

Where I'm coming from:

- I don't mean trouble.
- I'm not asking for you back.

- I'm not saying I can't forget.
- I'm not contorting myself in sadness.

Conditions on you:

- None.
- I don't mind where you've been.
- I don't mind if you make me sad.
- I don't mind not knowing where you slept last night.
- Not asking you to say yes or no.

Well, maybe one condition:

- Look at yourself in the mirror tomorrow morning. I wonder if you can see yourself as clearly as I see you.

Farewell, Angelina
Man leaves a woman
To get some peace and quiet.
He hallucinates.

I live in perpetual confoundment over the two Dylan songs containing the name Angelina. The first of the two, "Farewell, Angelina," is from the 1965 "Bringing It All Back Home" sessions. The second, "Angelina," from 1981, was left off the "Shot of Love" album. "Farewell,

Angelina" carries that same kind of sour-tongued fever-dream Book of Revelations daytime nightmare feeling as "Gates of Eden." Lyrically, it feels like a dress rehearsal for "Desolation Row" and its gallery of hallucinatory Fellini extras. I say that I am confounded because the songs don't yield their secrets easily. It might be that there are none, though I feel more confident saying that about the older song than the newer. Whatever Dylan thought of it, I don't know, but most of the exposure that the song has had to the public has been from Joan Baez, who named one of her albums after the song and has performed it often.

What Dylan must do: Go, follow the sound of triangles, leave, leave, be gone, go where it's quiet.
What the sky is doing: burning, trembling, folding, changing color, being embarrassed, erupting.

Other nouns and verbs: Bandits (stealing bells of the crown), triangles (tingle), trumpets (play slow), jacks and queens (left the courtyard), 52 gypsies (walking past the guards), deuce and ace (ran wild), cross-eyed pirates (shooting cans), neighbors (clapping for the pirates), King Kong and elves (dancing the tango on the roof-tops), makeup man (hands shut dead people's eyes), machine guns (roaring), puppets (throwing rocks), fiends (attaching bombs to clock hands), Angelina (calling Bob whatever she wants).

Sitting on a Barbed Wire Fence
Bob's temperature's up.
His dog bites a rabbit. His
Woman calls him Stan.

More wordplay on a half-finished song. That's the essence of "Sitting on a Barbed Wire Fence." It was recorded in 1965 during the "Highway 61 Revisited" sessions.

- He's paid, in two installments, $15 million + 1,272 cents, and $1,227.55. His dog bit a rabbit. His football sits on a barbed-wire fence.
- His temperature is up, his feet are slow. He got a shot from an Arabian doctor, but the doctor wouldn't give him a prognosis.
- He has a woman who fills him with her drive. She calls him Stan and Mr. Clive.
- You might think this song is a riff, but you would think otherwise if you had been inside a tunnel and fallen 69 or 70 feet over a barbed-wire fence... "all night!"

She's Your Lover Now
Guy's ex is trouble.
Why should he deal with her when
She has a new man?

I've seen some positive words written for "She's Your Lover Now," which Dylan intended for release on

"Blonde on Blonde" in 1966, but dropped from the album after he and the musicians spent multiple takes on the project without getting it right. I don't quite feel as positive about the song as others do. Songs like this sound like Dylan knew he had stumbled on a great idea with "Like a Rolling Stone," and he wanted to get that sound to work again. But what seems strong and fresh on "Rolling Stone" sounds flabby and rambling here. The lyrics sound more like a pastiche of Dylan than Dylan himself, relying on atmosphere, vinegar, and occasional symbols that don't quite do themselves justice.

The three verses of "She's Your Lover Now":

- I was in pain because you left me. I destroyed everything I had, and that just made the pawnbroker laugh and the landlord cry. Why did you do it to me? And you think I should remember something that you want to tell me that you forgot to say? As for you, fella, I see you're with her now, so you deal with her if you're lovers now.
- Now we're going to work out our problems like we were in court or in binding arbitration, I guess. Meanwhile, I never tried to change you, and you could always have just walked out if you wanted. What is it with forgive and forget? Why do you ask me to do that? And

your guy here keeps asking me to pass him ashtrays, and keeps saying everything twice. Why do you praise her every time she opens her mouth?

- I never asked you to be faithful. You should have left if you wanted to leave. Some nonsense about castle stairs and trips to El Paso and San Francisco that he can't remember. Meanwhile, this new lover finds he has nothing to say so Bob goads him, and suggests that it won't be long until the woman in question is standing on the bar wearing a fish head and carrying a harpoon and wearing a fake beard, and that it's up to him to stop this transformation into Captain Ahab or whatever it is that she's trying to be.

Santa-Fe
Bob's roaming around.
His woman says he can stay.
She's in Santa Fe.

This is a Basement Tapes song that seems to have little lyrical center or serious intent, and that's just fine.

Wallflower
"May I ride you home?"
Wallflower asks wallflower
For a late-night dance.

"Wallflower" first appeared on the 1973 album "Doug Sahm and Band" on which Dylan performed as a sideman. The song, which Dylan copyrighted in 1971, is a standard country-and-western love number.

- Wallflower, let's dance. I'm sad and lonely like you. As a matter fact, I'm falling in love with you.
- What are we both doing here? Let's dance.
- I took one look at you and, regardless of the smoke in this joint, I knew that you would be the one for me.
- The ending that most of us hope for in such circumstances: "Wallflower, wallflower, take a chance on me. Please let me ride you home."

Nobody 'Cept You
Nothing pleases him
Except you. You remind him
Of pretty church hymns.

Here's a sweet little outtake from the 1973 "Planet Waves" sessions with the Band.

The situation:

- He believes in nothing.
- Nothing is sacred for him.
- He tries for nobody.

- Nothing worth living or dying for to him.
- Nobody sees him.
- Nothing pleases him.
- Nothing hypnotizes him.
- Nothing holds him in a spell.
- Everything runs by him like water.
- Everybody wants his attention.
- Everybody wants to sell him something.

Things she does:

- Reaches him.
- Is admired by him.
- Sets his soul on fire.
- Matters.

Things she's like:

- A church hymn he used to hear.

And then there's this sweet, weird lyric:

"Used to play in the cemetery
Dance and sing and run when I was a child
Never seemed strange
But now I just pass mournfully by
That place where the bones of life are piled
I know somethin' has changed."

Call Letter Blues
Woman leaves, man stays.
Kids and friends ask, where's she gone?
She's with her new man.

This is a separate set of lyrics for the song that eventually became "Meet Me in the Morning" on the 1975 album "Blood on the Tracks." "Call Letter Blues," recorded during the sessions for that album, is a much more direct song. The singer's wife has left him, and he doesn't know what to tell friends who ask where she is, and the problem gets worse when the kids ask too. He tells them "Mother took a trip," and "I walk on pins and needles. I hope my tongue don't slip." Meanwhile, he keeps hoping he'll spot her in the crowd, but the last lines of the song make him realize that he could wait a lifetime for that moment, and it probably won't happen: "But the sun goes around the heavens, And another day just drives on through."

Golden Loom
Bob recalls his tryst
With a fisherman's daughter
Whom he failed to hook.

"Golden Loom" is of a piece with "Mozambique," that supreme piece of laid-back vacationland music from the 1976 album "Desire." This song didn't make it to that album. Fisherman's daughter shows up at just the right time, carrying a loom. It's a smoky, starry night in autumn. Boats in the bay, eucalyptus in the air. They wash their feet at the shrine, drink wine, she starts crying. She takes off in the summer. (The loom goes with her.) Later, he walks across the bridge "in the dismal light." Stripped cars and such. He sees a trembling lion with a tail made of a lotus flower. When he thinks he's kissing her, she's not really there.

Catfish
Catfish played baseball
And struck everybody out.
The freest agent.

I don't like songs about baseball. There are exceptions, but songs about sports generally leave me cold. "Catfish," a Jacques Levy-Bob Dylan collaboration that was recorded for the 1976 album "Desire," but ultimately left off, is no exception. The song is basic. Catfish Hunter is a great baseball player, nobody can play like he can. That's all very nice. The Dylan touches that make it a little more sly deal with Billy Martin grinning and Catfish's pinstripe suit and cigar and alligator boots.

Seven Days
Seven more days and
Bob's pretty comrade arrives.
He's tired of waiting.

"Seven Days" has some great moments, but generally it serves no purpose to my ear other than to get a shaggy band together to play shambling and disorganized rock music at top volume while Dylan sings cryptic lyrics. Though he didn't release it at the time, Joe Cocker and Ron Wood of the Rolling Stones did versions that resounded well with audiences.

The five verses of "Seven Days":

- She's coming in a week. I'll be at the station waiting for her. All I gotta do is survive.
- She's been gone since I was a child. I haven't forgotten her eyes.
- I've been good while waiting, though I've been known for hesitating.
- There's kissing, thieving, fighting, while I've been trying to be tender.
- She's my beautiful comrade from the North.

Ye Shall Be Changed
You work too hard and
You need a new beginning.
Go get born again.

This romp through Judgment Day promises that you shall be changed if you're able to hang on until then. The song was recorded in 1979 during the "Slow Train Coming" sessions.

You Changed My Life
I ate with the pigs
Until God gently told me:
Pay now, skip dessert.

This song from 1981 was part of the sessions for the album "Shot of Love." It's one of his more ponderous Christian songs, and it probably was a wise decision to leave it off the album, though I would have taken it over "Lenny Bruce" any day. Regardless of its middling nature, it has some good zingers in it.

Need a Woman
She's like salvation
And Bob needs her pretty bad,
Maybe more than God.

In the midst of his Christian music period, Bob Dylan wrote "Need a Woman." It was copyrighted in 1982, though recorded during the "Shot of Love" sessions in 1981. He avoids the God theme for most of the song, though suggests to her toward the end that religious belief is a private matter, quite the opposite of what he had been practicing in those years.

What Bob needs:

- Someone who can see him as he is.
- Someone who doesn't give a damn.

- Someone to be his queen.

His situation:

- Patience wearing thin, fire in his nose.
- Searching for truth the way God designed it, though he might drown before he finds it.

His research:

- He's been watching her for five years.
- She doesn't know him, but he knows her laughter and tears.
- She doesn't frighten him, though she does make his heart beat faster.
- She appears to be in need of a man.
- He's seen her boot heels spark.
- He's seen her in the day and in the dark.

Angelina
Bob discovers that
Converting Angelina
Isn't that easy.

This outtake from 1981's "Shot of Love" is a gnarled knot of Gnosticism. It sounds like an appeal to a woman, probably a fairly attractive one, whom he would like to see born again to avoid eternal hellfire and other pagan playtimes.

- He always takes chances. Right hand retreats, left hand advances. Monkey dances to a concertina tune.

- Blood in his hair as he sails. He knows why he's at your door. He thinks Angelina has seen him before.

- His eyes: two slits to impress a snake. His face could impress a painter. He worships a god with the body of a hot woman and a hyena's head.

- Does he need your permission to turn his cheek? Why should he speak if you can read his mind? You're looking for a man, but he doesn't know anything about him.

- Valley of the giants: where the stars and stripes explode. There were sweet peaches and milk and honey. A judge sent him along there with your subpoena.

- When you die, whose fault will it be? He tried to love you, but he's done playing the game. Your friend and his enemy are the same person.

- Black Mercedes in a war zone. Your servants are half dead and you're out of luck. He asks the tall men where they want to be conquered... perhaps Jerusalem? Perhaps Argentina?

- She's an orphan, she's full of vengeance – now satisfied – and everything she owns has been sold. He is surrounded by angels. She wears a blindfold.

- He has seen "pieces of men marching" in an attempt to take heaven by force. He sees an unknown rider on a pale white horse, death, of course. What do you want from him? He'll bring it to you. Just step into the arena.

- "Beat a path of retreat up them spiral staircases. Pass the tree of smoke, pass the angel with four faces, begging God for mercy and weepin' in unholy places." A reference to the prophecies of Ezekiel, perhaps.

Someone's Got a Hold of My Heart
Woman snares a man
Who's all wrapped up in intrigue.
He wants to get out.

This outtake from the sessions for the 1983 album "Infidels" appeared in a mostly rewritten form two years later on the 1985 album "Empire Burlesque," now known as "Tight Connection to My Heart (Has Anybody Seen My Love)."

Tell Me
Before I leave you,
Tell me if you love me
Or if you love him.

This could have been a high school slow dance song or a mainstream hit. The song was recorded during the sessions for "Infidels." A man knows that his lover loves him no longer, and he's wondering what's going on in her mind, and more specifically, who the guy is whom she must be seeing on the side.

Lord Protect My Child
Since people are mean
And because the world is bad,
Lord, protect his child.

What one might call a "big ask" from God, "Lord Protect My Child" combines a humble plea from Dylan for divine protection of his son with a sidelong request for world peace and justice. The song was recorded for "Infidels," but left off the final cut.

Foot of Pride
Pride's a deadly sin,
And just about everyone's
Out to break the law.

"Foot of Pride" barrels through its six-plus minutes on attitude and fine, lean pop music. What's it all about? The haiku contains the central message, while the song radiates in all directions with unrelated stories that begin and end in just a few seconds. The song was recorded for "Infidels," but was struck out. The first time I heard the song was when Lou Reed performed it for the Columbia

Records concert to celebrate Dylan's 30th anniversary on the label. You can hear the band and Reed struggling with the lyrics and the music, and you can't blame them. (Their version, which sounds unrehearsed, makes up for most of its infractions in raw power.) Dylan's lyrics are all over the place, and there are so many words that I would challenge anyone to try this in a karaoke bar just to see how it goes. But as far as flawed gems go in rock n' roll, I love this song. The keyboard keeps an appropriate two-chord drone going through the verses. The song conveys menace, humor, irony and apocalyptic warning, and sounds pretty cool all the while.

Blind Willie McTell
Blues singer frames
Stories of the South's decline:
Magnolias and slaves.

- Bob sees an "arrow on the doorpost" saying the land is condemned from New Orleans to Jerusalem, and wanders through east Texas where martyrs fell. And then the non-sequitur end of every verse: "And I know no one can sing the blues like Blind Willie McTell."
- Owl sings to stars above barren trees and "charcoal gypsy maidens" "strut their feathers well" as someone, presumably a circus crew, takes down tents.

- Plantations burn, slave masters crack whips, magnolia blooms, the ghosts of slavery ships sail. Tribes moan, undertaker's bell.
- Woman and man and a bottle of bootleg whiskey by the river. Chain gang on the highway. Rebels yell.
- All that's left of God's presence on earth is power, greed and "corruptible seed." Bob, meanwhile, is in the St. James Hotel, looking out the windows, and thinking about how nobody can sing the blues like McTell.

Series of Dreams
Interpreting dreams
Is hard. But just having them
Sometimes is harder.

It's a terrific song, and sounds very much of a piece with the rest of late 1980's pop as it was wending its way into the warmer sounds of the 1990's. It has a kind of glacial majesty that U2 achieved when they didn't ruin it with Bono's homilies to the brotherhood of man and the upper-class alienation of European cities and Wim Wenders films. And it has a good beat. I suspect that opening "Oh Mercy" with it, which was the original intent, would have not balanced well with the other songs, all of which are slighter in their production. I like this as a standalone. It's too much of a mountain to compete with a bunch of hills.

Series of dreams:

- Nothing comes to the top.
- Everything stops, wounded, at the bottom.
- Nothing specific. Someone wakes up and screams.
- No exit. Time and tempo fly.
- Umbrella is folded. Someone throws it in your path.
- Your cards are no good unless you're playing interstellar poker.
- Numbers were burning.
- He witnesses a crime.
- Running.
- Climbing.

Things he wasn't doing in the series of dreams:

- Anything too scientific.
- Making any great connection.
- Falling for intricate schemes.
- Anything that would pass inspection.
- Looking for special help.
- Going to great extremes. (He's already gone the distance.)

Good As I Been to You
Frankie & Albert; Jim Jones; Blackjack Davey; Canadee-i-o; Sittin' on Top of the World; Little Maggie; Hard Times; Step It Up and Go; Tomorrow Night; Arthur McBride; You're Gonna Quit Me; Diamond Joe; Froggie Went a-Courtin'

Frankie & Albert
Frankie kills Albert
After he cheats. She feels bad,
Goes to jail, and hangs.

Frankie & Albert is a variation on the song Frankie & Johnny. Or the other way around. The song might be a little more than 100 years old. Or nearly 200 years old. There appear to be hints of a rich history of wronged women killing their errant men, especially when they're out with other women.

- It's been covered something like 256 times.
- Murder: 212 Targee Street, St. Louis, Missouri. 2 a.m., October 15, 1899. Accused: Frankie Baker (1876-1952), 22 years old, shoots 17-year-old Allen/Albert Britt. Albert was out with Alice Bly, AKA Alice Pryor, at a "cakewalk." Their crime: dancing. Baker was acquitted and sent to a mental institution.
- Murder 2: Frances "Frankie" Stewart Silver. Murdered husband Charles Silver, Burke County,

North Carolina, 1832. She was executed, rather like the Frankie in Dylan's version.

Jim Jones

Criminal Jim Jones
Gets sent to Australia.
He plots his revenge.

"Jim Jones" is the tale of a British convict sent to Botany Bay, Australia. It sparkles like the sea with images of tall ships, pirates and the bushrangers and prisoners. The song was published in 1907.

The tale of Jim Jones:

- Judge sends him "across the stormy sea" to join an iron gang. Warns him that he'll hang if he steps out of line.
- While at sea, pirates attack convict ship. Five hundred convicts drive the pirates away. "But I'd rather have joined that pirate ship than gone to Botany Bay." In storms, he would rather have drowned than gone to New South Wales.
- Shackled in irons, sentenced to hard labor, awaiting only the promise of an unconsecrated grave. He plans to escape and join the bush rangers, also called rankers, such as Jack Donahue and his gang.

- He fantasizes about coming back in the middle of the night and shooting his jailers.

Blackjack Davey
Married woman flees
With lover Davey. Husband
Can't make her come back.

This is an old Scottish borderlands ballad of an aristocrat's teenaged wife who flees her life of leisure to live in the wilds with Blackjack Davey, her considerably sexier and possibly younger gypsy lover. This is one of the more popular ballads to survive the past 200 years or so, and has been covered by many singers. "Blackjack Davey" is one of my favorite Dylan songs, and he conveys in here the wild country of the moors, the old-time feel of the setting and the combination of romance, lust, bewilderment and fright that must have overtaken all three characters in the acting out of this drama. (In many of the original versions, Johnny Faa the gypsy is caught by the Earl of Cassilis, who hangs him and other gypsies from the Dool Tree, while Lady Jane Hamilton is confined essentially to purdah forever.)

Canadee-i-o
Girl at sea, disguised.
Captain saves her from sailors,
Boyfriend much chagrined.

"Canadee-i-o" is the story of a boy who sails to Canada, and dresses his girl up as a boy sailor so she can come too. At sea, she is unmasked. The other sailors try to throw her overboard, but the captain intervenes and saves her life. Not only that, he marries the girl and makes her a happy and wealthy bride once they make land. What of the boy sailor? The suggestion in Dylan's version of the song is that the boy is ready to accept her death sentence, or perhaps, as some versions of the song go, he tries to participate in her doom. Dylan's version doesn't mention his fate. There are other versions out there, known as "The Wearing of the Blue" and "Caledonia." The wind-swept, weary resignation in Dylan's performance makes this one of his best songs.

Sittin' on Top of the World
You might think I care
That you left me. Believe me,
I can't be bothered.

This is a blues chestnut from the Mississippi Sheiks, recorded for the first time in 1930. It's about a guy who can't be bothered that his girlfriend left him. Why?

- He can get a woman as quickly as she can get a man.
- He's not the begging kind so he won't ask for her back.

- He's not into worrying or craving in vain.
- He has plenty of work to do anyway.

Little Maggie
Gun-toting Maggie
Dropped me for another man.
I left, she's drinking.

I don't know much about "Little Maggie," but found one online source says that it's a "white blues" song from the isolated mountains and hollows of rural Virginia.

Inside the world of Little Maggie:

- She's standing around with a rifle on her shoulder and a six-shooter in her hand. Blue eyes shine like diamonds in the sky.
- I'd rather be stuck in a lonely hollow with no sunshine than see her with a man, especially knowing that she'll never be mine.
- I'm leaving the country thanks to my misery.
- Sometimes I have a nickel, or a dime, or 10 whole dollars and all I do is pay for Maggie's wine.
- Maggie's getting drunk in the bar. Why? She's upset about the other guy whom she wants, but can't have.

Hard Times
Remember the poor
While you're rich and having fun.
They're outside your door.

The full title of this song by American parlor music composer Stephen Foster is "Hard Times Come Again No More." The song is a plea to people wealthy enough to live comfortably to remember that the poor and their troubles are never far away. The music, like most parlor songs of the 19th century, is simplistic and sappy, but Dylan gives it a fine edge. Foster, the "father of American music," wrote a number of other well-known songs that became, and in some cases, remain well known to beginner piano students, including "Beautiful Dreamer," "Camptown Races," "Jeanie With the Light Brown Hair," "My Old Kentucky Home," "Oh! Susanna," "Old Black Joe" and "Old Folks at Home."

Step It Up and Go
She used to love him,
But she stepped it up and went.
That's what he does too.

Originally called "Bottle Up and Go." It's an old blues song from the 1930s. The version that most people seem to refer to online is Blind Boy Fuller's, though I see that John Lee Hooker has done it too.

- Little girl used to love me. She went.
- Got another little girl upstairs. She puts on airs, makes a living that way.
- What else can you do when the front door and back door are shut?
- Got a little girl named Ball. I gave her a little bit and she took it all.
- Walking down the street with my honey, talking about the chief of police.
- My woman's been gone. Tell her to come home. I haven't had any loving.
- I hear my woman calling me and I have to go.

Tomorrow Night
You loved me tonight.
But I'm beginning to doubt
If you will later.

Elvis Presley's version is the one you know best, but the song was written in 1939 by Sam Coslow and Will Grosz. Dylan's version aches with melancholy. Through his croak, you can hear the heat and lust and the confusion and expectation of loss that you know the narrator is going to feel once he discovers that last night was last night and that's all there's going to be, as Eve Kendall put it in "North by Northwest."

- Will you remember what we did tomorrow night? Or is it just one more memory that I will linger on?
- Your lips are tender, your heart is beating fast. You surrender to me, but what about tomorrow?

Arthur McBride

Arthur and cousin
Won't fight in France. They clobber
The draft recruiter.

This is an old Irish (or Scottish? British?) ballad, perhaps from the 17th century or later. British recruiters approach Arthur and his cousin on the beach as they walk on Christmas morning, and tell them how wonderful life is in the military and how they should suit up and go fight in France. Arthur and cousin don't take so well to the idea, whereupon the Brits replace cajolery with threats of stabbing them to death with their swords. Arthur and cousin express their desire for pacifism by beating the Brits with their shillelaghs and throwing the little drummer boy's drum and the other soldiers' swords into the sea.

You're Gonna Quit Me

Babe, if you leave me,
I'll kill you and go to jail.
You think I'm kidding?

"You're Gonna Quit Me" is a short, violent song about what most people would consider spousal abuse. It's by Blind Arthur Blake.

- You're gonna leave me, good as I been to you.
- Gave you money to buy shoes and clothes.
- You're going to evict me.
- I'm going to kill you because of this. A sentence to jail and the chain gang won't be fun, but they will be worth it.

Diamond Joe
Joe hires cowboy
Who hates his lying, cheap ways,
But Joe has him trapped.

"Diamond Joe" is a song about a cowboy hired by a Texas ranch baron who finds himself exploited beyond his wildest imagining. The oldest version that I can find is by Cisco Houston, but I see that Ramblin' Jack Elliott covered it too. Dylan's version is far more weary in its delivery than the other two, and is irresistible. I read on the website of California State University, Fresno that a man named Nicholas Hawes says that his father Baldwin "Butch" Hawes wrote it for a radio program for the BBC produced by Alan Lomax. The song appeared on "Chisholm Trail," the second of these "ballad operas" of life in the Old West. When the song appeared a decade later in Cisco Houston's repertoire in Sing Out!

magazine, it was listed as traditional, something that bothered Hawes and his wife, but they did not take issue with it.

- Diamond Joe has a big ranch in Texas. He carries his money in a diamond-studded jar and has no respect for the law.
- I signed on to his crew. He gave me a team of horses that were so old they could barely stand.
- I nearly starved to death working for him. I never saved a dollar while laboring under his hand.
- His bread was bad and his meat was tough. He couldn't feed me properly and never stopped talking.
- There was never such a rounder as Diamond Joe.
- I tried to quit him three times, but he always talked me out of it, so here I am punching cattle in the pay of Diamond Joe.
- "And when I'm called up yonder, and it's my turn to go, give my blankets to my buddies, give the fleas to Diamond Joe."

Froggie Went a-Courtin'
Froggie wants to wed.
He marries mouse, snake eats her,
And a duck eats him.

"Frog Went a-Courtin'," also known as "The frog came to myl dur," "A Moste Strange Weddinge of the Frogge and the Mouse," "King Kong Kitchie Kitchie Ki-Me-O" and other titles, has been around for nearly 500 years if not more. The story is straight, if not succinct, and it's a murder ballad. Premise: Frog asks mouse to marry him. She says she needs permission: "Without my Uncle Rat's consent, I wouldn't marry the president." Uncle Rat "laughed and shook his fat sides to think his niece would be a bride," and then he arranges a wedding party in the hollow of a tree.

Guests:

- Moth. Laid out table cloth.
- Juney bug. Brought water jug.
- Bumble-y bee. Put mosquito on knee.
- Broken black flea. Danced jig with bumble-y bee.
- Mrs. Cow. Tried to dance. Didn't know how.
- Little black tick. Ate so much, she got sick.
- Big black snake. Ate wedding cake.
- Old gray cat. Ate mouse and rat.

Conclusion:

- Frog escapes over brook. Lily-white duck swallows him up.
- "Little piece of cornbread laying on the shelf. If you want any more you got to sing it yourself."

World Gone Wrong

World Gone Wrong; Love Henry; Ragged & Dirty; Blood in My Eyes; Broke Down Engine; Delia; Stack A Lee; Two Soldiers; Jack-A-Roe; Lone Pilgrim

World Gone Wrong

You left and I said
I'd kill you. It's a bad world.
It's clearly gone wrong.

"World Gone Wrong," by the Mississippi Sheiks, is the source of the name that Dylan used for this album. The song turns a breakup into a biblical event, but in a sparing way.

- "Strange things have happened, like never before. My baby told me I would have to go. I can't be good no more, once like I did before. I can't be good, baby, honey, because the world's gone wrong."
- Feel bad now. No home.
- I told you if I didn't leave you, I would have to kill you.
- I tried to be loving, but you weren't loyal.
- If this happens to you, ask God to get her off your mind.
- When you are so irritated with her that you can no longer behave, show her the front door. Scratch that. Show *yourself* the front door.

Love Henry
Henry doesn't love her
So she kills him. That's one way
To keep your man true.

"Love Henry" comes from a tune called "Young Hunting," or folk ballad Roud 47, also catalogued as Child Ballad #68, and comes from 18th-century Scotland. Other titles include "Henry Lee," "Early Richard" and "The Proud Girl." Another similar song is a Child Ballad called "Young Benjie," with variants known as "Child Waters" and "The False Lover Won Back." A man tells his girlfriend that he loves another woman. She stabs him to death and dumps him in a well. She then promises a little birdie that she'll treat him kindly, in this version a parrot – presumably because it could tell the police about the murder. The parrot tells her that there's nothing doing, given what she just did to poor Henry. The interesting note in this song is her remorse after she kills Henry. "Get well get well, Love Henry!" she cried.

Ragged & Dirty
Dirty derelict
Asks woman for a quick one
To help pep him up.

This is an old blues song, and the lyrics haven't changed much over the years. The trouble is that I don't quite understand what's going on here. My view is that it's about a guy who caught his wife cheating on him with his best friend, so he's out on the road, and hungry and broke and so on. He runs into another woman and suggests that they have sex. She is married to someone else, but he suggests that they make it a quickie and he'll be gone before her man ever suspects what's going on. If that's not the story, then two men must be sharing the verses, as some of the lines are about Mr. Unlucky cursing the rotten turn of events, and others are about getting a quick crack at the lady while her man is out.

Blood in My Eyes
Man pays a woman
For a date. She won't be rushed.
He reclaims his cash.

Here's the story of a man who sees a pretty woman and asks if they can make love. To prove his attraction, he goes home and puts on his tie and brings her back all the money that he can find. She asks if he can slow down, but he says he can't wait. He begins to suspect that she's about to take the money and not hold up her end of the deal, so he asks for his money back.

Broke Down Engine
He's like a dead car.
She's probably the reason.
Bodywork might help.

It's the singer's engine that needs jumping. In this old blues song by Blind Willie McTell, a man is lonely so he blows all his money on gambling. When he runs out of cash, he pawns his pistol and his best clothes. Then he prays to God to give him back his woman, and promises to stop bothering God if he'll just do as he asks. Following this, he asks the woman to come back to him. He praises her dance skills and suggests that if she's a real hot mama, she can make his engine, whistle and bell work again (as I was saying about "bodywork"), and most importantly, relieve his weeping spell.

Delia
Curtis kills Delia
And goes to jail. Bob loved her
But couldn't save her.

Delia Green, as the story goes, was shot and killed by Mose Houston on Christmas Eve 1900. She was 14, he was 15, and they reportedly had a sexual relationship. According to the tale, he killed her after she called him a "son of a bitch." As Dylan and others have put it in the various versions of the story, Delia went underground and Houston, also known by other names, went to jail.

He got out after a few years, but died in New York in unknown circumstances. Some versions, like Johnny Cash's, tell the story from the point of view of the murderer. Bob's doesn't. He adds a number of details, likely fictional, to the story. More importantly, he adds himself as the self-pitying man who loved Delia, but knew that she had eyes for someone else – someone who would be the death of her. Every verse ends with him telling us that "All the friends I ever had are gone."

Stack A Lee
Stagger kills Billy
Over a Stetson hat theft.
Stag goes to prison.

This is an old tale, covered many times. A pimp in St. Louis, "Stag" Lee Shelton, shot an underworld buddy, Billy Lyons, in a bar fight that involved Lee's Stetson hat. That's the basic story. Everything else from the song's first known reference in 1897 to the present has been an embellishment or a variation.

- Hawlin Alley. Raining.
- Barroom. Stag asks for some beer. Asks Bill why he's here. Bill says he's waiting for his wife to arrive on a train.
- They fight about the hat. Stag plans to shoot Bill, who pleads for his life on account of his three children and wife. He calls Stag a bad man.

- Stag says he will take care of them, but he must kill Bill because he did something bad in regards to the hat. We don't know what.
- He shoots Bill in the head. Bill dies.
- The doctor cries, "What have you done?"
- Horses and a hearse take Bill to the cemetery.
- Stag runs away in the dark.
- Cops find Stag sleeping.
- Stag goes to jail.
- The ghost of Billy Lyons haunts Stag while he's in jail. "Jailer, I can't sleep. 'Round my bedside Billy Lyons began to creep."

Two Soldiers
"If I die, tell Mom,"
One soldier said to his mate.
But then they both die.

"Two Soldiers," also known as "The Blue-Eyed Boston Boy," is an old song from the Civil War, author presumably unknown. According to Lyle Lofgren, it likely is a story based on the battle of Fredericksburg in 1862. A blue-eyed boy and a tall dark man are fighting for the Union, and the boy asks the man to please tell his mother if he dies. He says he would do the same for the dark man. Both die in battle, and there is no one left to tell the boy's mother what happened, nor his blue-eyed girl.

Jack-a-Roe
Boy goes off to war.
Girl follows, dressed as boy. She
Finds him, they marry.

Another song of many titles: "Jack Munro," "Jackie Monroe," "Jack-A-Roe," "Jackaroe," "Jackaro," "Jackie Frazier," "Jack the Sailor," "Jack Went A-Sailing," "The Love of Polly and Jack Monroe." In this case, Jack could be the guy's name, or a reference to his life as a sailor, i.e., "Jack Tar." He goes to sea, and off to war. His girl can't bear to let him go and insists on coming with him. Unlike in many of these stories, both live, stay together and get married.

- Wealthy London merchant's daughter had plenty of suitors, but she wanted only Jackie Frazier.
- Father says he would rather lock up his daughter than give her to Jackie.
- She says too bad.
- She dresses up as a man and joins the navy. She tells the captain that they call her "Jack-A-Roe."
- The captain says she looks too much like a girl to be ready for combat. She says she's up for anything.
- There's a battle. She finds her Jackie among the wounded.
- She takes him to the doctor and he heals the boy. "The couple, they got married, so well they did

agree. The couple, they got married, so why not you and me."

Lone Pilgrim

Dead pilgrim in tomb
Tells man he died of disease
And went to heaven.

Here's a merry tune. "Lone Pilgrim" apparently dates back to 1838.

- I visited a place and found the grave of a pilgrim. I heard his ghost whisper to me.
- He said: be it storm or thunder, I'm at peace lying here and cry no tears.
- I caught the plague and died, my master called me home. "My soul flew to mansions on high."
- Please tell my family not to cry for me. "The same hand that led me through seas most severe has kindly assisted me home."

From **Bob Dylan's Greatest Hits Volume 3**
Dignity

Dignity
Dignity: it's more
Than a word. Everyone knows,
But really, they don't.

"Dignity" is the great Dylan anthem that wasn't. Like Sam Peckinpah's movies "The Osterman Weekend," "Pat Garrett and Billy the Kid" and "Major Dundee," I don't think there's one finished version that matches what Dylan was searching for in this song. Dylan and producer Daniel Lanois intended the song to appear on 1989's "Oh Mercy" album, but repeated takes failed to produce what they wanted. In Dylan's book, "Chronicles: Vol. 1," he says everyone eventually got fed up and abandoned the track. I heard it first on the 1995 "MTV Unplugged" album, and then on a single featuring various edits.

Who's looking for dignity and where:

- Fat man/blade of steel.
- Thin man/last meal.
- Hollow man/cotton field.
- Wise man/blade of grass.
- Young man/passing shadows.

- Poor man/painted glass.
- New Year's Eve party. (Somebody was murdered just after dignity phoned for a cab.)
- Bob/city-town-midnight sun.
- Bob/the police.
- Blind man/trance/pockets of chance/circumstance like pocket lint.
- Bob/Mary Lou's wedding. (She has a deadly secret and an aversion to being seen with Bob.)
- Bob/Where the vultures feed.
- Bob/asking the maid while the house is on fire, his debts go unpaid and the cold winds blow.
- Drinking man/crowded room with obscured mirrors/lost forgotten years.
- Bob/Prince Philip at the house of blues. (He speaks on condition that he gets paid and can speak off the record. He has a bone to pick with dignity.)
- Bob/sons of darkness and sons of light in the border towns of despair.
- Bob/in a river on a boat reading a note.
- Sick man/doctor/masterpieces of literature.
- Englishman/in the wind.
- Unidentified person with a photograph that he claims is dignity, but Bob says no one has taken a picture of dignity.
- Bob/the red and the black and the valley of dry bone dreams.
- Bob/the edge of the lake.

From **MTV Unplugged**

John Brown

John Brown

John Brown goes to war
And gets himself blown to bits.
How proud is Mom now?

"John Brown" is a grim tale penned by Dylan in 1963 about a boy who makes his mama proud by enlisting and going to war. She doesn't know quite what to do when he comes home disfigured by injury, but clutching all those medals that she was hoping that he would win. A particularly grim moment in which the soldier faces his enemy and discovers that they look just like the other is almost certainly lifted from one of the most dramatic and heartbreaking scenes from the 1930 Lewis Milestone film adaptation of Erich Maria Remarque's novel "All Quiet on the Western Front." The song appeared at the time under the pseudonym Blind Boy Grunt on a Broadside Ballads release. Its first appearance on a Dylan album was on 1995's "MTV Unplugged." Further versions have surfaced on commercial releases since then.

Time Out of Mind

Love Sick; Dirt Road Blues; Standing in the Doorway; Million Miles; Tryin' to Get to Heaven; 'Til I Fell in Love With You; Not Dark Yet; Cold Irons Bound; Make You Feel My Love; Can't Wait; Highlands

Love Sick

He loves you, but he
Wishes he'd never met you.
That's what "love sick" means.

"Love Sick," marked Dylan's official entrance into the house of old rockers. This song defined the path of Dylan's work and critical reaction to it up to the present. It's a morbid, mysterious and bitter song, and though I wasn't captivated when it came out, my opinion has changed. It's a good one. It's also noteworthy for appearing in a Victoria's Secret commercial.

- Walking on dead streets with you alive in his brain. Feet tired, brain wired, the sky is crying.
- He's in the midst of love and sick of it.
- He sees lovers in the meadow, silhouettes in a window. He hangs on to a shadow.
- Clock tick, love sick.
- Silence can be like thunder. Sometimes he's going under. He wonders if you could ever be true.
- Love sick = wish he'd never met you. Love sick = trying to forget you.

Dirt Road Blues

Bob's walking the road,
Hoping his baby comes back.
He'll hope forever.

Bob and his band play a grungy blues theme that hits the usual Dylan topics:

- Baby's gone, she won't come back.
- Bob goes wandering, hoping for a ride, just like Robert Johnson.
- He'll keep walking until his eyes bleed and he's been freed.
- He's looking for the sunny side of love, but getting rain and hail.
- He'll have to put up a barrier between himself and everyone else.

Standing in the Doorway

Woman breaks Bob's heart.
He shouldn't take her back, but
He probably will.

Many of Dylan's relationship elegies are masterpieces in how they reflect on the passage of time doing little to dim some torches that we carry. "Standing in the Doorway" is a less charitable song than some. In this one, the singer remains bitter about how the woman left him in the lurch years ago, "standing in the doorway, crying."

Million Miles
He tries to get close.
She's a million miles away.
And she stays that way.

Another grubby blues song. The refrain sums it up: "I'm trying to get closer, but I'm still a million miles from you." Physics and interstellar travel across the endless gulf between humans will get you every time.

Tryin' to Get to Heaven
I am done down here.
You're in the past, so I'll just
Rush off to heaven.

"I'm tryin' to get to heaven before they close the door." It's a great refrain for a country song, and Dylan, no stranger to country, seizes the moment for this excellent song.

- It's going to rain as I wander through the high water. It's hot. I'm beginning to forget you.
- I had to leave Missouri quickly. You broke my heart. Now the book is closed. I'm in the lonesome valley.
- People are waiting for trains. Their heartbeats are loud in my ears. I tried to give you everything. See what good that did.
- I'm going to New Orleans. I'm told everything will be all right. I remember riding in a

buggy with Miss Mary-Jane who has a house in Baltimore.

- I'm going to sleep in the parlor and relive my dreams. Is everything as hollow as it seems?

'Til I Fell in Love With You
I was fine until
You came along. Now I'm screwed,
And I'll have to leave.

This song has the nearly monotonous rhythm and melody focus of much of Dylan's more recent work, but it serves the single-minded purpose of the song, which is to drive home the point that – as he has often said in his recent work – life won't be the same now that he's met her, and boy is he sorry that he ever did. That's because she's like a drug.

Not Dark Yet
Bob is getting old
And the world has gotten worse.
And it's not done yet.

This melancholy look-back-on-life-at-dusk song defines Dylan's later-stage motifs: summing up the highs and lows of life and their union.

- Sunset. Too hot to sleep. Soul turned to steel, but still plenty of scars.

- No more sense of humanity. Pain accompanies every beautiful thing. She wrote him a letter, and she was nice about it while being honest.
- Bob's been to London and Paris, the river and the sea. He's been on the bottom in a world where everyone lies. He's not looking for anything from anyone. "Sometimes my burden seems more than I can bear. It's not dark yet, but it's getting there."
- You think he's moving, but he's standing still. He's numb. Not a murmur of a prayer.

The music soars under the able hand of producer Daniel Lanois, and despite its mere four verses, it's epic stuff. It's just not what you want on during your periods of bitterness, regret and your seventh wine spritzer. Or maybe it's exactly what you want on.

Cold Irons Bound
Wrong about my friends,
Wrong about you, wasted life.
And I'm still in love.

A recurring theme in Dylan's songs, particularly from 1997 onward, is this combination:

- I made lots of mistakes in life, particularly with leaving the right woman and staying with the wrong one.

- The future is bleak and my bones are old and I wish things had turned out better.
- I really blew it with you, but I love and miss you anyway, and there's nothing to be done about it.

This is one such song.

Make You Feel My Love
I'd abase myself
To make you feel my love, or
I could sing this song.

This song has been covered by a number of artists, most notably Adele. Garth Brooks also did it. The first person to sing it was Billy Joel, whose version came out earlier than Dylan's. It's not hard to see why the song has proven to be the most popular of Dylan's more recent hits. It's a straight-up love song, and as Paul McCartney said, some people want to fill the world with silly love songs – and what's wrong with that? I'd like to know. 'Coz here I go again...

What he can do for you:

- Offer warm embrace.
- Hold you for 1 million years.
- Would never do you wrong.

What he would do to himself for you:

- Go hungry.
- Go black and blue.
- Go crawling down the avenue.
- Everything.
- Make you happy.
- Make dreams come true.
- Go to ends of earth for you.

Can't Wait
I have looked for you
For years. I want you so bad.
Better find you soon.

More gut-bucket swamp-rock. Dylan in "Can't Wait" sings about how he can't wait for a former lover to change her mind. He wants her back, he can't live without her, he can't understand why this is and he can't wait because without her, he'll die. That all being said, he doesn't know what he would do if he saw her. He probably wouldn't be able to control himself. He concludes that he's the one as he goes "strolling through the lonely graveyard of my mind." When they parted, he left his life with her many years before. It's definitely not a situation you want to be in unless you make your living writing songs like this.

Highlands
All done with the world,
Paradise so far away,
Bob pretends he's there.

"Highlands" is Dylan's longest studio recording at 16 minutes and 32 seconds. At its most general the singer longs to be somewhere else. The good times are gone. People complain about this and that (he wants to play Neil Young on the stereo, but someone always is telling him to turn it down), other people seem to be in far more enviable positions. His conscience would trouble him if he had one. He wanders, nowhere to go, and lets things happen to him. It would be better if he could be in the highlands where none of this would matter. He concludes that he's there in his mind and that's good enough for now. And then there's the strange intermezzo that takes up a fair portion of the song: He goes to Boston, visits a restaurant. He asks the pretty waitress for boiled eggs. She has none to offer, and her tone becomes increasingly critical as she begins to suspect that he is mocking her. She asks him to sketch her. He does. She disagrees with the likeness. He says it most definitely is what she looks like. She accuses him of ignoring feminist literature. He says, no, he's read Erica Jong. He leaves while she's in the kitchen. He feels lonely and yearns for the highlands.

Single: **<u>Roving Gambler</u>**

Roving Gambler
Play your love like cards?
Don't be surprised if someone
Calls you on your bluff.

This gorgeous traditional ballad of a wastrel and the woman who deserves better has been done many times by many people. Dylan's version appeared as a song on the "Love Sick" single from the "Time Out of Mind" album.

The story:

- He's a roving gambler. He gambles, he travels. He can't stay away from a card game.
- He meets a pretty girl in San Francisco. She tells her mother she's in love with the gambler. The mother is upset. "How can you treat me so, leave your dear old mother, and with a gambler go."
- Lucky mother, unwise girl. He leaves his sweetheart in San Francisco and goes to Maine and gets into a poker game.
- He shoots the dealer for cheating.
- That's not considered a justification for murder so he goes to jail, whereupon the warden taunts him: "You've gambled your last game."

From **The Bootleg Series Vol. 4: Bob Dylan Live 1966, The "Royal Albert Hall" Concert**

Tell Me, Momma

Tell Me, Momma

What is wrong with her?
Something's on her mind, but she
Won't tell him what gives.

"Tell Me Momma" was released commercially only in 1998 on volume four of the Bootleg Series, a recording of him and the group that became the Band in concert at the Manchester Free Trade Hall. It uses a number of old blues references as a basis for the singer to ask his gal what's wrong with her.

- Ol' black Bascom. (Don't break no mirrors.)
- Cold black water dog. (Make no tears.)
- Don't you love me still? You have a steam drill and you want a kid to make it work for you like John Henry's hammer, so something is on your mind.
- Verse 2 has the weird stuff: "Spend some time on your January trips. You got tombstone moose up and your graveyard whips."

- Verse 3 contains an exhortation to "bone the editor," which I fully endorse. He's not reading, and his painted sled (Charles Foster Kane? Hearst?) is actually a bed.
- She's close to the window ledge, now why would she want to jump? "For I know that you know that I know that you know, something is tearing up your mind."

From **The Essential Bob Dylan**
Things Have Changed

Things Have Changed
The world can hurt you
If you let it in. Bob did,
But now things have changed.

This song from "The Wonder Boys" soundtrack earned
Dylan an Academy Award and a Golden Globe Award.
I like it best for its refrain, "I'm locked in tight, I'm out
of range. I used to care, but things have changed." This
is a song about growing a shell to keep the world at bay,
a lesson learned only after multiple rounds through the
wringer.

Selections from **Live 1961-2000: Thirty-Nine Years of Great Concert Performances**
Somebody Touched Me; Wade in the Water; Handsome Molly; Grand Coulee Dam

Somebody Touched Me
Somebody touched me.
Jesus testimonial?
Or police report?

This Christian country song was written by Leon Bowles and Tim Frye, and was recorded by the Stanley Brothers.

What the hand of the Lord was doing:

- While I was praying, somebody touched me.
- While I was saying glory glory glory, somebody touched me.
- While I was singing, somebody touched me.
- While I was preaching, somebody touched me.

Wade in the Water
Should kids be wading
If God troubles the waters?
Songwriter says yes.

Here's a spiritual-style song that was recorded in 1961.

"Wade in the water
Wade in the water, children
Wade in the water
God's a-gonna trouble the water
God's a-gonna trouble the water."

Handsome Molly
When Molly leaves you,
You'll be sorry, just like the
Next fellow will be.

Fiddler Gilliam Banmon Grayson and guitarist Henry Whitter brought us the song "Handsome Molly," which was the B-side to their hit single "Train 45." I don't know if they wrote it. The song appeared in 1927 or 1928. Grayson died at the age of 43 in a car accident in rural southwestern Virginia in 1930. Whitter died of diabetes at 49. "Omie Wise" and "Little Maggie" are two other songs that Grayson recorded that found their way into Dylan's repertory.

- I wish I were a sailor, and while I sail, I'd think of Molly.
- Molly left me after accepting my offer of marriage.
- My heart's broken; she should go with whom she pleases.

- She has a roving eye now. I saw it when I went to church last Sunday.
- I go out at night when everyone's asleep and cry for Molly at the riverbank.

Grand Coulee Dam
They're dam fine wonders,
Columbia River and
The Grand Coulee Dam.

Dylan and the Band recorded this Woody Guthrie song at a tribute to the folksinger in 1968. There's an album of the concert, but it wasn't released under Dylan's name so I didn't include his two other performances, "Dear Mrs. Roosevelt" and "I Ain't Got No Home." It's a tribute to the dam as a modern wonder of the world, a particularly useful and relevant, contemporary thought during the time of the WPA and the Great Depression.

Love and Theft

Tweedle Dee & Tweedle Dum; Mississippi; Summer Days; Bye and Bye; Lonesome Day Blues; Floater (Too Much to Ask); High Water (For Charley Patton); Moonlight; Honest With Me; Po' Boy; Cry a While; Sugar Baby

Tweedle Dee & Tweedle Dum

Tweedle Dum and Dee:
Not exactly the best of friends
As the world ends.

Tweedle Dee and Tweedle Dum might have started off as the inhabitants of a farcical poem from the 18th century, but they became best known as the twins in "Alice's Adventures in Wonderland" and "Through the Looking-Glass" by Lewis Carroll. Dylan transforms them into a sinister duo who are more sick of each other than Lewis and Clark must have been by the time they reached the western slopes of the Rockies.

Mississippi

Guy makes a wrong choice,
Has no woman or future,
But he's doing fine.

"Mississippi" is one of Dylan's latter-day hits, a song of regret and bad choices. It also contains contrition from

Dylan when it comes to broken relationships. That's pretty rare, and all the more precious for that.

- Our days are numbered. We muddle by, and are trapped in our own prisons.
- Trapped in the city, raised in the country, working in the town, in trouble wherever I go.
- My ship is sinking and I'm drowning in poison. No future, no past. Still, "my heart is not weary, it's light and it's free."

Summer Days
Bob's rolling along.
They say he's a washed-up star.
He thinks he's feisty.

"Summer Days" is undoubtedly a fine song, though it seems to be a collage of stories that form some new shape when viewed from afar rather than one narrative.

- He has a house on the hill and pigs in the mud. His girlfriend has royal Indian blood.
- He's standing on the table, proposing a toast to the King with a capital K, like Elvis the king, or maybe he's the Indian king.
- A bunch of girls tell him he's a worn-out star as he drives the flats in his Cadillac.

- You can't see the land, the fog's so thick. By the way, what good are you if you let some old businessman bully you?

- Wedding bells and a choir. What looks good by day can look bad by night.

- Is this his wedding? She's looking at him and holding his hand and saying, "You can't repeat the past." He quotes F. Scott Fitzgerald: "You can't? What do you mean you can't? Of course you can!"

- Someone asks him where he's from and where he's going. He says he doesn't need to tell them. He refers to his lifelong position of living defensively, then suggests sarcastically that she "break his heart one more time, just for good luck."

- His dogs are barking. Someone must be near the house. His hammer is ringing, but his nails aren't going in. I can only assume that this is a sex thing.

- Want to say something? Say it or shut up. If you want to know about him, go ask the chief of police.

- He's leaving in the morning as soon as the dark clouds disperse. He's going to burn his house down before he goes, just as a "parting gift."

Bye and Bye
Old man still can dance.
With age comes wisdom. He knows
You're his only love.

I saw an interview with Joni Mitchell on CBC in which she said Dylan told her that he hadn't written a song for 20 years, but was putting together pieces of older songs to make new ones. "Bye and Bye" is that kind of song. The narratives wander, sometimes declining to connect from one verse to the next. Only the mood is constant. In "Bye and Bye," the band shuffles through a 1940s-style tune as Bob grabs whatever from the songbag fits his fancy, and doesn't forget a few jokes here and there like, "I'm sittin' on my watch so I can be on time."

Lonesome Day Blues
This guy's all alone
And wistful. He didn't sleep
With his hot roommate.

Musically, "Lonesome Day Blues" is a barn burner. Lyrically, it reads just how you think it would. This song is meant to be played nice and loud.

- Sad day, mind million miles away.
- People dancing the double shuffle, sand on the floor. I left my girl while she stood in the door.
- Dad died, brother was killed in the war. Sister got married. Never heard from no more.
- Samantha Brown lived in my house for about four or five months. I never slept with her, regardless of what the neighbors think.

- Road's washed out, it's raining. I have observed that things that are hard to part with are things you don't need.
- I'm driving to or from the mill, listening to the radio. I wish my mother were still alive.
- Your lover, who is rotten, a thief and a coward, is coming across the barren field.
- I have a captain who's schooled, skilled and decorated, and not the least bit sentimental about all his buddies who have been killed.
- I listened to the wind last night. It brought an omen of approaching something or other, but nothing ever comes.
- I'm going to spare people whom I've defeated, and plan to hold a public address. The plan is to teach peace to the conquered and to tame proud people.
- Rustling leaves, stuff falling off the shelf. "You gonna need my help, sweetheart, you can't make love all by yourself."

Floater (Too Much to Ask)
When you get this old,
You get less sentimental
About everything.

"Floater (Too Much to Ask)" is one of those old-fashioned songs that could have come out 80 years ago, though the lyrics are decidedly modern. The song contains 16 verses, none of which seem to relate to each other, other than a recurring reference to living like a contrarian when people try to get the singer to do one thing or another. The title comes from the last verse when Dylan observes that it's not easy to kick someone out (of your home, I guess), and that it's unpleasant task. Sometimes, he says, someone wants you to give something up, and even if they cry about it, "it's too much to ask."

Other contrary stuff in the song:

- Sometimes old men around here get on bad terms with the young men, but age doesn't mean anything anyway.
- One of the boss's hangers-on tries to bully you and inspire you with fear, but it has the opposite effect.
- His father is like a feudal lord and has more lives than a cat. He's never argued once with his wife, and as Dylan says, "Things come alive or they fall flat."
- Romeo tells Juliet her complexion makes her look old. Juliet replies: "Shove off if it bothers you so much."
- Bob says that if you interfere with him or cross him, your life could be in danger. He's not as cool or forgiving as he sounds, he says.

High Water (For Charley Patton)
These flood-water blues
Don't pick and choose. Just? Unjust?
You will get rained on.

"High Water" is a pastiche of old blues song lines (dust my broom, Bertha Mason, the cuckoo is a pretty bird...). It's a strong, compelling song, full of the dark foreboding of storm clouds and rising flood waters. It also contains one hell of a banjo part.

How the high water is making things (note that each line is sung before the words "High water everywhere"):

- Nothing standing there.
- It's tough out there.
- Things are breakin' up out there.
- It's rough out there.
- It's bad out there.

What's happening:

- Gold and silver being stolen.
- Big Joe Turner made it to Kansas City. He's thinking dark thoughts on the corner of 12th and Vine. High water.
- Shacks are falling.

- People leaving.
- Possessions lost.
- Bertha Mason says, "You're dancin' with whom they tell you to or you don't dance at all."
- Coffins dropping in the street.
- Water in Vicksburg.
- The judge is looking for Charles Darwin trapped out on Highway 5.
- The cuckoo is a pretty bird.
- Fat Nancy isn't feeding Bob like he asked.
- Bob's thinking about dusting his broom in the morning, like Robert Johnson said.
- Thunder over Clarksdale, Mississippi.
- Bob can't be happy if you're not happy.

Moonlight
It's pretty tonight.
Man meets woman in moonlight.
They cross the river.

"Moonlight" is another combination of elegy to the day and the seasons and the defiance of an old man who still has something to offer the world, not to mention a woman.

Honest With Me
If you knew my mind,
You'd be honest. I love you,
But I waste my time.

- Stranded in New York City, avoiding some of the women who give him the creeps. His memories could strangle a man.
- Came ashore in the middle of the night. Quotable line: "Lots of things can get in the way when you're trying to do what's right."
- Not sorry. Happy to have fought. Wish he'd won. PS, the Siamese twins are coming to town. They're expecting a crowd
- Never want to go back home.
- My gal's face: like a teddy bear, though she's tossing a baseball bat in the air. As for the meat, you couldn't cut it with a sword. He's crashing his car.
- Me: My eyes are pretty. Smile: nice. Available for reduced price.
- I won't keep bothering you if you prefer that I don't. I could hop the Southern Pacific railroad at 9:45. Did you know that it's hard to believe that some people were alive?
- Stark naked, don't care. Gonna hunt naked in the woods.
- Why I'm on earth: to create an industrial empire/do what circumstances require.
- My parents' advice to me: don't waste your years. Everyone since then has been giving me advice.

Po' Boy
Poor boy's working hard,
A step ahead of the law.
Things will work out fine.

"Po' Boy" is a curious collage built from sources including the Marx Brothers and "Confessions of a Yakuza" by Japanese author Junichi Saga. In between there are references to Blind Willie McTell songs and Shakespeare's "Othello," along with a "knock knock" joke to round it out. It's not a palette that I ever would have thought of, but I'm not Dylan. I can't crack the nut of this song, but I was game to go along with it because its charm sells itself.

- Poor boy shows up. Me: who are you looking for? Him: Your wife. Me: She's in the kitchen, cooking. Don't make me tell you again.
- I'm at the store, buying something. The guy there wants $3. I offer him $4.
- I'm working on the main line, and working hard.
- Othello to Desdemona: I'm cold, I need a blanket, and "by the way, what happened to that poison wine?" Desdemona to Othello: "I gave it to you, you drank it."
- "Calls down to room service, says send up a room," like Groucho Marx did.

- My mother: daughter of a wealthy farmer. My father: traveling salesman. (Dylan's first traveling salesman joke in a song since 1964's "Motorpsycho Nitemare.") I didn't know my father. When Mom died, an uncle who ran a funeral parlor took me in, did lots of nice things for me, and I won't forget him. This is the Yakuza reference.

- Guy says, "who are you?" I say, "Freddy." He says, "Freddy who?" I say, "Freddy or not, here I come."

Cry a While

My tear supply's done.
You have plenty yet to shed.
Time to make you cry.

You made him cry, now it's your turn. That's the message that ends every verse of this song, though the little stories that precede the refrain are an intriguing display of the Dylan rhyme machine at work.

Sugar Baby

You're fine without me.
Why bother reuniting?
I don't see the point.

Another fine song in the ever-growing catalogue of Dylan songs about a lost lover going down the road who probably should just keep moving because there's no sense in getting back together – even if it's something they want. It's another in several of his recent songs in which he sings about bright sunshine and light, and how he needs to turn his back to it because it's too intense.

From **The Bootleg Series Vol. 5: Bob Dylan Live 1975, The Rolling Thunder Revue**

The Water Is Wide

The Water Is Wide
Hope my boat floats.
I know wood sometimes fractures,
Like your love for me.

Who knew that the unhappy marriage of the 2nd Marquis of Douglas and Lady Erskine in 16-whatever would produce a song that people sing today? "The Water Is Wide" is the distillation of many folk songs that stem from a common source, a reconstituted version of the lament of the marchioness. The point of the song? True love flies away and it doesn't come back, and doesn't that just suck for you.

- Situation: The water is wide.
- Problem: No wings to fly.
- Solution: Build a boat for two and my love and I will row across.
- Conundrum: Our ship is loaded deep, but not as deep as the love I'm in, so I don't know if I sink or swim.

- Once: I leaned my back against a young oak, which I thought would be trusty. But he wasn't, so he broke and plunged me into metaphor.
- Moral: "Love is a jewel while it's new. But love grows old and waxes cold and fades away like the morning dew."

Selections from **The Bootleg Series Vol. 7: No Direction Home: The Soundtrack**

When I Got Troubles; Rambler, Gambler; This Land Is Your Land; Dink's Song; I Was Young When I Left Home; Sally Gal

When I Got Troubles

Begone, my troubles.
I'm gonna swing them away
And leave them behind.

I think that "When I Got Troubles," from 1959, is Dylan's first "solo" recording to be commercially released.

- Got trouble on my mind. I plan to leave it behind.
- Swing your troubles away.

Rambler, Gambler

Leave me alone if
You don't like me. Write to me
If you should need me.

This one, from 1960, begins with the chorus that anyone who has spent a drunken evening at an Irish bar will know: "I'm a rambler, I'm a gambler, I'm a long way from my home. If the people don't like me, they can leave me alone."

This Land Is Your Land
This land is our land,
Never mind what the records
At City Hall say.

This is one of Woody Guthrie's most famous folk songs.

- It's your land from California to New York.
- I affirmed this while walking down the highway and looking up at the beautiful blue sky and the golden valley.
- I've been all around this country from the beach to the desert. This is definitely your land and my land.
- I walked while the sun shone and the wheat waved and the dust rolled and the fog lifted, and someone told me this was our land.
- I saw a sign that said "no trespassing," but on the other side it said nothing at all. You know what that means: this land is our land.
- I saw my people by the steeple, waiting in a bread line during the depression. They were hungry and wondered if the land was made for you and me. (It is.)
- I can go wherever I want and be as free as I want and no one can stop me.

Dink's Song (Fare Thee Well)

Man knocks up woman.
He used to want her a lot,
But not anymore.

"Dink's Song," better known as "Fare Thee Well," gained some prominence in recent years after it made an appearance in the Coen brothers movie "Inside Llewyn Davis." It provided apt accompaniment (and echoed the plot) to the sour, depressing film, about a selfish folk singer in Manhattan in the 1960s who was good enough to hold his own, but he was not the genius he thinks he is. The music is bright, but the lyrics are longing. It's about a woman whose lover leaves her when he get her pregnant. Not only does he abandon his responsibility, he loses his interest in her when she begins to show.

I Was Young When I Left Home

He rambled while young.
While boozing, he hears Mom died,
But he can't go home.

- Guy leaves home, never writes to his parents.
- Collects his pay, runs into a guy who tells him his mother's dead and his sister's "all gone wrong," and dad needs him home immediately.
- He doesn't have enough money, clothes and, apparently, reputation to do this.

- You can gauge how far he is from home by the sound of the train whistle.
- He needs to pay his debt to the commissary, pawn his watch and chain, and go home.
- He misses his mother. He doesn't like being out in the windy plains, even though he thought he would before he went out roaming.

Sally Gal
Sally gal, don't doubt
Dylan's gonna soon find out
What you're all about.

"Sally Gal" is an outtake from the 1962 sessions for the album "The Freewheelin' Bob Dylan." It is an extremely simple song as you can see:

- I'm gonna get you, Sally Gal. (x4)
- I'm a rambling kind of guy and I come and I go. Sally says it happens all the time.
- I'm gonna get you, Sally Gal. (x4)

Selections from **Live at the Gaslight 1962**
Rocks and Gravel; The Cuckoo; Cocaine; Barbara Allen; West Texas

Rocks and Gravel

How to build a road.
This lesson followed by: how
To find my girlfriend.

Dylan recorded "Rocks and Gravel" during the 1962 sessions for "The Freewheelin' Bob Dylan," but its first appearance in a commercially released format was this live take from the Gaslight concert. The studio take appeared on the rare "50th Anniversary Collection." It also appeared on the TV show "True Detective" in the first season. It's a short song, and it contains the following pieces:

- To build a solid road: you need rocks and gravel.
- To satisfy my soul: you need a good woman.
- By the way: have you ever been down on the Mobile and K.C. line? If so, have you seen my girlfriend?
- And here is a refrain that he took and altered for the song "It Takes a Lot to Laugh, It Takes a Train to Cry" – "Don't the clouds look lonesome shining across the sea? Don't my gal look good when she's coming after me?"

The Cuckoo
Gambler builds a house
To watch his girl and cuckoo
As they go riding.

Versions of the cuckoo song have come and gone for a few hundred years, from what I can tell. I wouldn't be surprised if that 1,000-year old song "Sumer Is Icumen In" didn't provide a root for the song, what with its verse to the cuckoo singing in the summer. Dylan's version contains more references to the "newer" older versions of the song. The cuckoo fulfills its purpose of being a harbinger of summer. Meanwhile, a man wants to gamble his way into some winnings, then use that money to build a house so he can get his girl (as she goes riding by), because he doesn't have the poetic gift to woo her with his words alone.

Cocaine
Cocaine's bad for you,
Causes trouble, makes you sick.
Try a little more.

There must be a whole barrel of songs about cocaine use in the pop and blues worlds. This one comes from the Reverend Gary Davis, who said he learned it in 1905 from a traveling carnival musician named Porter Irving.

- My girlfriend and I go out on the town, high on cocaine. Policeman knock us down.
- You need to help me. This cocaine is making me sick. It's running all around my brain.
- My girlfriend has a shotgun, says she's going to kill me.
- I got high on cocaine at 4:30 in the morning.
- Cocaine's for horses, not for me. Doc said it will kill me, but we don't know when.

Barbara Allen

Young boy is dying.
Barbara spurns him, then dies too.
He's the rose, she, thorn.

Originally known as "Barbara Allen's cruelty: or, the young-man's tragedy. With Barbara Allen's lamentation for her unkindness to her lover, and her self." Barbara Allen spurns the love of a man, or a boy, as there are many versions of the song out there since its first known reference by Samuel Pepys in 1666. The boy dies of heartbreak, whereupon Barbara regrets her decision to deny a man life through her lack of love. At this late juncture, she falls in love with him, and dies. From his grave comes a rose, hers the briar, and through their intertwining they discover fidelity and love.

West Texas
Going to Texas,
Looking for adventure, and
I'm not coming home.

- Going to Texas, going to find a fortune-telling woman.
- Will avoid western Dallas streets so as to preserve life.
- Going to Jack Rabbit's place.
- You'll miss me when I'm gone.
- Tell mama I won't be home tonight.

Modern Times

*Thunder on the Mountain; Spirit on the Water; Rollin'
and Tumblin'; When the Deal Goes Down; Someday Baby;
Workingman's Blues #2; Beyond the Horizon; Nettie Moore;
The Levee's Gonna Break; Ain't Talkin'*

Thunder on the Mountain

His soul's expanding:
Bob thinks of Alicia Keys,
Love, mercy and work.

"Thunder on the Mountain" is a great, luxurious over-
ture to the album. It feels like Dylan is ready for act five
of his life, and it's beginning with a fine period of renew-
al, humor and drive. Nothing has happened for ages, and
finally something is about to. He wonders where Alicia
Keys is, he thinks he'll forget his own problems and see
what other people need, and by the way, he doesn't give a
damn about your dreams. He also plans to raise an army
of "tough sons of bitches."

Spirit on the Water

She's the one for Bob.
He might be over the hill,
But that's no problem.

This is a lovely, loping song. This one has perhaps more
verses than it needs to get to the point, which is that
there's a woman he's in love with, in spite of the ways she

tries him, and he's ready to tolerate her transgressions as long as she sticks around. The title, and the first few words, "Darkness on the face of the deep" refer to the world just after the biblical account of how God created it. Before anything else, there was nothing but God's face moving over the deep water, it says in the book of Genesis. It's a powerful image.

Rollin' and Tumblin'

"Slut" charms Bob. He dreads
Early sorrow and pines for
His long-gone lover.

The original "Rollin' and Tumblin'" was recorded by Hambone Willie Newbern in 1929, though the ones that most contemporary audiences know are by Muddy Waters and Cream.

- I rolled and tumbled all night long.
- I have troubles. "Some lazy slut has charmed away my brains."
- The landscape is glowing in the day's golden light. I'm going to say whatever I want from now on.
- I tried to keep from thinking about you. I paid my dues, but my heart still suffers.
- I get up every morning and go lie down outside. I can do whatever I want.

- This latest girlfriend of mine was such a trouble-some woman that, "I swear I ain't gonna touch another one for years."
- It's getting warm and the buds are beginning to bloom. (I think I know what's going on here.) I continue to try to satisfy my woman.
- The sun came up again, as always. Oh, you're going to burn in hell one of these days.
- Shadows and doom: I'm raising the souls of the dead from their decaying tombs.
- Let's settle our past differences.

When the Deal Goes Down
Life is short, death long.
He'll be with you when you go
Because he loves you.

"When the Deal Goes Down" means "when you die." It's a compassionate, touching song.

Someday Baby
You worry me now,
But you won't worry me long.
I'm making you leave.

"Someday Baby" is based on a number of older songs done by Muddy Waters, Sleepy John Estes and others. It netted Dylan a Grammy award. The essence of the song is a description of a troublesome lover.

- Do what you want, say what you want, go away as long as you want.
- You took my money, you leave me full of doubt.
- I used to like to drive, but now you drive me crazy.
- I'm dwelling on the same thoughts and feeling uptight.
- I overlooked the good things in life for the sake of you, and I'm hooked.
- I'll wring your neck as a matter of self respect.
- Pack your clothes and take off. Don't come back.
- I tried to be nice, but now I'm kicking you out.

Workingman's Blues #2

Finding work is hard.
Finding love is harder still.
I hope we can work.

This tip of the hat to Merle Haggard and his "Workingman's Blues" is a wonderful song. Despite my enthusiasm for it, I find it a hard one to analyze. I put it down to love and work, the things that we spend most of our time doing.

- Chorus: "Meet me at the bottom, don't lag behind, Bring me my boots and shoes. You can hang back or fight your best on the front line. Sing a little bit of these workingman's blues."

- Sailing, ready for the storm-tossed deep. I'll take my enemies to hell and sell them to *their* enemies. Think I'll sleep the rest of the day and sustain myself on thoughts. "Sometimes no one wants what we got. Sometimes you can't give it away."

- Enemies are everywhere, some deaf and dumb. When will sorrow come? Outside: the night birds. Inside: lover. Sleeping in the kitchen, feet in the hall. This must be what death is like. The feet evoke the image of the corpse in Wallace Stevens's poem, "The Emperor of Ice Cream."

- People worry all the time. I don't think of them at all. I just think of you. You hurt me with your words, but that won't last.

- Bruised and down on my luck. I will give you another chance. Please come and dance me away. I have a new suit, a new wife and I can live on rice and beans.

Beyond the Horizon
Love you till we die,
And once we are dead and gone,
We'll still be in love.

This one takes its structure from "Red Sails in the Sunset." He works in notes about meeting someone just in time and yet being blue. For some reason, perhaps because of the "horizon" mention in the title, it makes me think of those aviation films of the old days, Chuck Yeager and the test pilots of "The Right Stuff," and those romance-and-flyboy books like "The Crowded Sky" by Hank Searls. I sometimes wonder if these references to the Eisenhower years are intentional. Dylan's early years spanned the Truman and Eisenhower administrations, a time of a broad, modern aesthetic in design, furniture, the arts, typefaces and technology that is hard to define but impossible to unlearn once you get an idea of its existence. I wouldn't be surprised if he were trying to sprinkle some of that essence in this song.

Nettie Moore
Nettie Moore is gone,
Bob's getting along somehow
In his lonely hours.

"Nettie Moore" is 12 verses and a chorus. It's a tangled, deep but spare song that builds itself on a pastiche of blues song references and other literary sources. Some say Dylan plagiarized other songs and other works, given its similarity to an old poem of the same name. I see a mix and match of inspiration. For every obscure line from someone's book or song or folk tale that ends up in here, there are explicit references to source material, from the Robert Johnson "blues falling down like hail" line in this song and the further adventures of Frankie and Albert, to a hat tip to Merle Haggard on "Workingman's Blues #2." The song doesn't tell a linear story, though Dylan keeps returning to missing Nettie Moore and having no one with whom he can share his feelings. He sings the song gently, slowly, with minimal drumming that almost suggests a funeral, though the tone is light and wistful instead of muffled and dark.

The Levee's Gonna Break
Forget the levee.
Blocking floods isn't my job,
But loving you is.

Two things are happening here. One is that Dylan's favorite metaphor, the flood, is threatening to overwhelm the levee. Then there's the state of Bob's love life.

Ain't Talkin'
You see Bob walkin',
Silent, resistant, vengeful.
Love lost, primed to fight.

Songs from this album and others that followed it flow like those old rivers of the plains states. They're sidewinders, long and meandering, and you can't tell where they're shallow or where they're deep. "Ain't Talkin'" lasts nearly nine minutes. Like many of his songs in the last 20 years, they rely on simple riffs or melodies, often taken from much older country-and-western or blues songs, played dozens of times in a row and sometimes without a chorus or a bridge. The words are where the variety lies, and Dylan packs each verse with seemingly unrelated stories, at least in the narrative. It's the feeling in the words that links each verse to the next, and the feeling is usually downcast. "Ain't Talkin'" is just such a song, and rather than trying to condense every event into 17 syllables or sounds, I tried to look at it as a picture. What you don't get in this second period of Dylan verbosity (and I mean that in a positive way, despite the connotation of the word) is the Rimbaud-style surrealism of his work in the mid-1960s. It's more of a combination of references from 2,000 years of history provided in a manner that is simple, yet as I said about the river, you'd be hard pressed to get accurate soundings as you sail. It's better to just let the river run.

- Walking in the mystic garden. Wounded flowers on vines. Cool/crystal fountain. Someone hits him from behind.
- Walking through weary world of woe. Heart is burning and yearning. No one knows.
- Prayer can help, but evil dwells in human hearts. Trying to love my neighbor and do right, but it's not going well.
- Burning bridges. No mercy for losers.

- Worn out from crying. Dry lips. Ready to slaughter my opponents if I catch them sleeping.
- People will crush you with wealth and power. Could happen at any moment. Making hay while the sun shines. Ready to avenge father's death.
- Back in the mystic garden - hot day, hot on the lawn, I tell this woman that the gardener is gone.
- Walking toward the end of the world.

Selections from **The Bootleg Series Vol. 8: Tell Tale Signs: Rare and Unreleased 1989-2006**
Red River Shore; Tell Ol' Bill; Dreamin' of You; Huck's Tune; Marchin' to the City; 32-20 Blues; Can't Escape From You; The Girl on the Greenbriar Shore; Miss the Mississippi; The Lonesome River; 'Cross the Green Mountain; Duncan & Brady; Mary and the Soldier

Red River Shore
Boy pines for a girl
Who said she was not for him.
He never forgets.

Boy falls in love with girl from the Red River shore, despite the pretty maids all in a row lined up outside his cabin door. He wooed and courted her, but she said to him "Go home and lead a quiet life." He never ended up with the girl, and even though the dream of having her died a long time ago, he has never been able to shake her from his mind. There is no way for him to be happy except to be with her, so when he returns to the old town to find her, everyone says that they don't know who he is talking about. This song, along with a few others in this collection, was slated for the "Oh Mercy" album, but didn't make the cut.

Tell Ol' Bill

Bob's beset by doubts.
He can't sleep, she's not helping.
Someone's after him.

This is a dark and stormy night song. It appeared on the soundtrack to the film "North Country," starring Charlize Theron, Frances McDormand and Woody Harrelson.

- River whispers, heavens near, body glowing, not a penny.
- I sing to myself, wondering if the tempest will drown me. (Feels like a nod to Prospero.)
- Stranded in a foreign place, can't sleep, can't find a smile.
- Why do you torture me?
- Remember me. I wish we could share our emotions.
- You trampled me and left me a cold comfort kiss. But I'm not afraid anymore so I have no reason to talk to you.
- I can't sleep. I walk by tranquil lakes and streams.
- The ground's hard and the stars cold as you speak. It's going to be a long night.
- Bleak rocks, bare trees, iron clouds, snow, gray and stormy sky.
- Sundown. Dark woods, dark town, you're going to get dragged down.

- Tell ol' Bill that anything is worth trying, and that Bob isn't alone. It's time to do or die.

Dreamin' of You
He still dreams of you
After a life on the stage.
He's going insane.

"Dreamin' of You" is another in the series of autumnal Dylan songs – bittersweet, lonely, searching kind of stuff. The music video, starring Harry Dean Stanton, centers on the old alterna-rock myth of a lonely man wearing a suit, driving in the desert. It's not Stanton's first road-trip through the hipper-than-thou wastes of the southwestern United States. Wim Wenders cast him in the unlovable loser role in the film "Paris, Texas" from 1984, but here he stumbles across an old stash of Dylan records in a garage, rather than Nastassja Kinski in a peep show booth.

Huck's Tune
A queen in Bob's deck
Might make a good hand, but he
Folds early and leaves.

Earlier in this volume, I said I didn't care for most songs about baseball. The same goes for horse racing, boxing, billiards and cards. Leave those to Nelson Algren, Damon Runyon and Walter Tevis. I also don't care much about gambling. "Huck's Tune" is a song that rests, in the end, on a deck of cards, and was used in a movie about poker, "Lucky You," with Eric Bana, Drew Barrymore and Robert Duvall.

Marchin' to the City
Now that he's been dumped,
He's going to the city.
No girl? Try plan B.

- Sitting on a wooden chair in church where I won't be found. Sorrow and pity rule the earth and skies. Not looking for anything from anyone.
- I had a woman. Did me wrong. Going to the city. Won't be long.
- Snow falling heavy like lead. Only you can heal me.
- The more people you're around, the lonelier you are. Chained to the earth like a slave. Trying to break out of death's cave.
- Boys playing in the street. Girls flying away. Carrying roses from someone. Looking for paradise.
- Go to London? Maybe Paris. Go along the river to the sea. Hoping to drink from pleasant dreams and clear streams.
- Weak weaker. Strong strong. Train keeps rolling. Girl looks at me with a fantastic smile.

- House on fire. No rain coming. You'll remember me when I'm gone. I'm going to be rich and famous.

32-20 Blues
Gonna shoot my gal.
My gun's bigger than hers is.
(She has a new boyfriend.)

The "32-20 Blues" is about a gun, which an angry man uses to shoot his woman because he's upset with her for cheating again. It's based on the "22-20 Blues" about the same thing. Robert Johnson performed the former, Skip James the latter.

Can't Escape From You
I can't tell if I
Love you or hate you. One thing
I know: I miss you.

Here's another song of trains, shadows, sunlight, loss, the memory of sweet days and the reality of the cold present. The singer laments for his former, and obviously current object of desire.

- Hope rides away on a train. Joy and love have faded. Hills dark, falling stars. He pretends he's not sad, but his heart's miles away. He can't escape from her memory.

- Why does he suffer? He did no wrong.
- She didn't behave well. She wasted her power, withered like a flower, played the fool. She tried to bring him down. He's not sad or sorry like he said he was before.
- Actually, he is sorry after all. They should have lasted forever, they had lovely days together, they had good times. Now she's with someone else, God knows who, and still, he can't escape from you.

The Girl on the Greenbriar Shore

Go with Greenbriar gal?
You'll be sorry, Mama said.
She wasn't lying.

This song, which the Carter Family performed, is the simple tale of what happens when a boy chooses a girl against his mother's wishes. Dylan performed the song live in 1992.

Miss the Mississippi

He'd rather be home
On the big river with you
Than in the city.

This is an old Bill Halley song made famous by Jimmie Rodgers in 1932. Bob Dylan recorded it in 1992 at Acme Recording in Chicago for an album that he decided not to release.

- Tired of big-city lights and glamour and the sights. Wishing I were back in Mississippi.
- Sad, weary, far from home.
- Everywhere I go, I think of you and the Mississippi river.
- Thinking of happy memories: mockingbirds singing around the cabin door, etc.

The Lonesome River
Pledge love eternal,
And you'll soon discover it
Probably won't last.

This is a song by Ralph and Carter Stanley, one of those high-lonesome bluegrass tunes about abandoned love. He sits on the river banks, accompanied by the lonely wind and the high water. He's too lonely to cry and has no one to love or kiss him goodnight because the woman he loves left him this morning. Once they swore to each other that they would stay together and be happy forever. Then she fell in love with someone else.

'Cross the Green Mountain
Civil war soldiers
Die on the battlefield.
Brothers fight brothers.

Civil War movies are more impressive than affecting to me. I feel the same way about "'Cross the Green

Mountain," which appeared on the 2003 soundtrack to the film "Gods and Generals." It's a song about the tragedy and waste of war, but it leaves me unmoved.

Duncan & Brady
Brady wants to kill,
But Duncan gets the first shot.
Too bad for Brady.

Brady the cop is looking for someone to kill. He goes to the bar and decides Duncan's the man, but Duncan shoots first. These events apparently are true, and have remained consistent over most of the versions of the song performed since the incident occurred in St. Louis, Missouri, in 1890. This song comes from sessions recorded in 1992 at Acme Recording in Chicago.

Mary and the Soldier
She will go to war
Because she loves her soldier.
First they get married.

Remember the scene in "History of the World, Part I" when Madeleine Kahn makes her selection of Roman centurion studs for an evening of partying with the Vestal Virgins? Mary of "Mary and the Soldier" pursues her quest for a man with similar élan.

"They march so bold and they look so gay
The colours fine and the bands did play
And it caused young Mary for to say
'I'll wed you me gallant soldier'."

She viewed the soldiers on parade and as they stood at
their leisure
And Mary to herself did say: "At last I find my treasure…

'But oh how cruel my parents must be
To banish my true love away from me
Well I'll leave them all and I'll go with thee
Me bold and undaunted soldier'."

The song is an outtake from the 1993 album "World
Gone Wrong."

Together Through Life

Beyond Here Lies Nothin'; Life Is Hard; My Wife's Home Town; If You Ever Go to Houston; Forgetful Heart; Jolene; This Dream of You; Shake Shake Mama; I Feel a Change Comin' On; It's All Good

Beyond Here Lies Nothin'

Stay with your old man.
Let's consider our future
And forget the past.

"Beyond Here Lies Nothin'" opens the album, which I suppose is a joke because there's plenty that lies beyond this song, and all of it is good. In this one, Dylan's an old man, he's singing songs of love to a woman, whether she's the same one who has so often abandoned him or whether she's someone new. Either way, he's old, mistrustful, bitter and reminiscing, while at the same time new vistas for life open up. Whether she's with him or without him in this song is up to the listener to guess.

Life Is Hard

I made it alone,
But I find that life is hard
When you're not with me.

Everybody knows what a bummer it is not to have your sweetheart by your side.

My Wife's Home Town
My wife is trouble.
She makes me do bad things, and
Her home town is hell.

- She makes you steal.
- She makes you rob.
- She gives you hives.
- She makes you lose your job.
- She makes things bad.
- She makes things worse.
- She has more potent poisons than a gypsy curse.
- She will make me kill someone.
- She makes me lose my reason.
- She ensures that I love only her.

If You Ever Go to Houston
Bob's Houston advice
Should keep you safe from the cops,
But not loneliness.

"If You Ever Go to Houston" is another one of Dylan's recent rueful songs of lessons learned late. It borrows the title line from the song "Midnight Special," but heads in its own direction. It's a time-warp trip through the oil city of today and the old days of the Texas republic, steeped in barbeque sauce and regret:

Instructions for Houston trip:

- Walk right.
- Hands in pockets.
- Don't look for a fight.
- Watch out for the sheriff at the corner of Bagby and Lamar.
- Know where you're going or stay where you are.

Instructions for Dallas trip:

- Say hello to Mary Anne.
- Tell her I've still got my finger on the trigger.
- If you see her sister Lucy, apologize for my absence.
- Tell her sister Betsy to pray for this sinner.

Why Bob knows all this:

- He nearly got killed there in the Mexican war.
- Something keeps him coming back.
- He knows about restlessness and having to keep moving forward.

Instructions for policeman:

- Please find my gal.
- She was last seen at the Magnolia Hotel.
- Be my friend.

Instructions for trip to Austin, Fort Worth and San Antonio:

- Visit the bar rooms I used to get lost in.
- Send me home my memories.
- Put my tears in a bottle. Seal fast.

What's at the corner of Bagby and Lamar in real life, according to Google Maps (at the time of this writing):

- Deloitte & Touche human resources office.
- Houston Public Library - central branch.
- Sam Houston Park.
- The Heritage Society.
- Tudor, Pickering, Holt & Co.
- Société Générale.
- Houston Volunteer Lawyers.
- METRO bus stop for routes 40 and 41.

Regarding Bagby and Lamar:

Who was Thomas Bagby (1814-1868)? He was a businessman and civic leader from Virginia who moved to Texas. He petitioned the legislature to emancipate a black female slave in 1847, but his petition was rejected. He was a Mason, a Presbyterian and an alderman of Houston's Fourth Ward.

Who was Mirabeau Buonaparte Lamar (1798-1859)? He was the president of the Republic of Texas, born near Louisville, Georgia. He played an instrumental role in repulsing the Mexican army at the Battle of San Jacinto, and called for the execution of Antonio Lopez de Santa Anna. His two opponents for presidency of the republic killed themselves on the same day, providing him with an easy win. He later died of a heart attack, having survived the death of his daughter.

Forgetful Heart
When the heart forgets
How it used to love, the mind
Is doomed to recall.

"Forgetful Heart" is regret and loss in fifth gear.

- Heart forgets the good times. Of all the organs, which would remember them better? That's a tragedy.
- Heart and I used to laugh. Heart was the answer to my prayer. Now it's just one day to the next.

Jolene
This is a decree
From the king: You are informed
That Jolene is queen.

"Jolene" – not the Dolly Parton song of the same name – makes one major assertion:

"Baby, I am the king and you're the queen."

Jolene's noteworthy qualities include walking down High Street in the sun, making dead men rise because of her charms, making Bob get a gun and sleep by your door, making Bob willing to sacrifice himself for you, making Bob want to possess you, making him keep his hands in his pockets and move along, steering Bob toward thoughts of gambling, her big brown eyes that set off sparks and her ability to make a pessimist feel like an optimist.

This Dream of You
I dream just of you.
It's the reason I'm alive.
But you're not around.

"This Dream of You" is another "she keeps haunting me" song. It's also yet another one where he describes his photophobia. "I wonder why I'm so frightened of dawn. All I have and all I know is this dream of you which keeps me living on." I start to wonder after a while if he's portraying himself as a vampire or a ghost, so torn and worn thin by love that he can't stand the day and must haunt the night.

Shake Shake Mama

Young sexy mama
Is worth a little heartbreak
For an old codger.

More photophobia appears here too.

- He gets the blues for you when he looks at the sun. Come back so you both can have some fun.
- It's early evening and he's walking up heartbreak hill.
- Shake like a ship going out to sea. You took his money and gave it to Richard Lee.
- Judge Simpson's walking down by the river. Old Simpson, that clown, shocks him more than anything.
- Some women really know their stuff, but oh dear, those torn clothes and rough language.
- He has no mother, father or friends.
- Mama ought to raise her voice and pray, and when she goes home, she had better go the shortest way.

I Feel a Change Comin' On

We're gonna be friends,
Lovers together at last,
Now that I am old.

"I Feel a Change Comin' On" feels like a valedictory, the finale to the album, whereas the last song, "It's All Good," is more like an epilogue. This song is an invitation to an old man's sweetheart to take the relationship one step further. As Bob sings, "If you want to live easy, baby, pack your clothes with mine." The repeated reference to the "fourth part of the day," which is "already gone," sounds like the beginning of Act V, often the last act in a Shakespeare play. And of course, all the world's a stage, so it's easy to see this sweet, sentimental song as a preparation for death.

It's All Good
It's all bad, really.
People make trouble and fight.
But why worry now?

"It's All Good" is a catalogue of misery, topped by Dylan's insistent refrain. It feels like combination of up-tempo blues and Cajun music.

- Talk about me. Stir the pot. I'd do it too.
- Politicians tell lies. Restaurant kitchen has flies.
- Wives leaving their husbands. I wouldn't change it.
- You could drown in a teacup.
- People on the land are sick. They would move away if they could.

- Widow cry. Orphan plea. More misery everywhere you look. Come with me, baby.
- Killer stalking the town. Cop cars at a crime scene. Buildings falling down.
- I'll remove your beard and throw it in your face. I'll be eating your lunch tomorrow.

Christmas in the Heart

Here Comes Santa Claus; Do You Hear What I Hear?; Winter Wonderland; Hark the Herald Angels Sing; I'll Be Home for Christmas; The Little Drummer Boy; The Christmas Blues; O Come All Ye Faithful (Adeste Fideles); Have Yourself a Merry Little Christmas; Must Be Santa; Silver Bells; The First Noel; Christmas Island; The Christmas Song; O Little Town of Bethlehem

Here Comes Santa Claus

Hide in your beds, kids.
Santa will come in your house
With a gift for you.

Horse opera star Gene Autry wrote this in 1947.

Do You Hear What I Hear?

Wind tells lamb tells boy
Tells king tells the people that
Jesus will bring peace.

The song comes from the time of the Cuban Missile Crisis.

Winter Wonderland

Bob and Parson Brown
Take this jingle-jangle tune
For a brand new spin.

Music by Felix Bernard, words by Richard B. Smith. Perry Como and the Andrews Sisters are but two of the many who have recorded this one.

- Sleigh bells, snow, a walk in the winter wonderland.
- No bluebird. Instead new bird. Sings love song.
- We'll build a snowman, call him Parson Brown, and he can marry us.
- We'll snuggle up by the fire and make plans for the future.
- We can build another snowman, pretend he's a clown, and have fun with him until the kids knock him down.
- It's fun to be outside in winter, though your nose gets cold.

Hark the Herald Angels Sing
The angels have news
About a new birth in town.
You'd better listen.

"Hark! The Herald Angels Sing" is a song by Charles Wesley from 1739. Dylan's version loses the exclamation point on the back cover of the album sleeve.

I'll Be Home for Christmas
Bob says he'll be home
For Christmas. But we all know:
He's always on tour.

The song was written by Kim Gannon and Walter Kent, who wanted to write a song about anyone who couldn't be with their family at Christmas time. Bing Crosby recorded the song in 1943, and it became a big hit for military personnel abroad during World War II, as well as their families.

The Little Drummer Boy
Bing, Bowie and Bob —
They all do the drummer boy.
It must be the drum.

"The Little Drummer Boy" was written by Katherine Kennicott Davis in 1941, and represents one of the best examples of "ear worms" in popular music. There is no way to remove the "pa rum pum pum pum" refrain from your ears except for repeated applications of lye and death metal. So the experts say. The famous versions of this song include the ones by the Von Trapp family singers, the Harry Simeone Chorale, and the bizarre Christmas TV special version with Bing Crosby and David Bowie from 1977.

- New king born. We bring gifts for him because he's the king.
- I'm a poor boy and have no gift for the king so I'll play him my drum.
- Mary conducts the orchestra of the boy and the ox and lamb.
- Drummer boy plays his best. The kid smiles at him.

The Christmas Blues

Christmas time sucks if
You have no friends or lover
To buy presents for.

This bluesy Christmas carol was written by Sammy Cahn and David Holt. Jo Stafford released a version in 1953, as did Dean Martin.

O Come All Ye Faithful

Come to Bethlehem.
You'll never believe what's there.
Or maybe you will.

"O Come All Ye Faithful," otherwise known as "Adeste Fideles" is the only time I can think of when Dylan sang in Latin. This song is ascribed to John Francis Wade, who lived in the 18th century, though others have been associated with it.

"Adeste fideles læti triumphantes,
Venite, venite in Bethlehem.
Natum videte
Regem angelorum:
Venite adoremus (3×)
Dominum."

Have Yourself a Merry Little Christmas
Have a good Christmas.
Even if things suck, they will
Be better next year.

This Christmas carol comes from the 1944 movie "Meet Me in St. Louis." The writers Hugh Martin and Ralph Blane changed some lyrics under pressure to make the song lighter. In particular, they changed "Have yourself a merry little Christmas/It may be your last/Next year we may all be living in the past" to the line, "Let your heart be light." Frank Sinatra, in his version, asked Hugh Martin to change "Until then we'll have to muddle through somehow" because the name of his album for which he recorded the song was "A Jolly Christmas." "The name of my album is A Jolly Christmas," he reportedly said. "Do you think you could jolly up that line for me?" This is where the "highest bough" line comes from.

Must Be Santa
Beard, red cap, red nose.
Please issue an APB;
It must be Santa.

"Must Be Santa" is a polka-style German drinking tune done as a call-and-response to identify Santa Claus. The original song, by Hal Moore and Bill Fredericks, was first recorded by Mitch Miller. Dylan mixes the names of post-war U.S. presidents into the list of reindeer. The video, if you haven't seen it, is a must. It starts off as a Christmas party and ends as an inexplicable chase scene involving a reveler who turns out to be some kind of villain. Both song and video are much fun. See if you can keep up with the rapid-fire recitation: Eisenhower Kennedy Johnson Nixon Carter Reagan Bush and Clinton...

Signs that the guy you see must be Santa:

- Beard that's long and white.
- Comes around on a special night.
- Boots and a suit of red.
- Long cap on his head.
- Big red cherry nose.
- Laughs this way: HO HO HO.
- Will soon come our way.
- Eight little reindeer pull his sleigh.
- Reindeer: Dasher, Dancer, Prancer, Vixen, Comet, Cupid, Donner and Blitzen.
- "Reindeer sleigh, comes our way, laughs this way, cherry nose, cap on head, suit of red, special night, beard that's white: Must be Santa, must be Santa, must be Santa Santa Claus!"

Silver Bells
What Christmas is like
In the city: silver bells
And red light green light.

First performed by Bob Hope and Marilyn Maxwell
in the movie, "The Lemon Drop Kid." Written by Jay
Livingston and Ray Evans. Bing Crosby made it famous.

The First Noel
News flash: Jesus born.
Three kings confirm the story.
We repeat the facts.

Dylan rumbles through it like a road paver.

Christmas Island
Tropical Christmas.
Santa drops in by canoe.
Let's go there sometime.

It's ridiculous, though Bob's in good company with other
performers of the song, notably the Andrews Sisters and
Bing Crosby.

The Christmas Song
Christmas is coming.
Kids aged 1 to 92:
It's coming for you.

This is the "chestnuts roasting on an open fire, Jack Frost nipping at your nose" song, and it was written by Bob Wells and Mel Torme in 1944. Jack Frost is Dylan's producer pseudonym, by the way.

O Little Town of Bethlehem
Bethlehem is nice,
Especially at Christmas,
Its big holiday.

This Christmas carol was written by Phillips Brooks in 1868.

- Bethlehem: you're sleeping, dark and dreamless under the stars, but there's a lot of hope and fear that the people are thinking about, and something you have is about to shine a light on them.
- Jesus is the silent infiltrator of salvation and blessings.

Selections from **The Bootleg Series Vol. 9: The Witmark Demos: 1962-1964**

Poor Boy Blues; Ballad for a Friend; Standing on the Highway; Long Ago, Far Away; The Death of Emmett Till; Bound to Lose, Bound to Win; All Over You; I'd Hate to Be You on That Dreadful Day; Long Time Gone; Farewell; Hero Blues; Whatcha Gonna Do?; Gypsy Lou; Ain't Gonna Grieve; Guess I'm Doing Fine

Poor Boy Blues
Poor boy cries a lot.
Everyone and thing he sees
Produces fresh tears.

"Poor Boy Blues" contains nine tiny songs over nine verses, all with the same refrain: "Cain't ya hear me cryin'? Hm hm hm."

Bob Dylan and nine stories:

- Where did you sleep last night?
- What's wrong with you, baby?
- Let me jump on this train.
- I'm old enough for you to serve me a drink, bartender.
- I run at the sound of the police whistle.
- Don't charge me for this call, long-distance operator.

- No difference between ashes and diamonds.
- Court hears about my general condition.
- Mississippi River she sure do run swiftly.

Ballad for a Friend

My friend went out west.
He left home on a truck, but
Came back in a box.

Bob sings about an old friend from Minnesota who went wandering on the open road, and either was hit by a truck or else someone else hit him after a truck dropped him off by the side of the road in Utah. They brought him back to the North Country to bury him.

Standing on the Highway

Bob's standing around.
Trying to thumb himself a ride.
His life rolls on by.

Here's another lonely thumb-a-ride song that Dylan recorded as a demo for the Witmark publishing company in 1962. It's the old lament of blues singer Robert Johnson: Standing on the highway, trying to bum a ride, but nobody knows him, and everyone passes him by. The second verse is more metaphorical: he's trying to be brave, as he notes that one road goes to "bright lights" and the other goes to the grave.

Long Ago, Far Away
Crucifixion, slaves,
War, murder... Out of fashion?
Don't you believe it.

This demo reminds listeners that evil deeds of the past aren't just history so we're not absolved from thinking about them and worrying about the evil deeds of today.

The Death of Emmett Till
Two angry white men
Torture and murder Emmett.
They are acquitted.

Emmett Till was a black teenager, murdered by Roy Bryant and J.W. Milam in 1955 because they took offense when he spoke (or perhaps flirted) with Bryant's wife, 21-year-old Carolyn. They beat him in a barn, gouged out one of his eyes, shot him in the head and dumped him in the Tallahatchie River. They tied a 70-pound cotton gin fan around his neck with barbed wire. His mother insisted on an open casket at the funeral to bring attention to the brutality of the crime and the racism that spurred it. A jury acquitted Bryant and Milam, who later told Look magazine that they killed Till.

It's one of Dylan's "journalism songs," in the same vein as "The Lonesome Death of Hattie Carroll" or "Who

Killed Davey Moore?" Or, for that matter and much more loosely, "Hurricane." He lets his indignation show, and accuses his listeners of apathy.

Bound to Lose, Bound to Win
Gonna be walking
Whichever way I'm bound for.
I might win or lose.

"Bound to Lose, Bound to Win" is another in the big book of Dylan songs about people who ramble like hobos, and generally reflects the Woody Guthrie spirit of the age that he embraced for a few years.

All Over You
Bob's gonna get you.
Will he love you or kill you?
Remains to be seen.

I've seen the title of this song written as "If I Had to Do It All Over Again, I'd Do It All Over You."

- I'd wait 10,000 years if I had to.
- Dog have bones, cats have lives, King Saud has 400 wives. Everybody has something they look forward to. I know what I look forward to: doing it all over you.
- I would do a lot of calisthenics just for fun if I could.

- Little David got his chance against Goliath and Samson took the building down. Everybody gets a chance to do the thing they want to do. I know what I would do.
- I don't need money. When I think about the bad things you did to me, I think about the bad things I'll do to you.
- I'm going to do what I need to do to you after I smoke my last cigarette, drink my last drink and bury all my dreams.

I'd Hate to Be You on That Dreadful Day

Get right with Jesus;
Judgment Day is no picnic
For lifelong sinners.
Here's what happens if you don't:

- St. Peter will tell you it's too late when your clock stops and you visit him.
- Sweats and nightmares.
- The pills you will want that day will cost too much to buy.
- You'll walk instead of drive. Everybody will know just who you are.
- Wine's 5 cents a quart. You only have 4. (A preview of "Subterranean Homesick Blues.")
- You should have listened when you had a chance.

Long Time Gone
Good boy turned hobo
Gets heart broken, scorns others,
Wanders forever.

Hobos, hobos and more hobos.

Farewell
He's leaving his girl
For no particular place,
And he will miss her.

"Farewell" is the straightforward tale of a man who is:

- Leaving at sunrise for Mexico. Or maybe California.
- Promising to meet his true love at another time.
- Sad at the thought of missing his true love though he's the one with restless feet.
- Lamenting the weather. (Wind and rain, and eventually hail.)
- Looking to get lucky out west.
- Saying he'll write her letters and travel with his true love in his heart.
- Preparing to tell her stories of the road as he passes by incognito.
- Ready for the friendly, discreet and non-judgmental people of Mexico.

Hero Blues
You want a hero?
It ain't me. Try someone else.
Like Napoleon.

"Hero Blues" was recorded for the 1963 album "The Freewheelin' Bob Dylan," but was left off. You can hear the seeds of "It Ain't Me Babe" in the lyrics. Both songs are about a woman who wants her man to be things that he's not.

- She wants him to be a hero so she can tell her friends.
- She begged, cried and pleaded for him to go out and start a fight with a stranger.
- She reads too many books and watches too many movies.
- She needs a different kind of guy, perhaps Napoleon Bonaparte.
- When he's dead, she's more than welcome to call him a hero while she stands over his grave.

Whatcha Gonna Do?
When death comes for you,
What do you think you will do?
Because I can't help.

"Whatcha Gonna Do?" is a standard warning to folly-indulging sinners to repent before death comes for us and it's too late to say we were good. Think about Hieronymus Bosch and his "Death and the Miser," or any of the other paintings you've seen in galleries of people having a good time as the clock strikes its memento mori. Or "The Masque of the Red Death" by Edgar Allan Poe.

Gypsy Lou
Elusive girlfriend:
The pursuit of Gypsy Lou
Is a full-time job.

The singer searches the country to find her. He tires out his feet. You would too. She's been to:

- Old Cheyenne.
- Denver town.
- Wichita.
- Arkansas.
- Gallus Road, Arlington. (I'm assuming this refers to Gallows Road in Fairfax County, Virginia.)
- Washington.
- Oregon.
- A Memphis calaboose. (Prison.)

Her itinerary ends in the calaboose. One of the boys she left behind committed suicide.

Ain't Gonna Grieve

Don't waste time grieving.
Equality is coming
Despite obstacles.

This is one of those classic folkie protest songs, full of the line, "Ain't gonna grieve no more no more." The theme is civil rights.

Guess I'm Doing Fine

"Guess I'm Doing Fine" is a fair enough ballad of the archetypal annoying optimist whom you encounter in the soppier shelves of the folk song library. Predating "Moonshadow" by a few years, the song lists a host of unfair omissions and grievances, but it always bounces back with the "yes, but at least I have X" resilience of the irritating happy-go-lucky itinerant folksinger.

- No childhood, no friends. But I have my voice!
- No money. But I'm still around!
- Trouble on my mind. But other people have more trouble than I do!
- No armies. But I have one good friend!
- People have kicked me, whipped me, trampled on me and shot at me. But I'm alive!
- Rocky road. Stones cut my face. But at least I have a road!

Tempest

Duquesne Whistle; Soon After Midnight; Narrow Way; Long and Wasted Years; Pay in Blood; Scarlet Town; Early Roman Kings; Tin Angel; Tempest; Roll on John

Duquesne Whistle

Hear that whistle blow?
That's the train I'm waiting for,
Coming right on time.

There's no doubt that this train is blowing loud and fast into town, its little red light blinking. Could it be death? It's blowing in a way that's impossible to ignore. And it makes me think of those old blues songs where the train takes away dead lovers.

- Blows like it's going to sweep his world away.
- Blows like she's never blown before.
- Blows like she's at his chamber door.
- Blows like she isn't going to blow anymore.
- Blows like the sky's going to blow apart.
- Blows like his woman's on board.
- Blows like it's going to blow his blues away.
- Blows like it's going to kill him.
- Blows like she's blowing right on time.

Soon After Midnight
Bob's on the night shift.
He's singing your praises and
Wants no one but you.

"Soon After Midnight" sounds like a love song. It is, but it contains its share of violence. It even has a body count.

- It's just after midnight, and Bob's day has begun. He's looking for phrases that can help sing your praises.
- A young woman took his money.
- His heart is cheerful and unafraid.
- Bob has a date with the fairy queen. Charlotte the harlot dresses in scarlet. Mary dresses in mink.
- These ladies chatter and chirp, while Bob promises to drag the corpse of Two-Time Slim through the mud.

Narrow Way
Heaven's a hard climb,
So if I get tired, Jesus,
Come down and see me.

Biblical epic.

- Walk across the desert until sane. (Exodus of the Jews.)

- Leave everything behind. (Sodom and Gomorrah.)
- It's a long, narrow way. (Book of Matthew: Walk the straight and narrow.)
- "If I can't work up to you, you'll surely have to work down to me someday."
- You: drinking from an empty cup. (Last Supper.)
- You: buried and dug up. (Resurrection.)
- Lost your head for bread and wine. (Last Supper again.)
- Death washed its hands of you. (Resurrection.)
- Too many lovers wailing at the wall.
- About a thousand tongues, I couldn't count them all (Martin Luther hymn: "Oh dass ich tausend Zungen haette," or "If I had a thousand tongues.")
- The moving finger is moving on. (Apparently from the Rubaiyat of Omar Khayyam, rather than the Bible, unless it's a reference to the handwriting on the wall that Belshazzar saw. *(See the entry for the song "Belshazzar" in the "Basement Tapes Complete" section of this book.)*

The song from which Dylan borrows his chorus is "You'll Work Down to Me Someday" by the Mississippi Sheiks, and in that case, the singer definitely is addressing a woman. I hear a bit more of "In My Time of Dyin'," however, in which the singer asks Jesus for a new pair of wings if the pair he's using now don't get him high enough on the path to heaven.

Long and Wasted Years
Couple stays married
For years after they break up.
Wasted tears and years.

I don't think that "Long and Wasted Years" is all that easy to follow, but it is a heartfelt song. Whether these two were married or whether Dylan is getting at something else in this song, I don't know.

- We loved each other a long time ago.
- Heard you talk in your sleep last night. What you said was downright criminal.
- What can we do about our relationship?
- Haven't seen my family in 20 years, since they lost their land. They might be dead by now.
- My enemy with the iron heart died in shame and ignominy.
- I wear dark glasses to keep the secrets in and the sun out. I am sorry if I hurt you.
- We were like two trains running side by side. You don't have to go.
- So much for tears.

Pay in Blood
Bob plans his revenge
Against those who did him wrong,
And there will be blood.

This song could have been called the "Cranky Bastard Blues." "Pay in Blood" is six verses of Dylan nearly losing his temper as he counts the ways that he's going to make somebody sorry for hurting him. He wants revenge, but not before he lists the wrongs that this unnamed villain has committed against him as well as the ways that he has transcended all of them, though not enough to forgive.

- I'm grinding away each day through this life of toil and pain. I've been through a lot and survived it all, but I could stone you to death or put you in chains for your crimes.
- Every new day strips away a few more of your hopes. All that dying just makes me live on, mainly because "I got dogs could tear you limb from limb."
- Life dealt me a bad hand, but I'm going to play it anyway. I might obey God's laws, but if I do wrong in my quest for satisfaction, then by all means put me in front of a firing squad.
- "You got the same eyes that your mother does. If only you could prove who your father was."
- I've been through hell, but I survived. "What good did it do? You bastard! I'm supposed to respect you?"
- And of course, a Shakespeare twist: "I came to bury, not to praise."

And the end of each verse: "I pay in blood, but not my own."

Scarlet Town
It's bad times in town.
The end is near, good's in fear,
Bob's vision is clear.

The roots of "Scarlet Town" are easy to see. It's the setting of the old English ballad of grim death and love (but I repeat myself), "Barbara Allen," known to some as the tale of the red rose and the briar. A young man falls for Barbara who scoffs at his love. Then he takes sick and dies. She, realizing what she has thrown away, dies too. Out of their graves come the rose and the briar, forever entwined with the beauty and fragrance of the petals inseparable from the harm of the thorn. "Scarlet Town" takes off in different directions.

In Scarlet Town:

- There's ivy and thorn, streets with names you can't pronounce, gold whose value has fallen on the market. It's full of people dancing and asking if you're going their way. Uncle Tom still works for Uncle Bill, or as you would say more plainly, the whites still control the blacks.
- Sweet William Holme is dying as Mary lies by his side and prays for him. Bob would weep for Sweet William as Sweet William would for him. Little Boy Blue comes to blow his horn.

- Scarlet Town is under the shadows of palm trees during the hot day. There are beggars and there is too little help for everyone, too late. They pray in the graveyards there. Bob touched the garment, which I take to mean the garment of Jesus, but found that the hem was torn.
- The signs of apocalypse – as seven wonders – manifest in Scarlet Town. Evil and good are neighbors. If you wear your heart on your sleeve – or place it on the platter – someone will take a bite out of it. Nobody will hold you and kiss you goodnight. Crying won't do you any good, as the blues song goes.
- In Scarlet Town, children fight their father's battles, with whiskey, morphine and gin. There is a woman there with legs that could drive a man mad. Through all this, you would wish you had stayed in Scarlet Town.
- And in spite of all the ills that plague Scarlet Town, people still have a good time at night, and heaven comes a little closer to the ground.

Early Roman Kings
I might be old,
But I'm a tough gangster type
Like those Roman Kings.

The early Roman kings to whom Bob seems to refer are the street gang as well as the early kings of Rome.

The song is a combination of allusions to both groups of kings, and a comparison between Bob's physical (particularly amatory) skills and the toughness of the gangs, even though he's going on 200 or 300 years old.

- Roman Kings were an early gang, based in Chicago and New York, tough S.O.B.'s who ruled the place. Don't mess with them.
- The early Roman Kings, and the Romans in general, took care of business. They even put a pretty major dude to death on a Friday.
- Classic blues singer bragging. Don't mess with me baby, I'm like an early Roman King, and I'm tricky.
- Oh, by the way, when I said "I," I was talking about myself, the devil. Satan. Beelzebub. Death. Whatever it is you fear, that's me. I'm evil.
- The apocalypse is coming, and I'm going to enjoy it.

And here are your early Roman Kings:

- Romulus (mythical): 753-715 BC. Rape of the Sabine women.
- Numa Pompilius: 715-673 BC. His adviser was a nymph. Peaceful reign.
- Tullius Hostilius: 673-642 BC. Destroyed the Alba Longa. His name was his calling card.
- Ancus Marcius: 642-617 BC. Expander of Rome, founder of Ostia.

- Tarquinius Priscus: 617-579 BC. Not Roman, but Etruscan. Built the Cloaca Maxima, laid out the Circus Maximus. Conquered stuff.
- Servius Tullius: 579-535 BC. Set up the class system based on wealth. Built a wall around the city.
- Tarquinius Superbus: 534-510 BC. He irritated the people. His son Sextus outraged Lucretia, who was married.

Tin Angel
Man steals woman.
Husband tracks them down. Then they
Slaughter each other.

They all die in the end. That's your spoiler for "Tin Angel," a variation on the "Blackjack Davey" ballad.

- Wife runs off with younger lover.
- Husband pursues, upset.
- Husband confronts the lovers. Passionate words ensue.
- Lover shoots husband dead.
- Wife stabs lover to death, saying just because she was unfaithful didn't give her lover the right to kill the husband.
- Lover learns too late the real price of commitment.
- Wife kills herself to return the favor she did her lover.

Tempest

Titanic goes down,
An unscheduled appointment
For sixteen hundred.

An epic and a tragedy and a repository of somber humor. The most obvious evidence of humor is the reference is to Leonardo DiCaprio, one of the stars of the James Cameron film about the sinking of what the Onion called "the world's biggest metaphor." There also is a kind of destiny detachment in the words, noting that this terrible event was like any other distraction, only on an enormous scale. The refrain in the song that makes it most interesting is the watchman dreaming that the Titanic is sinking, almost a desire for it to be nothing more than a nightmare. At the time it spawned many songs, particularly among blues singers doing their version of journalism. As Dylan noted, he wanted to record his version too.

Some flotsam and jetsam from the wreckage:

- Bob calls the sinking "the promised hour."
- Watchman dream #1: Titanic sinking into the underworld. Note the use of the word "watchman," the same word that the King James Bible uses in the book of Isaiah for the guard in the dream who hears from the heralds that Babylon has fallen. This is the image that Dylan used in

"All Along the Watchtower," and the title that Harper Lee used for her second novel, "Go Set a Watchman." This watchman sees inundation coming, not all that separated from Dylan's repeated references in his music to the big flood, whether it's the one in the Bible or the ones on the Mississippi River – either way, they herald the fall of old empires and the beginning of new ones.

- Leo's on board with his sketchbook.
- Cupid breaks his bosom and falls into a woman's lap.
- Leo thinks there's a problem on board.
- Leo walks into the whirlwind.
- The universe opens for the passengers. The angels do not intervene.
- Dead bodies.
- Exploding engines, dead propellers, overloaded boilers. Bow splits.
- Passengers weary as they try to escape death.
- Watchman dream #2: The Titanic is dropping to her knees.
- Wellington puts on his pistols.
- Alarm bells ring to hold back the water, just like King Canute commanded the waves to go back.
- Love and pity send prayers to mothers and daughters in the icy ocean.
- Some gamblers remain behind in a friendly game as they sink.

- Fights and murder.
- Lifeboats: too few. Murder, betrayal, lies.
- Bishop reminds God: "The poor are yours to feed."
- Davey the pimp dismisses his girls. "Saw the water getting deeper, saw the changing of his world."
- Jim Backus, who can't swim, gives his lifeboat seat to a child. (I suppose that he ended up surviving and cast away on "Gilligan's Island" where he played Thurston Howell III.)
- As he dies, he sees rampaging death, but his heart is at peace.
- Leo tries to hold back the water.
- Watchman dream #3: He tries to warn people that the Titanic is sinking.
- Captain sees the compass needle pointing down down down.
- Captain reads the Book of Revelations.
- Ship sinks. The loveliest and the best die. "Those whom the gods love..."
- The newswires report.
- Watchman dream #4: The Titanic is now part of the deep blue sea.

Roll on John
Hear the sad story
Of John Lennon, Bob's old friend
And tragic hero.

This eulogy to John Lennon 32 years after his murder has a way of bringing it all back. Dylan and Lennon had an interesting relationship, and to hear the way Dylan looks back on it is affecting. The song "Roll on John" finishes the album on an emotional note, even as Dylan reserves his feelings and sings the song straight. There are multiple references to Lennon's life, the Beatles and songs from his solo career as well as the ones credited to him and Paul McCartney.

Selections from **The 50th Anniversary Collection**

Going Down to New Orleans; (I Heard That) Lonesome Whistle; Baby, Please Don't Go; Milk Cow (Calf's) Blues (Good Morning Blues); Wichita Blues; That's All Right, Mama; I Rode Out One Morning; Ballad of Donald White; Deep Ellum Blues; Stealin'; Hiram Hubbard; Two Trains Runnin'; Ramblin' on My Mind; Muleskinner Blues; Motherless Children; Kind Hearted Woman Blues; Black Cross; Ain't No More Cane

Going Down to New Orleans
You don't understand.
I'm going to New Orleans.
I have some troubles.

"Goin' down to New Orleans" is an early track, mostly a variation on Muddy Waters's "Louisiana Blues." Waters focuses on a mojo bag that he'll use to impress the ladies. Dylan is more concerned with some trouble that is chasing him. He had an idea that this would happen after visiting the fortune teller, who tells him that he's all right, but he's cursed by bad luck. Of course, his wandering means he must leave a woman.

(I Heard That) Lonesome Whistle
Guy gets in trouble,
Leaves gal in Carolina,
Gets jailed in Georgia.

This is a Hank Williams song that Bob Dylan played a few times in the early 1960s in studio rehearsals. It's an outtake from the sessions for "The Freewheelin' Bob Dylan."

- Knocks up girlfriend, has to hop a train.
- He was young and stupid. He also broke his girlfriend's heart and presumably committed a crime, as he was sent to prison in Georgia.
- He's ashamed, just a number, not a name. He listens to the lonesome train whistle as the train rolls by.
- He'll be in prison for life.

Baby, Please Don't Go

New Orleans: You know
It's a place where Bob would
Prefer you don't go.

The old blues song that everyone and their brother has done. In Dylan's performance, he's on the Parchman Farm, otherwise known as the Mississippi State Penitentiary in Parchman, Mississippi. The song is a "Freewheelin'" outtake.

Milk Cow (Calf's) Blues (Good Morning Blues)

The milk cow's missing.
If you see her, send her home.
Someone needs a suck.

A Sleepy John Estes song became a Robert Johnson song and eventually reached its way to Dylan, who recorded several takes of it for "The Freewheelin' Bob Dylan" album during 1962. This is a standard blues, combining sickness, sex and cheating. The metaphors barely hide the subject matter. (Though to explain the blue milk: this is a fungal spread.)

- What's wrong with you, milk cow? You have a little calf and your milk is turning blue.
- Your calf needs a suck, but with that blue milk, I believe he's out of luck.
- I want to milk, but my cow won't come. I want to churn the milk and it won't turn. I'm crying. If you see my milk cow, please send her home.
- My milk cow has been wandering all over the place. Why does she suck on some other man's bull cow in that strange man's town?

Wichita Blues
Son leaves Wichita.
Dad says, "You might catch TB."
Son runs out of cash.

"Wichita Blues," also known as "Goin' to Louisiana," is a "Freewheelin'" outtake.

- Leaving Wichita, it's cold. Dad says I might get TB.

- Arriving in West Memphis. No money for public transportation. Tears in my eyes.
- Looks like it's going to rain.
- Going to Louisiana, and it looks like my traveling is just beginning.

That's All Right, Mama

Mom doesn't approve
Of son's girl. He doesn't care,
Even if she's bad.

This song, made popular by Elvis Presley in the '50s, got the Dylan treatment during the "Freewheelin'" sessions. They said back then that Father knows best, and in this case, the singer doesn't believe it. He's not listening to his mother's advice either.

- Mama can say what she wants, and so can Pop, but the girl I'm fooling with *is* good for me.
- As a result of this parent-son discord, I am leaving town and then you won't have to worry about me anymore.

I Rode Out One Morning

Man can't find a "friend,"
Like, "ladyfriend." He's dirty,
He'll need a bath first.

"I Rode Out One Morning" is a folk-blues pastiche, the story of someone who goes out wandering to find a friend, and then laments how hard it is to be lonely. It comes complete with mournful ostinato on the guitar, changing only its chords. I don't buy a bit of the sad boy attitude. I think he's in the mood and needs to find himself some female companionship. He notes that he rides out one morning, trying to make a friend, but can't find one in the city. He then notes that his hands are dirty and his hair is messed up.

This song comes from recordings taped at the home of Eve and Mac MacKenzie in the fall of 1962.

Ballad of Donald White
I steal and murder.
You made me this way. Shoulda
kept me in prison.

Dylan fans will recognize the tune that formed the basis of "I Pity the Poor Immigrant" six years after he performed this song. "Ballad of Donald White" is a song of societal ills too, but in a different vein. Ol' Donald sings the sad story of his life just before he hangs for murder. He came from Kansas, ended up in Seattle and everywhere he went he was an anti-social loser who couldn't fit in. He had no education and stole to support himself. He wound up in jail where, rather like some of Jean Genet's homosexual criminals, he found his real home.

Trouble is, the jails and institutions were too crowded so he was set free. He begged to go back where he felt he belonged, but no one would incarcerate him without reason so he killed a man on Christmas Eve 1959. Naturally, they took him back, but only for a short stay. Then they hanged him. Don's last question was whether "boys that come down the road like me, are they enemies or victims of your society?"

Deep Ellum Blues
This part of Dallas,
Is thick with thieves. Your daddy
likes to hang out there.

Deep Ellum is a neighborhood in Dallas, not far from the Baylor University Medical Center. It's an arts and entertainment spot these days, but a century ago it played host to more bawdy forms of the arts (theft, and so on) and entertainment (drugs, gambling, etc.). It was also a hot spot for blues musicians from Blind Lemon Jefferson to Robert Johnson to Bessie Smith. The song "Deep Elm Blues," or "Elem" or "Ellum," depending on how people spelled it, is an ode to – or warning about – the fun, sinful side of town. Les Paul, Jerry Lee Lewis and the Grateful Dead have performed versions of this song.

Dylan's version, which he performed in New York in the early 1960s, contains advice and news, namely:

- Keep your money in your shoes while in Deep Ellum.
- Notice to pretty mama: your daddy has the Deep Ellum blues.
- When Bob went to Deep Ellum, it was on a one-way track. He took his money and never gave it back.

This song was recorded on April 16, 1962 at Gerde's Folk City in New York.

Stealin'
Some people don't change.
They say they will, but they go
Back to what they were.

She doesn't believe that he loves her. She doesn't believe that he's sinking (and needs her). He's gradually turning back into the same kind of person that he used to be, which is not such a good kind of person. Evidence: the woman whose love he needs is married, so you can be sure that she treats him properly. It reminds me of that old movie title, "I Could Never Have Sex With Any Man Who Has So Little Regard for My Husband."

Hiram Hubbard
Despite alibi,
Firing squad shoots Hiram H
Dead without a will.

I don't know much about "Hiram Hubbard," but was able to find one or two references online. It's a mountain murder ballad, most likely from eastern Kentucky, and coming from the days of the Civil War. Jean Ritchie, who performed the song before Dylan, indicates that Hiram was likely arrested and shot by rebel soldiers, though for what crime we don't know. Aiding the enemy, perhaps. Dylan's version doesn't clarify, though Ritchie's includes this verse:

"While travelling through this country
In sorrow and distress,
The rebels overhauled him,
In chains they bound him fast."

In her version, they shoot him with 11 bullets, though Dylan's version uses "three," presumably the better to rhyme with "tree." Dylan performed his version at the Finjan Club in Montreal on July 2, 1962.

Two Trains Runnin'
This is a Muddy Waters song.

- Two trains run in this direction, with one leaving at midnight and the other at dawn. (This is not a math problem.)
- These trains are symbols for women, as you would expect in a blues song. One of these trains appears to be another man's wife.

- He's going to find another woman who rides like a Cadillac car.
- The woman he's with has put him on top of the shelf.

Ramblin' on My Mind

Angry man rambles.
He hates to leave his woman,
But she is unkind.

This is an old Robert Johnson blues song that Dylan recorded in 1962 at the Finjan Club.

Muleskinner Blues

Muleskinner likes work.
He finally finds some, then spends
Payday cash on girls.

Dylan performed this old Jimmie Rodgers song in 1962 at the Finjan Club. It's a yodel about a mule skinner, as you might expect.

- Good morning captain. You don't need another mule skinner on your new road line.
- I like to work. I like mule punching.
- Hey little waterboy, bring some water. If you don't like your job, drop the bucket.
- I'm working on a new road for $1.10 a day. I plan to spend it on three women this Saturday night.

Motherless Children

Mom dies, kids get by.
Dad will try, sister will fly.
On Jesus don't rely.

Eric Clapton's version of this song, the opener on "461 Ocean Boulevard," is the one that most people these days know. The original was called "Mother's Children Have a Hard Time." Dylan's version comes from a show at the Gaslight Cafe in October 1962.

- Motherless children run a hard road when your mother is dead.
- Father will do the best he can when your mother is dead.
- Some people say your sister might do when your mother is dead. But she'll get married and turn her back on you.
- Jesus won't be no mother to you when your mother is dead.

Kind Hearted Woman Blues

His "kind-hearted" gal
Packs a .32, but he
Thinks he might shoot first.

"Kind Hearted Woman Blues" is another song in the long series of woman-hating songs by blues artists. This one, which Dylan performed at the Gaslight Cafe in 1962, is based on blues master Robert Johnson's first studio recording from 1936. His song was based on other blues songs by other people from that time.

Black Cross
Literate black man
Out-theologizes priest.
They hang him for this.

"Black Cross" is the story of Hezekiah Jones, written by Joseph S. Newman in 1948 and performed by Richard "Lord" Buckley in 1959. Dylan performed the song in 1962 at the Gaslight Cafe. Hezekiah Jones is a black farmer who reads too much for his own good in a country full of ignorant bigots. One day a priest comes to his house to ask him if he believes in God and the Church. Jones sports with the priest, using humor and irony, and turns the priest's questions back on him. The white people hang Jones because, as they say, "the son-of-a-bitch never had no religion."

Ain't No More Cane
Cutting cane's hard work
For Texas prisoners on
The Brazos River.

This is an old prison work song about sugarcane cutters. They didn't have a happy life:

- Cane's been ground to molasses after the prisoners cut it all down.
- Speaking of which, you should have been around in 1910 and seen what a rough life these cutters had.

Selections from **The Bootleg Series Vol. 10:**
Another Self Portrait (1969-1971)

Pretty Saro; Annie's Going to Sing Her Song; Railroad Bill;
Thirsty Boots; This Evening So Soon; These Hands; Working
on a Guru; Bring Me a Little Water; Tattle O'Day; Wild
Mountain Thyme

Pretty Saro
Man must leave woman
Whom he can't afford. He dreams
About her and moans.

"Pretty Saro" is an 18th-century English ballad that
survived in the Appalachian mountain region. It's one
of Dylan's most tender vocal performances. The gist:
poor man loves Sarah, but she would prefer a freehold-
er with house and land. He knows he can't afford what
she wants, so he can't have her. He wishes he were a
poet so he could write her a poem that would make her
fall in love with him, but he can't write a poem, so he
wanders the riverbank and dreams of Sarah wherever
he goes.

Annie's Going to Sing Her Song
You should hear Annie.
She leaves, then begs to come back.
I always let her.

The premise to the tune, which was released on Tom Paxton's album "6" in 1970, is this: Annie leaves her fella, then she cries and begs to come back. This happens a lot. He always takes her back. Paxton introduces the song by inviting us to have a few drinks because we're going to need them as we hear about this dysfunctional relationship. Every time he describes the situation, he gives us a stage wink, the detachment that says, "yeah, I know, this sucks, but what do you want me to do?" I would hate to be poor Annie, humiliated nightly as Tom complains about her in front of everyone.

Railroad Bill
I fear Railroad Bill.
He'll take whatever he wants
And kill everyone.

Here's a portrait of a bad man named Bill who rides the railroad like the mean old hobo he is.

The crimes of Railroad Bill:

- Never worked.
- Never will.
- Mighty mean.
- Shot the midnight lantern out of the brakeman's hand.
- Took my wife, threatened to kill me if I resisted.

The revenge of the singer:

- He bought a .38 and is taking it out west, presumably to find Bill and shoot him.
- As the singer notes, "Honey honey honey, think that I'm a fool? Think I would quit you when the weather is cool? Ride ride ride..."

Thirsty Boots
One crash pad needed
For a civil rights worker
Who's returning home.

This is a song by Eric Andersen about a civil rights activist returning from the field.

- You've been on the road, in the rain, in jail, here and there. Clothes are dirty. The jail cell you were in soon will be razed. Hang out for a little while and take it easy before you rush off again.
- Take off your boots and relax your dogs. I'll entertain you for a while.
- Tell me about how the Civil Rights struggle has been treating you.

This Evening So Soon
Bill is dead because
He chased downtown girls around.
We told him not to.

This song was called "Tell Ol' Bill" when Bob Gibson did it in 1958. That is the same title as a Dylan song on the eighth volume of the Bootleg Series, but this is not that song. The phrase "This morning, this evening, so soon," is the chorus, and is the title of the song as Carl Sandburg called it in 1927 in "The American Songbag." The song, likely originating in the 19th-century American South, admonishes ol' Bill to "leave the downtown girls alone." In the rest of the song, you hear that ol' Sal was baking bread when she found out her man Bill was dead. They bring him home in a "hurry-up wagon," and his "arms, his legs and feet were dragging." That's the secret life of ol' Bill that Sally finds out only too late.

These Hands
My workingman's hands
Can vouch for me even if
My track record can't.

Eddie Noack wrote this song while on guard duty in the Army in Texas. It was meant as a patriotic song, but Johnny Cash's version turned it into a working man's praise.

These hands:

- Aren't a gentleman's hands.
- Are calloused and old.
- Raised a family.
- Built a home.

- Praised the Lord.
- Won a heart.
- Fulfilled their task.
- Worked their fingers to the bone.
- Brought me more happiness than those that are attached to the arms of so many strivers.
- Didn't do all they planned, but they did what they could to clasp in prayer to God to hear his plea on Judgment Day.

Working on a Guru
It's raining outside
And I need an umbrella.
So does the guru.

This is a guitar workout between George Harrison and Dylan, recorded during the "New Morning" sessions. The words don't mean much, but they're fun anyway.

- Rain, windshield wipers. I don't feel like groovin'. Working on a guru instead.
- I need an umbrella. I'm that kind of fella. I need a guru before sunset.
- That guru could be you.

Bring Me a Little Water
With Sylvie around,
Bob lacks for nothing, but he
Still wants some water.

This appears to be a variation on the title "Bring Me Little Water Sylvie," which I think was written by Leadbelly. Sylvie is a nice girl from Florida who lacks for nothing in the department of serving her man:

- Sylvie came up in April to spend some time with me.
- Would you bring me some water, Sylvie, for my tired brow?
- She arrived on Wednesday at dawn.
- She says she loves me all the time, and often helps me when I can't get things done on my own.
- She brings me: beer and honey, slop and beans, coconuts and candy, and turnip greens.

Tattle O'Day
Man buys animals
That can't possibly exist.
Then he plays with them.

I think that "Tattle O'Day" was meant as a children's song. Eric Andersen wrote it.

- A little brown dog. He can whistle, sing, dance and run. His legs are 14 yards long, allowing him and the singer to go around the world in 12 hours.
- A four-inch-tall bull whose lowing shakes London to the ground.

- A flock of all wethers (castrated sheep) who produce wool and feathers. They also bring him lots of "increase" as they give birth to lambs and geese every autumn and every time the moon changes.
- A four-acre box that the singer carries in his pocket, having filled it with silver and guineas that he saved up to buy himself a trip to Turkey.
- A speckled hen who sits on an oyster until out springs a 15-hands-high hare.

Wild Mountain Thyme
If you ask your girl
To pick thyme, and she says no,
Just ask another.

"Wild Mountain Thyme" is a song by Francis McPeake of Belfast, and is a variant on an old Scottish song called "The Braes of Balquhither." Dylan and the Band performed it at the Isle of Wight festival in 1969.

- Summer's coming, leaves are coming in, and the wild mountain thyme blooms around the purple heather.
- Go with me, lassie, to pull up the thyme.
- If you won't go, I'll find another lassie to go.

- I'll build my love a tower at the base of the mountain, and I'll fill it with flowers. Come on, lassie, be that woman.
- The spring's coming, the birds are singing, and the thyme is blooming.

Selections from **The 50th Anniversary Collection 1963**

New Orleans Rag; Lonesome River Edge; Back Door Blues; Honey Babe; Goin' Back to Rome; Ramblin' Down Through the World; Hiding Too Long; Dusty Old Fairgrounds; James Alley Blues

New Orleans Rag
Bob's friend refers him
To a call girl. Evidence
Suggests she's lethal.

This is a silly song recorded during the sessions for "The Times They Are a-Changin'" in 1963. Bob's in New Orleans, feeling low and mean and all the usual blues feelings, when a guy suggests that he visit a woman who can fix him up. But here is what happens to the men ahead of him in line for room 103:

- Couldn't walk, linkin' and a-slinkin', couldn't stand up, moaned, groaned, shuffled down the street.
- Wiggled and wobbled, could hardly stand, frightened look in eyes as though had fought a bear.
- Long legs, couldn't crawl, muttered and uttered, broken French, looked like had been through monkey wrench.

Lonesome River Edge
He holds her hand
And kisses her lips and leaves
Her on the river.

This is an abbreviated performance that Dylan played at
Gerde's Folk City in 1963.

Back Door Blues
You would be blue too
If your girl split, and then a
Big coffin arrived.

In reality, the singer would rather have a coffin show up
at his back door than have his girl leave, but it seems am-
biguous enough to me when I explore the words that I
thought it was OK to fool around with the order of things.

Honey Babe
So long, honey babe,
You don't do me like you did.
That's enough of you.

There's not much to this song, which pops up briefly on
a recording of a concert at Gerde's Folk City in 1963, and
it's arguably not worth including as a haiku, but I figured
that the "honey babe" line that he used here must have
later found a home in the song "Don't Think Twice, It's

All Right," which led me to steal a line of that song for this haiku.

Goin' Back to Rome
You can have New York.
I'll take the Colosseum
As I'll be in Rome.

"You can keep Madison Square Garden, give me the Colosseum." This wisp of a song, "Goin' Back to Rome" got one performance live in 1963.

Ramblin' Down Through the World
I'm just a rambler.
Ramble happy, ramble sad.
Ramble good or bad.

This is a song that Dylan performed live in 1963 at Town Hall in New York. In the song, we learn that the singer is just one of those rambling boys, rambling and making noise. Sometimes he's lonely, sometimes he's blue, and nobody knows it better than you. He's just a rambling pearl.

Hiding Too Long
Racists and bigots
Say they are patriots though
We know they are not.

Dylan performed "Hiding Too Long," also known as "You've Been Hiding Too Long," in 1963 at Town Hall in New York. It's a rant, though a well intended and blunt one, and falls right into the middle of his protest song catalog.

Dear phony super-patriotic people who say hate and fear are the way:

- You're thinking of your sales, not of me.
- You're not thinking of George Washington or Thomas Jefferson. You say you are, so you lie and mislead. You use their names for your advantage.
- Don't talk about patriotism when you throw southern black men in prison and say "the only good niggers are the ones that have died."
- I'll never stand on your side.
- You make it hard for me to love. I'll never be one with you.
- Go out and say what you say openly so everyone can see what a hypocrite you are.
- You hide behind the American flag.

Dusty Old Fairgrounds
Melancholy clowns
From one fairground to the next
Ride the blue highways.

"Dusty Old Fairgrounds" is a rarity from 1963. Dylan performed it at Town Hall in New York City in April 1963. It's a tale of ratty fair roustabouts and performers. Dylan traces their ride to bring others fun, from the winter grounds in Florida to Michigan, Wisconsin and other places. They entertain the kids in cow country and in Montana. They're friends with one another in a union no one else can understand. They're free of the rules and conventions of normal society. Then they go back to St. Petersburg for the winter. Life is fleeting, joys are fleeting, love is fleeting...

James Alley Blues
I'm a graveyard man.
I need an undertaker
Girl to bury me.

Dylan performed a version of the "James Alley Blues" in April 1963 at the home of Eve and Mac MacKenzie. It sounds nothing like the original by Richard "Rabbit" Brown, taking only the first line of Brown's song. Essentially: 1. Times aren't what they used to be. People are hard to please. 2. Take me if you can, but not if you want a fortune-telling man. 3. I'm walking down the road on my way to the graveyard. What I need is an "undertaking woman to drive me six feet underground."

From **The 50th Anniversary Collection 1964**
Bob and Eric Blues #1; Black Betty; Johnny Cuckoo; Money Honey; More and More; Susie Q; Glory, Glory; Dr. Strangelove Blues; Stoned on the Mountain; Denise

Bob and Eric Blues #1
Bob and Eric ask
Betsy to hang out with them
Over at her place.

This song was sung by Eric von Schmidt and Dylan at von Schmidt's Sarasota, Florida, home. It's an improvised courtship of sweet Betsy, with Bob and Eric content to fight politely over her in her parlor. The two men switch identities toward the end.

"Well now I know
It don't cause no disgrace
Cause neither one of us are here,
We just take each other's place."

Black Betty
Betty's a pistol,
But she shoots her mouth off and
Annoys the captain.

Old folk song, apparently about a gun or a bottle of whiskey or a prison whip or something. In this version, as with Nick Cave's version, Betty is a woman.

Johnny Cuckoo
Dirty Johnny wants
To join the army on a
Cold and stormy night.

Johnny had a strange notion to join the army in the middle of the night.

"Here come long Johnny Cuckoo
One cold and stormy night
Well, what did you come for?
I come for to be a soldier
Well you look so black and dirty
Well I'm just as clean as you are."

Money Honey
Landlord wants money,
So guy wants it too. He asks
His woman for some.

This is a Jesse Stone song, recorded by Clyde McPhatter and the Drifters, Elvis Presley and others.

More and More
Know why I feel good?
Because I'm forgetting how
It sucked when you left.

This song was written by Merle Kilgore, and sung by
Webb Pierce.

Susie Q
Susie's qualities
From her walk to her talk make
Me love her true.

A stoned home recording of a famous song written by
Dale Hawkins.

"Oh Susie Q
Baby I love you..."
I like the way you walk, talk, etc.

Glory, Glory
So much for burdens.
I'm laying mine down, then I'm
Going to heaven.

It's a spiritual.

Dr. Strangelove Blues
Some like it hot and
Some like it cold, but Strangelove
Likes it very weird.

Ridiculous improvised song.

- He might be a man or a woman. He might like
  it cold or hot. He might like it skinny or tall. Or
  short and small. Or not at all.
- He put me in bed with Charles Laughton when
  he turned out to be King Lear.

Stoned on the Mountain
On the mountain, in
The valley, or wherever,
You might end up stoned.
A song about smoking pot by two stoned guys.

Denise
Denise's facial
Cues suggest she has something
She keeps to herself.

Here's the piano tune that became "Black Crow Blues"
from the 1964 album "Another Side of Bob Dylan."
Here, it has another title and other lyrics. "Denise" did
not make the album.

"Denise, Denise,
You're concealed here on the shelf.
I'm looking deep in your eyes, babe,
And all I can see is myself."

Selections from **The Bootleg Series Vol. 11: The Basement Tapes Complete**

Edge of the Ocean; My Bucket's Got a Hole in It; Roll on Train; Mr. Blue; Belshazzar; I Forgot to Remember to Forget; You Win Again; Still in Town; Waltzing With Sin; Big River; Folsom Prison Blues; Bells of Rhymney; Under Control; Ol' Roison the Beau; I'm Guilty of Loving You; Cool Water; The Auld Triangle; Po' Lazarus; I'm a Fool for You; Johnny Todd; Tupelo; Kickin' My Dog Around; See You Later Allen Ginsberg; Big Dog; I'm Your Teenage Prayer; Four Strong Winds; The French Girl; Joshua Gone Barbados; I'm in the Mood; Baby Ain't That Fine; Rock, Salt and Nails; Song for Canada; People Get Ready; I Don't Hurt Anymore; Be Careful of Stones That You Throw; One Man's Loss; Baby, Won't You Be My Baby; Try Me Little Girl; I Can't Make It Alone; Don't You Try Me Now; Young But Daily Growing; Bonnie Ship the Diamond; The Hills of Mexico; Down on Me; One for the Road; I'm Alright; I'm Not There; All American Boy; Sign on the Cross; Get Your Rocks Off; Don't Ya Tell Henry; Bourbon Street; My Woman She's A-Leavin'; Mary You, I Love You Too; Dress It Up, Better Have It All; Silent Weekend; What's It Gonna Be When It Comes Up; 900 Miles From My Home; Wildwood Flower; One Kind Favor; She'll Be Coming Round the Mountain; It's the Flight of the Bumblebee; Wild Wolf; Gonna Get You Now; If I Were a Carpenter; Confidential; All You Have to Do Is Dream; 2 Dollars and 99 Cents; Jelly Bean; Any Time; Down by the Station; Hallelujah, I've Just Been Moved; That's the Breaks; Pretty Mary; Will the Circle Be

*Unbroken; King of France; She's on My Mind Again; Goin'
Down the Road Feeling Bad; On a Rainy Afternoon; I Can't
Come in With a Broken Heart; Next Time on the Highway;
Northern Claim; Love Is Only Mine; Silhouettes; Come All
Ye Fair and Tender Ladies*

Edge of the Ocean
On the ocean's edge,
Something is on its way
When the seagulls come.

Dylan was experimenting with words as sounds and
rhythm, and creating feelings out of words that weren't
necessarily arranged in sentences that you could dia-
gram. Here are some of the lyrics:

> "Upside down....we're living on the edge of the
> ocean with a mockingbrew
> ready to frown...with a fleet right over my win-
> dow...well, always ocean round
> well, ever up on every morning...brother, brother
> was in my sound...but let me tell you,
> brother, it won't be when the seagulls cross over
> town."

My Bucket's Got a Hole in It
I can't buy no beer.
My beer bucket has a hole.
I'm going to scream.

This is an old song by Clarence Williams, the jazz pianist, composer, singer and publisher (notably of "race records" in the first two decades of the 20th century) of songs with fascinating titles such as "I Ain't Gonna Give Nobody None o' This Jelly Roll," "I Wish I Could Shimmy Like My Sister Kate," "You Missed a Good Woman," "I Can Beat You Doing What You're Doing Me" and "Cake Walkin' Babies From Home."

The most well known version is by Hank Williams. The haiku contains a reference to a scream, one of which Bob lets loose during the song.

- My bucket has a hole in it, therefore I cannot buy beer.
- I saw crabs and fishes in the sea while I stood on the mountain. They were doing the be-bop-bee.
- I don't need to work hard because I have a woman in the boss man's yard.

Roll on Train
This train is rolling,
This train is out of control.
This train rolls all night.

It doesn't sound like the Elton Anderson song of the same name, but who knows...

Mr. Blue

I wish you loved me.
You're painting the town red and
I'm painting it blue.

"Mr. Blue" is a song by the Fleetwoods from 1959. It epitomizes white "rock and roll" that seemed, at least to me, to be an attempt by the music industry to cater to mainstream white radio listeners who thought that Elvis and Jerry Lee were too raunchy and "black." The song was written by Dewayne Blackwell. His other songs include "I'm Gonna Hire a Wino to Decorate Our Home," recorded by David Frizzell, and "Friends in Low Places," made famous by Garth Brooks.

- Our guardian star turned from silver to blue and stopped glowing on the day I lost you.
- I and he both believe that your love is not true.
- If you are looking for me, call me Mr. Blue.

Belshazzar

Babylon's king paid
The price for screwing the Jews.
Writing's on the wall.

Belshazzar had a big feast, and being short on glassware, they used the golden cups and other vessels from the Jews' temple. While Belshazzar probably did plenty of things to offend God, this seems to have presented an occasion for the big man to show up at the party. At this point, a hand writes on the wall, "Mene mene tekel parsin." Daniel, the prophet from the Old Testament, is brought in to explain what this could mean, as Belshazzar feels the cold breath of eternity on his neck. He has seen the writing on the wall, as the saying goes. Daniel's interpretation of the message: Belshazzar was weighed in the balance and found wanting, and his kingdom will be given to the Medes and the Persians. Belshazzar came to an unhappy end, as did Babylon. It fell to the Persians, led by Cyrus the Great in 539 BC.

A short note on the words:

- They were written in Aramaic and without vowels. Not everyone could read them. Daniel could, and he saw:
- MENE = Mena = 60 shekels. Non-literal interpretation: numbered.
- Tekel = shekel. Non literal: weighed and found wanting in balance to the 60 shekels.
- Parsin = half pieces, but also a pun on Persian. Non-literal interpretation: divided kingdom, a kingdom that cannot stand.

I Forgot to Remember to Forget
Now he remembers:
He forgot to remember
To forget they met.

Dylan does Elvis. The song was written by Stan Kesler
and Charlie Feathers. Elvis recorded it in 1955.

- I forgot to remember to forget her.
- I thought I would never miss her, but I do.

You Win Again
Every time you cheat,
I can't bring myself to go.
So you keep winning.

This Hank Williams song shows you what happens
when you let your spouse cheat.

- They say you're running around. I should leave,
  but I don't.
- I shouldn't have trusted you. Everybody knew
  that but me.
- You're going to do to the next guy what you did
  to me.
- You're shameless.

Still in Town

He tried to leave you
By leaving town. The problem?
He never got out.

Imagine "By the Time I Get to Phoenix" where the singer
never gets farther than El Monte. That's Hank Cochran's
"Still in Town." The song is about a guy who can't be with
his lover anymore. I'm assuming that she left him, though
I began the haiku with the words "He tried to leave you."

Waltzing With Sin

Waltzing with sin is
Not the dance ticket you want.
It's not good for you.

I don't know who wrote "Waltzing With Sin." I've seen
it credited to truck-driver songwriter Red Sovine as well
as Mr. Hell-Raiser/Womanizer/Drinker/Born-Again
Christian preacher Sonny Burns.

- Someday you'll find out that the world dropped
  you from its to-do list.
- You partied and socialized too much and were
  waltzing with sin all the while.
- You're like Satan in disguise. Unfaithful, unwor-
  thy, unwise.
- The next guy will regret being with you just as
  I do now.

Big River
I followed my girl
Way down the Mississippi,
Crying all the way.

Where would we be – and I include Bruce Springsteen,
Joni Mitchell and Johnny Cash in this – without rivers to
skate away on? This Johnny Cash river metaphor song
made an appearance during the Basement Tapes sessions:

- Guy meets a woman near the headwaters of the
  Mississippi River. He follows to the Quad Cities.
- She's not there. He follows her down the river to
  St. Louis.
- And to Memphis.
- And to Baton Rouge. And New Orleans...

The cycle of life being what it is, his inability to find
her leads him to cry copious tears which of course keep
the Mississippi full of water, allowing women like her to
continue to elude guys like him.

Folsom Prison Blues
Man shoots some dude
For no reason. Now he whines
Because he's in jail.

"Folsom Prison Blues" is what happens when your
train song meets your prison song. In this case, Johnny

Cash put them together while he was stationed in West Germany at the Landsberg Air Base. It's a famous tale: guy is stuck in prison, sentenced for shooting a man in Reno "just to watch him die." His mother told him when he was young not to play around with guns, and it turns out she was right. Meanwhile, people on the train passing by the prison are rich and enjoying the good things in life. If our hero got out of prison, he would buy the train and move it down the line from prison.

Bells of Rhymney
Welshmen get pissed off,
Strike against the mine owners,
Then go back to work.

Idris Davies wrote this poem as part of his book "Gwalia Deserta" ("The Wasteland of Wales"). The former coal miner-turned-poet wrote about depression and despair in Wales in the 1920s, but it was Pete Seeger who took the words and made a song of them in 1957. The Byrds made it a pop hit in 1965. In the song, the bells of various cities stand in for the tongues of the poor, depressed and dispossessed of Wales, with their coal miners beaten down by the failure of the British 1926 general strike as well as a coal mine disaster.

Under Control
She's under control.
She doesn't need her hand held
As she's hard to hold.

If I could understand the lyrics better, I would have had this haiku under control.

Ol' Roison the Beau

Roison plans his wake.
There will be lots of drinking,
Hogsheads of whiskey.

Here's a drinking song about drinking. And death. And drinking after you're dead.

- I'm ol' Roison the Beau and I've been all around the world. Now I'm going to die and go to hell, but that's all right because I know they have a nice place laid out for me there.
- When I'm dead and on the slab, you'll hear me crying up from hell to send me a hogshead of whiskey.
- Make sure you get 12 fellows, get them drunk, then take me out to the field and bury me.
- Put some barrels there with me and write my name on them with a diamond ring.
- I hear death coming! Time for one more drink. Let's toast to death!

I'm Guilty of Loving You

He knows the verdict
When it comes to loving you:
Completely guilty.

The lyrics are scanty... basically Bob shouting about how he's guilty of loving you and what can he do.

Cool Water
If you and your mule
Were stuck in the desert, you'd
Want some water too.

One of the great country-and-western songs, "Cool Water" was written by Bob Nolan in 1936. I know the song because of the version that Marty Robbins did on the album "Gunfighter Ballads and Trail Songs." I love the passing reference to this song in "Old Dirt Road" by Harry Nilsson and John Lennon on Lennon's "Walls and Bridges" album.

The Auld Triangle
Irish prisoners
Live monotonously with
Mice in their jail cells.

Dominic Behan's song for brother Brendan Behan's 1954 prison play "The Quare Fellow."

- In my prison cell. Mice squeaking, I'm hungry. The triangle jingle jangles.
- Warden screams to get up.
- Prisoner weeps for his lover.

- Prisoner dreams, seagulls soar.
- Prisoner wants to be with the 70 women in the women's prison.

Po' Lazarus

The deputy's task:
Find Lazarus, bring him back.
How? Dead or alive.

> "Oh where the high sheriff told his deputy
> Go out and bring me Lazarus
> Dead or alive."

"Po' Lazarus" was recorded by Alan Lomax and Shirley Collins, and sung by James Carter while he was a prisoner on the "Parchman Farm," part of the Mississippi State Penitentiary. It's a work song and an "African bad-man ballad." It's a work song that four men would sing to keep time while chopping down trees.

I'm a Fool for You

Being your fool is
Hard work for Bob. He can't sleep.
He can't count either.

The lyrics sound like they were written more as place-holders than a final version. It's too bad that this one didn't go anywhere. It sounds like it would have been a good one with the right amount of practice and polish.

> "It's all right in my head, but I can't slumber
> and it's too high for me to count, I can't get the number
> I'm a fool for you."

Johnny Todd

Johnny Todd went to sea.
He left his girl, and she
Married someone else.

Here's an old ballad for the boys who took a notion to go wandering and leave their girls behind. I'm guessing that Dylan heard it from the Clancy Brothers and Tommy Makem.

- Johnny Todd wanted to go sailing on the high seas and left his gal waiting in Liverpool.
- She wept and moaned until she met another sailor.
- He's a smart character: he proposes to her and says she can get instant satisfaction now instead of waiting for Johnny. He promises linens, a wedding ring and a gilded baby's cradle.
- Johnny comes home and finds out what went on while he was gone.
- Moral of the story: Don't be like Johnny. Marry her before you ship out.

Tupelo
A big flood arrives.
People must flee Tupelo
Because it's submerged.

One of the stranger treats you could give yourself in life is listening to Dylan drawl his way through "Tupelo," the old John Lee Hooker boogie blues song about a big Mississippi River flood. He can't bring any of Hooker's easy gravitas to the song, but there's something hokey and funny about it, and it sounds pretty good.

Kickin' My Dog Around
Those boys gotta stop
Kickin' my dog around when
I go into town.

This eternally weird song is one of my favorites. Also known as "Ya Gotta Quit Kickin' My Dog Around," this song was an old-timey music hit in the 1920s for the country music fiddling act Gid Tanner & His Skillet Lickers. Apparently its roots go back to the early 19th century. I'm guessing that Dylan knew the song in part because the sheet music was published by Witmark, the company for which he recorded so many demos from 1962 to 1964. The premise of the song is a question that remains unanswered: every time he goes to town, the boys kick his dog around. Why? In Dylan's version, the Band echoes his "dog dog dog" line with "bark bark bark." He switches to "duck duck duck," followed by the response, "quack quack quack." It's funny if you listen to it.

See You Later Allen Ginsberg
Bob and the Band
Say adios to Ginsberg
Over and over.

This is a completely ridiculous Band/Dylan sing-along. It goes like this:

> "Crocagator (See you later, crocagator)
> After a while, smockawhile (See you later, Allen Ginsberg)
> See you later alligator (See you later, crocagator)
> After a while, crocodile (In a while, Allen Ginsberg)
> See you while, crocagator (See you later, crocagator)
> After a while, crocodile (In a while, crocodile)
> Allen Ginsberg, later gator (See you later Allen, Ginsberg)
> Later later, Allen Ginsberg (See you while, alligile)
> Allen Ginsberg, later later (Later, later on the Nile)
> Allen Ginsberg, after a while (See you later if you're wild)

Allen Ginsberg, Allen Ginsberg (See you later, crocagator)
Allen Ginsberg, after a while (See you later, crocagator)."

Big Dog
Come home, you big dog.
You squeeze me and please me, but
You're just teasing me.

"Big Dog" barely deserves inclusion in the haiku series because it is 22 seconds long, a fragment from the Basement Tapes sessions rather than a serious attempt at a complete song. That said, it has enough words that an eager haiku smith can't help but give it a shot.

I'm Your Teenage Prayer
I'm your teenage prayer,
Just the kind of boyfriend that
You always wanted.

A ridiculous stab at 1950s rock and roll. This one lurches along like the clay about to fall off a potter's wheel.

Sample:

> "Take a look and when it's cloudy all the time
> All you gotta do is say you're mine
> I come runnin' anywhere
> Take a look at me baby
> (Just take a look at me baby)
> I'm your teenage prayer."

Four Strong Winds
Canada drifter
Invites girl to Alberta,
But halfheartedly.

If you're not listening closely to the words in this Ian & Sylvia song, you get the impression that it's a weepy song about lost love and the pain of enforced separation of lovers. But it's not. It's a far more ambiguous song about the selfish singer and the lover whose affections seem real, while his are suspect.

The song begins with the brilliant beginning of the repeated chorus:

> "Four strong winds that blow lonely, seven seas that run high.
> All these things that don't change, come what may."

And then...

> "But our good times are all gone,
> And I'm bound for moving on.
> I'll look for you if I'm ever back this way."

You can tell that he's not into it anymore, so he's looking to light out on the road. To where? The middle of frigging nowhere. And he leaves her with a promise. "I'll look for you if." If. Whatever it's all about, it's a lovely song, and it hits you with the heartbreak of the big sky and the prairie just like a good song should.

The French Girl
French girls are trouble.
They will love you and leave you.
Au revoir? Jamais.

This is a song from Ian & Sylvia's 1966 album "Play One More." It's a bittersweet tale of what happens when you hook up with a French girl who won't tell you her name. She's undoubtedly bent on maintaining her independence, as you can see:

- She wears three silver rings on the crazy Saturday night that you spent at her place.
- But first: Saturday morning! It's raining, you go walking on winding roads back to her house.

- You drink red wine at her place. You get it on, fall asleep.
- She wakes up and you make small talk. You have to go, but you promise to meet her. She names a place.
- When you go to the French café, nobody there speaks English so they can't tell you where she is. (This is Canada, presumably, so I'm assuming that the inability to find a single person to speak English when so much is at stake is stretching it.)
- You tell another guy that he might run into this girl in Canada, and that the chances of managing to keep her are low because she's too much for you.
- After your affair with her, you'll never be the same.

Joshua Gone Barbados

Joshua says he'll
Back the sugarcane strikers,
But he bails instead.

Breaking news from St. Vincent in the Caribbean: Ebenezer Joshua, head of the labor union, goes on vacation while the sugar cane workers strike. Three men die as a result. Or so says Eric von Schmidt, who wrote this song about the trade union leader and later politician, assemblyman and chief minister of this poor island nation. Supporters of Joshua say this reading is erroneous.

I'm in the Mood
Do you know this mood?
If you can't tell already,
I'm ready for love.

It's a John Lee Hooker song. Dylan and the Band stumble through it.

- I'm in the mood, baby, I'm in the mood for love.
- I said night time is the right time to be with the one you love.
- You know when night comes baby, God knows, you're so far away.
- I said yes, my mama told me, to leave that girl alone.

Baby Ain't That Fine
This song compares love
To good fried food, Georgia pines,
Birds, bells and sunshine.

This is a Dallas Frazier song that scored a hit for Gene Pitney and Melba Montgomery in 1965. The haiku is just about what you'd expect from a song in which lovers tell each other how happy they'll be. In fact, they say their love will "sizzle and fry."

Rock, Salt and Nails
Man reminisces
Over his lying ex and
Thinks he might kill her.

Too many songs about jilted lovers end with the man thinking he might kill his ex out of heartbreak and jealousy. I prefer my music to be a little less homicidal when it comes to breakups, but other than that, it's a pretty good song. It was written, apparently, by one Bruce "U. Utah" Phillips.

- The weeping willows and I are hanging out by the river. The birds are warbling and moaning. It was here that you first lied to me about your feelings for me.
- I can't get you out of my mind when I lie awake at night. You wrote me a letter and you were ashamed of yourself, and I hope your conscience continues to bother you.
- Not being able to sleep while being heartbroken is a major drag. I go outside and look at the sky. I can't cry, I can't sing.
- If women were blackbirds and thrushes, I'd go out to the marsh and wait for them to fly by so I could shoot them. If women were squirrels, I'd load my gun with rock, salt and nails.

Song for Canada
Why two Canadas?
We're much better off as one.
Isn't that enough?

I'm assuming that the river in question is the St. Lawrence as well as the gulf that separates Quebec from the Maritime and Atlantic provinces, but in a more profound sense, it's about the gulf between Quebec and the rest of Canada. I think it is, anyway. The song, written by Ian Tyson of Ian & Sylvia with Peter Gzowski, sounds like an appeal to Quebec to remain part of Canada despite a desire among some of its citizens to seek independence.

- Why can't we talk to each other? We're both changing. We've been together too long and we still share a lot.
- Mostly, we share this great big river flowing to the sea/eternity.
- Two nations, one river. Not so bad?
- Why do you pretend I don't exist? Why are you so bitter lately? I never held you down.
- I'm glad that you're proud and I know you made it on your own. But your new pride should let you know that you don't have to stand alone.

People Get Ready
Salvation by train.
The ride is free, Jesus pays.
Thank God for the trip.

This 1965 song by Curtis Mayfield appeared on one of his albums with the Impressions. It's a song about freedom, using the Underground Railroad as its anchor, though the song is as much about spiritual salvation, the way that I read it. I used for the haiku the main refrain, "People get ready, the train is coming. Don't need a ticket, you just get on board." And the only thing that you have to say for riding this train to freedom is, "Thank the Lord." It's a gorgeous song. Dylan also recorded a version of it for the 1989 film "Flashback."

I Don't Hurt Anymore
Nothing is better
Than forgetting the woman
Who tossed you aside.

"I Don't Hurt Anymore" was a country-and-western hit for Canadian singer Hank Snow, one of Dylan's frequent sources for country cover songs. It was written by Walter Rollins (who co-wrote "Here Comes Peter Cottontail," "Frosty the Snowman" and "Smokey the Bear") and Don Robertson (co-writer of "Does My Ring Hurt Your Finger," "Love Me Tonight," "I Love You More and More Each Day" and another Dylan cover, "Ninety

Miles an Hour (Down a Dead End Street)"). The song is one for breakup victims on the mend:

- No more hurting, teardrops dry, no floor pacing, no burning inside.
- Time has freed him, though he once wanted to die. He's fine, you're out of his mind, and God bless his good luck.

Be Careful of Stones That You Throw
You know this lesson,
The one about glass houses.
Don't throw stones in them.

Bonnie Dodd wrote this one in the late 1940s. Dion, Hank Williams and others recorded it. The singer tells the story of a neighbor who shows up while he's gardening. She says she wouldn't let her daughter near the bad girl down the street who drinks and no doubt engages in other anti-social activities. Not long afterward, the singer hears the screeching brakes of a car, and discovers that the bad girl down the street saved the gossipy neighbor's daughter from being run over. The bad girl dies.

One Man's Loss
Dating and trading
Are similar. If you're long,
Someone else is short.

I think that the connection between love, loss and capi-
talist trading structures is more than clear.

> "Better come down easy or don't come down
> at all
> You don't try and please me, somebody's gonna
> fall
> One man's loss always is another man's gain
> Yes, one man's joy always is another man's pain."

Baby, Won't You Be My Baby
The world has problems,
But my main concern is that
You be my baby.

As far as semi-coherent songs from the Basement Tapes
sessions go, this is one of the more intelligible ones. That
doesn't mean it makes much sense.

- Bob looks east and west and sees "all mankind in
  misery," but is more concerned with asking a girl
  to be his baby.
- He doesn't see what he likes the best. Then the
  girl again.
- She should drop her heavy load.
- Fire in the east, fire in the west.
- He's trying to save her time and not trying to
  mess with her.

Try Me Little Girl
Try me, little girl.
Let's have ourselves a family.
Be with me, not them.

"Try Me Little Girl" is a suggestion to get together with the singer and raise a family instead of being with other guys.

I Can't Make It Alone
Woman is no help
To guy who says he loves her
And needs her with him.

Yet another unpolished song.

Don't You Try Me Now
Don't you play with him.
You might enjoy breaking hearts,
But yours might be next.

One more song about a guy warning a girl not to mess around with his delicate heart.

Young But Daily Growing
Girl marries young boy
Half her age. They have some kids.
He's dead at 18.

"Young But Daily Growing," also known as "The Trees They Do Grow High," "Daily Growing" and "Bonny Boy is Young (But Growing)," dates back at least to the 18th century. The Wikipedia entry for this song says it was found in a 1770s manuscript collection of Scottish anthologist David Herd. It also formed the basis of the Robert Burns poem, "Lady Mary Ann" from 1792. The song is about a boy who is married to a girl who is a bit older than he is. He's usually 11 or 12. It's a moving, haunting song.

Here are the lyrics to one version, also taken from the Wikipedia entry:

> "The trees they grow high, the leaves they do grow green
> Many is the time my true love I've seen
> Many an hour I have watched him all alone
> He's young, but he's daily growing.

> "Father, dear father, you've done me great wrong
> You have married me to a boy who is too young
> I'm twice twelve and he is but fourteen
> He's young, but he's daily growing.

> "Daughter, dear daughter, I've done you no wrong
> I have married you to a great lord's son
> He'll be a man for you when I am dead and gone
> He's young, but he's daily growing.

"Father, dear father, if you see fit
We'll send him to college for another year yet
I'll tie blue ribbons all around his head
To let the maidens know that he's married.

"One day I was looking o'er my father's castle wall
I spied all the boys a-playing at the ball
My own true love was the flower of them all
He's young, but he's daily growing.

"And so early in the mornin' at the dawning of
the day
They went out into the hayfield to have some
sport and play;
And what they did there, she never would declare
But she never more complained of his growing.

"At the age of fourteen, he was a married man
At the age of fifteen, the father of a son
At the age of sixteen, his grave it was green
Have gone, to be wasted in battle.
And death had put an end to his growing.

"I'll buy my love some flannel and I will make a
shroud
With every stitch I put in it, the tears they will
pour down
With every stitch I put in it, how the tears will flow
Cruel fate has put an end to his growing."

Bonnie Ship the Diamond
Whaling ship sets sail
On a long, crappy voyage.
Not so bonnie, boys.

This is an old song about whale hunting in Greenland, though Dylan changed the lyrics when he and the Band test-drove the song. Dylan's takes the action south to Veracruz, but gets in all the negative stuff.

- The Diamond was a good ship.
- Sword and rope and my buddy John, we went fishing for whales.
- We had a hard time controlling the ship at night and we felt bad.
- Rise up, let your hearts never fail! We're going fishing for the whales.
- We're down in Veracruz. Also Cape Fate and Cape Horn.

In the original lyrics, the Diamond sailed from Peterhead for the Davis Strait between Greenland and Ellesmere Island in Canada. The girls watch the men leave and the men bid them not to cry.

The Hills of Mexico
Trust me when I say
You can find safer jobs than
Buffalo hunting.

"The Hills of Mexico" is known by other titles and variations, notably "Trail of the Buffalo" or "On the Trail of the Buffalo" or "Buffalo Skinners." It's an old 19th-century song warning of the hazards of going buffalo hunting, which was such a big business that we managed to kill most of them.

Down on Me
I feel really bad.
Everyone is down on me.
Not one exception.

There is little thinner source material to work from. At 42 seconds long, "Down on Me" barely exists. The only lyrics that I can catch are, "Seems like everybody in the world is down on me." You could argue that it's too scant for use. Still, the song is twice as long as "Her Majesty" by the Beatles.

One for the Road
Time for one more drink.
One for me and one for her.
She's gone? I'll drink both.

"One for My Baby (And One More for the Road)" is a Harold Arlen/Johnny Mercer song written for the musical, "The Sky's the Limit," and is best known as a Frank Sinatra song. Dylan's song "One for the Road" appears to be a different song, using only the title. In Dylan's version, you get a sense that the song wasn't finished yet.

"I cry alone at night
There is no friend in sight
I love getting back at night
But I wish I don't.

"This bottle is dried up too
And I'll be all cried up soon
I can't see no God on the moon
It's a long way to go."

I'm Alright
I was blue before,
But I can tell you now that
I'm doing all right.

This is another barely-begun track with the Band.

"Now when I call her by her name, you know,
She don't come
She don't lead me down easy child
But I don't
I'm gone, the man he's standing on is
Maybe some
But I don't have a leak and
'Cause she knows she don't."

I'm Not There
Bob tells this girl
That he's not there at all, though
She's looking for him.

There are lots of people who make lots of hay about "I'm Not There," Which came to mainstream prominence in Todd Haynes's film of the same name. Some people point to the profound lyrics and stair-climbing melody, and say it's a lost masterpiece, a mysterious beauty from the shadows of Dylan's undiscovered (at the time) catalogue. I don't get it. I think it goes on too long and the words seem more like placeholders than anything coherent. I don't mind Dylan's arbitrary choice of words to hold down a pattern as a re-hearses a song, but whatever people think is there, it's not there at all.

All American Boy
Boy joins a rock band,
Makes music, meets pretty girls,
Winds up on a farm.

This song was a Bobby Bare hit in 1959, a pastiche of sorts of Elvis Presley's rise to fame and his subsequent drafting into the Army. Dylan and the Band kept the basic structure, but it sounds like wine, whiskey and weed, along with the relaxed atmosphere and Dylan's penchant during the sessions for trying out all kinds of nonsense lyrics, produced a new song:

"Well, I bought me a guitar, put it in tune
Went out there the month of June
'Twas a hot dog night and a stick in a roar
Everybody was a-down on this side.
There was a holy cow (holy cow)
Mean cow (mean cow)
Double jaw (double jaw)
Cow (cow)."

Sign on the Cross
That sign on the cross
Worries Bob something fierce.
It won't disappear.

"Sign on the Cross" is one of those songs that long-time
bootleg-trading fans of these sessions say is one of the
high points. And it is, musically speaking. The religious
tinge to the grand arpeggios makes me think of songs like
"Everybody Hurts" by REM, and Dylan's impersonation
of an old-time radio preacher sounds powerful and stirring
until you realize that he's just bullshitting. This isn't so much
of a song of religious striving as it is a satire on the same.

Get Your Rocks Off
Everywhere you go,
Everybody says one thing:
Get your rocks off me.

Most people know what "get your rocks off" means. I think that Dylan and the Band knew what they were saying when they recorded this silly blues number, but the way they use the phrase is altogether different.

- Old maid 1 says to old maid 2 as they're lying in bed: Get your rocks off of me.
- Man 1 says to man 2 up on Blueberry Hill: Get your rocks off of me.
- Man 1 says to man 2 down on Mink Muscle Creek: Get your rocks off of me.
- Children shout at Bob and company as they drive by in a Greyhound bus: Get your rocks off of me.

Bob at one point begins to cackle as he sings, which makes this bizarre track charming. Whoever in the Band does the bass voice accompaniment ("Get 'em off!") is a clown.

Don't Ya Tell Henry
Cows, chickens, me and
You say it: "Don't tell Henry –
Apple's got your fly."

This appeared on the 1975 "Basement Tapes" album, but sung by the Band.

Bob goes to the river to "see who's born," which, I'm assuming, means people who've just been baptized and born again. The chicken tells him the cryptic message about what not to share with Henry. Bob goes to the corner to look around. He says it's 10:30. He runs into the woman he loves, who shares with him the cryptic message about what not to share with Henry. Bob goes to the beanery at 12:30 to look around and see himself. He is distracted by a horse and a donkey, and then looks for a cow. He finds several, all of whom share with him the cryptic message: don't tell Henry. Bob goes to the whorehouse one night, again, just to look around. He looks for a tree, then goes upstairs and sees himself, and receives the cryptic message again. Henry makes no appearance in the song.

Bourbon Street
I no longer live
On Bourbon Street, but there are
Some nice girls who do.

Complete chaos. Bob and the boys sing a woozy, boozy New Orleans Dixie-style song that sounds like they made up the words as they played. The story concerns a man singing about how he used to live on Bourbon Street, but he doesn't live there anymore, but should you happen to be going there, you should take care to note that there are lots of nice women there who will show you a good time.

My Woman She's a-Leavin'
Woman's hard to please.
Her man is a rolling stone,
And now she's leaving.

Entertaining background music.

Sample:

> "Reason on the panda mama's kitchen
> But she's all messed up with desire
> Well I hate to be no streetin'
> But my woman she's a leavin'
> And my feel no stand she's no liar."

Mary Lou, I Love You Too
I want to leave you,
But my heart wants to stay, so
I'll leave it with you.

This is a fairly well-formed rehearsal track, but it never went anywhere.

Dress It Up, Better Have It All
She's beautiful, but
She can't light a cannonball.
Not every girl can.

More Basement Tapes variety pack:

- Most people can't see that I've grown.
- She's a fine beauty but she can't light a cannonball.
- Honey I'm making a hard to road.
- Ended up leaving, but it's a heavy load.
- Dress it up, some people have it all.
- Sitting on a trail, can't find nails.
- I hope it come easy, I hope it come hard.
- Sitting in the barnyard in the chicken yard.
- Henry, get the boy home, he's been gone too long.

Silent Weekend
Bob's girl ditches him
For a weekend of parties
And other guys.

- My baby is giving me a silent weekend. She's off partying somewhere and telling me I have to put up with it. I am in misery.
- She surprised me with her decision to go rockin' and rollin' and swingin' with some other guys.
- I wish Monday would come. She's uppity, rollin', in the groove and strollin' over to the jukebox, and not with me, but with the aforementioned other guys.

- I've been thinking about cheating, and maybe I did cheat some. And here comes the weird stuff: "But I just walloped a lotta pizza after makin' our peace, puts ya down on bended knees."
- I hate this silent weekend. "Man alive, I'm burnin' up on my brain. She knows when I'm just teasin', but it's not likely in the season to open up a passenger train."

What's It Gonna Be When It Comes Up

Animal instinct:
If Bob were a chicken, he'd
Want to hear his sneeze.

Strange caricature of a lounge singer performance...

"Oh there's... one-room Cadillac.
Taking me in the breeze
If I was a chicken now, I'd just want to hear myself sneeze
Mmmmm, somethin' sure looks good goin' down, boys
Bb-b-b-b-bba-ba-boo
mmmmmm."

900 Miles From My Home

I'll come back home
If you don't want your husband
To be a hobo.

An old folk song updated with some Dylan twists.

"If I get down by the bank
And the river still does run
Yes and everything I see turns to foam
Even down on the ocean side
No she don't wade in just to bang my pride
Cause I'm 900 miles from my home."

Wildwood Flower
He said he loved me,
Called me flower. He left me
To my darkest hour.

"Wildwood Flower" is an old song by the Carter Family.
So recently in love with a charming swain, so cruelly
abandoned.

- I put lilies and roses and myrtle in my hair.
- I danced and sang and laughed and was happy
  and charmed all the hearts.
- But when I woke up the next day, my love went
  away.

She'll be Coming Round the Mountain
Around the mountain
She comes on six white horses,
Whenever she comes.

It's not actually about a girl. It turns out that the song is based on a spiritual referring to the return of Christ. The "she" refers to the chariot. The children's version appeared in Carl Sandburg's "The American Songbag" in 1927. In Dylan's version, it's really a she, as in a girl. She'll be driving six white horses, wearing pink pajamas and carrying three white puppies. We'll kill a rooster and have chicken and dumplings when she comes.

It's the Flight of the Bumblebee
Mean old bumblebee,
He keeps taking my candy
Right from my front door.

Here's an utterly weird song. "It's the Flight of the Bumble-bee." It is nearly unrelated to the "Flight of the Bumblebee" classical music tune by Nikolai Rimsky-Korsakov.

Wild Wolf
Wild wolf, holy books.
Pharaoh's armies made of bread.
No one cares for me.

"Wild Wolf" is an interesting, semi-intelligible song in progress. I'm not sure there is that much depth for the mining.

"Now the ruins are barely rolling
And the nations can't agree

On all that all the nations
But nobody feels very sorry for me…"

Gonna Get You Now
This is not a threat,
It's a promise: Bob will come
And get you right now.

"Gonna Get You Now" sustains itself purely on good atmosphere and strange words.

If I Were a Carpenter
Does my job matter
To you in deciding if
You'll have my baby?

This is a fairly coherent yet still rough version of Tim Hardin's "If I Were a Carpenter." You can tell that they're not taking it too seriously, particularly with the shouts of "yes!" when Dylan asks the boys if they would marry him if he were a carpenter. It's about what it sounds:

- If I were a carpenter, would you marry me and let me make babies with you?
- What if I were a tinker?
- I'd like it if you would do this. I'm lonely and full of sorrow. I'd give you anything.

- What if I were a miller?

Confidential
Don't tell anyone
How much he's in love with you.
It's confidential.

This is a 1956 hit single by Sonny Knight.

Ways in which his love for you is confidential:

- Like a church at twilight. (Assuming there's nobody there around that time.)
- Sentimental as a rose in the moonlight. (What could be more so?)
- A mother's prayer. (For relief from her nagging children, no doubt.)
- A baby's cry. (Something that's not normally confidential.)
- A lover's sigh. (Nearly always confidential.)

Why is it confidential:

- It's too beautiful for other hearts to share. (As it should be.)
- It's our secret. (We're not swingers.)
- There's no need for prying eyes. (Maybe we're married to other people?)

All You Have to Do Is Dream
Bob invites his girl
To love him in his farmhouse
And to blow his horn.

"So, poor little girl, come blow this horn
Hard as any horn might seem
It's very easily done, actually,
All you have to do is dream."

2 Dollars and 99 Cents
Making some change.
Let's start with $2.99.
Your sister has it.

Complete nonsense.

Jelly Bean
One in the morning
And Bob's baby's upside down,
And Bob is crying.

It's not about a jelly bean.

Any Time
Anytime at all,
You need me to want me to
Be your loving man.

The static on the vocal tracks, combined with his unpredictable and sometimes nonsensical word choices of some of these songs, makes understanding what's going on difficult, and perhaps highlights the pointlessness of some of the Basement Tapes tracks, other than to mess around. This is one of those songs.

Down by the Station
Young and ruthless man
Makes indeterminate plans
To meet his woman.

This is another of those songs.

Hallelujah, I've Just Been Moved
I have just been moved.
Was it because of God or
Was it your daughter?

The song mostly sticks to the straight-and-narrow idea of being born again, but there's a sly reference to a daughter buried in the improvised singing that gave me the direction for this haiku.

That's the Breaks
I wish you'd love me,
But I don't think that you will.
That's the breaks of life.

Breaking up is hard to do…

Pretty Mary
Don't be long, Mary.
Don't be blue either because
I'm coming to you.

> "But I'm coming with midnight
> And the cold winds in twilight
> And the dream of the world
> Of Pretty Mary."

Will the Circle Be Unbroken
Family's mother dies.
They're all sad, but happy that
She's gone to heaven.

"Will the Circle Be Unbroken" is a popular folk song from the Carter Family.

- Standing by the window on a cold, cloudy day, watching the hearse taking my mother away.
- I'm told that God has promised her a better home in the sky.
- I was pretty sad when they put her in the grave, though I tried to put a good face on it.

King of France
The king of France, he
Comes to America. He
Can't be understood.

The recording quality is so bad that some of the words
are hard to make out against the distortion. It wouldn't
feel out of place on "White Light/White Heat" by
the Velvet Underground. I've often wondered whether
this song has its roots in the Dauphin character from
"Huckleberry Finn," but it's anybody's guess.

She's on My Mind Again
It's before sunrise.
She's on his mind again.
He is packing up.

This is nearly all guesswork.

Goin' Down the Road Feelin' Bad
If you're feeling bad,
You should go somewhere warmer
Where water's like wine.

This blues song has been around a long time. Dylan's ver-
sion with the Band, sounds like a campfire sing-along.
There are other versions out there, including ones from
Woody Guthrie and the Grateful Dead. The lyrics cen-
ter on wandering poor folks and hobos who are tired of

being treated as such, and looking at moving somewhere like Florida or elsewhere where the water tastes like wine and the temperature is more accommodating to outdoor activities.

On a Rainy Afternoon
It sounds like she's gone,
Leaving Bob hanging around
On a rainy day.

This is not the song of the same name that Dylan recorded with Robbie Robertson in a hotel room in 1966 (and which appears on volume 12 of the Bootleg Series). This is a song about a dreary, rainy afternoon when the girl went out without the guy.

I Can't Come in With a Broken Heart
Here's a simple rule:
No broken hearts allowed here.
Don't come in with one.

Someone went to the trouble on the Internet to post the lyrics as well as they could understand them. Thank goodness because I had a hard time with them.

Next Time on the Highway
Several highway trips
Seem like several too many.
They might be fatal.

After the second verse of this chaotic jam, Dylan starts ragging on Richard Manuel of the Band, then starts singing again, then stops.

Samples:

> "Third time on the highway
> It was nineteen and ten
> They was treating the women
> Just like they was treating the men."
> (This is taken from the song "Ain't No More Cane.")

"Yes, listen to Richard play that piano. Go on, Richard, just play that piano, that shit [inaudible]. Just on the fucking piss on that shit..." (Another website says Dylan exclaims, "Go on Richard, just play that piano, all shit-faced." I don't hear that.)

Northern Claim

Only clouds and rain
Are all that I find in this
Dreary northern claim.

A poor recording of a fragment of a song, "Northern Claim" has the makings of a real song, but it never got past this rough recording. I don't know what a north-ern claim is. I wonder if it's a homestead claim, such as the pioneers received as they moved west in the 19th century.

Love Is Only Mine
Love is only mine
When I'm this far from the sea
And feeling lonely.

Dylan and the Band hack through the beginnings of a song that apparently never ended up going anywhere.

Silhouettes
Guy goes bananas.
He thinks his gal is cheating.
She probably should.

This doo-wop song appeared in 1957 as performed by the Rays. There are other notable versions, including ones from Herman's Hermits and the Four Seasons, not to mention Cliff Richard. The song, by Bob Crewe of the Crewe-Gaudio hit factory ("The Sun Ain't Gonna Shine Anymore") contains some ridiculous lyrics. This stalker-style song is of a piece with "No Reply" by John Lennon, not to mention "Run for Your Life," and could have been the blueprint for Martin Scorsese's crazy cameo in "Taxi Driver."

- Walked by your house, saw silhouettes through the shades.
- Saw you guys kissing and I cried.

- I rang the bell and said I was angry enough to beat down the door.
- It turns out that I was at the wrong house. Whoops.

Come All Ye Fair and Tender Ladies

Bob warns the ladies
That men will love them and
Leave them afterward.

Watch out, ladies, those men can be dawgs.

- They're a summer's morning star. They're here and gone, telling loving stories, saying they love you. Then the next day they're telling another girl the same story.
- You once did that to me. "You could make me believe with the falling of your arm that the sun rose in the west."
- If I were a sparrow, I could escape you as you love me, but I'm not so I must sit here and live in grief and sorrow. "If I had known before I courted that love was such a killing thing, I'd a-locked my heart in a box of gold and fastened it up with a silver pin."

Shadows in the Night

I'm a Fool to Want You; The Night We Called It a Day; Stay With Me; Autumn Leaves; Why Try to Change Me Now; Some Enchanted Evening; Full Moon and Empty Arms; Where Are You?; What'll I Do; That Lucky Old Sun

I'm a Fool to Want You

It's wrong to want you.
Every time I leave, I wish
I had you again.

By Frank Sinatra, Jack Wolf and Joel Herron.

- I'm a fool to want you
- You can't be true, at least not for me alone.
- The devil knows your kiss.
- I said I'd leave you and I did, but I always came back. "Take me back, I love you."

The Night We Called It a Day

It's the end of us:
The moon and stars went away,
The sun didn't rise.

- Cloud on the moon. You kissed me and left.
- The lament of the planets.
- An owl in the dark. Sad as I was. Maybe I was sadder.

- The moon set, the stars set, the sun didn't rise. There was nothing left to say.

Stay With Me
If I lose my way,
If I wander and do wrong,
I hope you stay close.

By Jerome Moross and Carolyn Leigh.

- God, be with me when I'm vain, blind and foolish.
- I'm like a lamb in the spring, wandering too far from home.
- I get lost, I get cold, I get tired. I sin, I look for shelter and cry. Grope and blunder.
- I'll keep walking. I hope that you stay with me.

Autumn Leaves
Had you in summer,
Missed your sunburned hands in fall,
Winter's worst of all.

By Joseph Kosma and the French poet Jacques Prévert. English lyrics by Johnny Mercer.

- Falling leaves in red and gold. Your lips, your kisses, sunburned hands I don't hold anymore.

- Since you're gone, the days are getting longer even though as winter comes they should be getting shorter.

Why Try to Change Me Now
I have strange habits,
But I love you so who cares?
I'm not gonna change.

- You know I have funny habits: walking in the rain, saying I'm going up to the corner and winding up in Spain.
- I daydream all the time and smoke and let the ashes fall on the floor, leave the key in the door when I go away on the weekends.
- Why try to change me now?
- Why can't I be more conventional? What do you want me to do?

Some Enchanted Evening
If you find true love
Laughing in a crowded room,
Don't leave her; seize her.

By Oscar Hammerstein II and Richard Rodgers. From "South Pacific."

- You see her first as a stranger in a crowded room.
- You'll hear her laughter in your dreams.

- Who knows why? Not fools. Wise men don't try.
- Grab her while you can and don't let her go.

Full Moon and Empty Arms
Wish upon the moon
And it might bring what I want,
Which, of course, is you.

Written by Buddy Kaye and Ted Mossman in 1945. The song's melody comes from the allegro scherzando movement of Sergei Rachmaninov's Piano Concerto No. 2 in C Minor. The lyrics are simple.

- Singer and moon: present. Lover: absent.
- It's a nice night. A kiss might not be there just to build a dream on, but a memory too.
- Singer wishes on moon.
- The wish is: you'll appear by the light of the next full moon.
- Singer wishes on moon again.
- He repeats the wish.

Where Are You?
No happy ending,
I can't believe we're apart:
My dear, where are you?

- I thought you cared about me. Where are you?
- What happened to us? Why did we say goodbye?

- Was this all in vain? Where is my happy ending?

What'll I Do

I know we split up,
But I wonder whom you kiss,
And where you are now.

- So much for our romance. But what will I do when you're far away and I'm sad?
- What will I do when I wonder who is kissing you?
- Who will talk to me? Not this photograph of you.

That Lucky Old Sun

I work my ass off.
I'd rather roll around like
That lucky old sun.

- I fight with my wife and work for my kids and sweat my life away.
- God, help me out here. I want to be like the sun, which has nothing to do but roll around heaven all day.

Selections from **The Bootleg Series Vol. 12: The Cutting Edge 1965-1966**
Remember Me (When the Candlelights Are Gleaming); Blues Stay Away From Me; Weary Blues From Waitin'; Lost Highway; I'm So Lonesome I Could Cry; I Can't Leave Her Behind; On a Rainy Afternoon; If I Was a King; What Kind of Friend Is This; Positively Van Gogh; Don't Tell Him, Tell Me; If You Want My Love; You Don't Have to Do That; California; Medicine Sunday; Lunatic Princess; Long Distance Operator

Remember Me (When the Candlelights Are Gleaming)
After we parted,
You restarted. Your new love
Won't last. Think of me.

"Remember Me" and the other songs listed here are from a 5,000-copy limited edition of volume 12 of the Bootleg Series. They are from the last disc of an 18-disc collection and were recorded in hotel rooms between Dylan's tour stops in the USA and Britain in 1965 and 1966.

This song is by Scotty Wiseman. He and his wife were known as the duo Lulu Belle and Scotty, christened "The Sweethearts of Country Music." Their big hit was "Have I Told You Lately That I Love You." (Not the one that you know by Van Morrison and popularized by Rod Stewart.)

Blues Stay Away From Me
Blues plague lonely guy.
He asks them to stay away,
But they never do.

This is an old country hit by the Delmore Brothers, and despite the title of the song, the blues never stayed away from them. One died young. The other had a heart attack and lost his father and daughter in quick succession.

Weary Blues From Waitin'
Women goes away,
Giving her lover the blues.
He wants her back home.

This Hank Williams single was released after he was found dead in his Cadillac on New Year's Day 1953. Dylan echoed the line, "Through tears I watch young lovers as they go strolling by" in another song many years later.

Lost Highway
Dissipated man
Blames wine, women and card games
For all his troubles.

This is another Hank Williams song, written and first recorded by country singer-songwriter Leon Payne in 1948.

I'm So Lonesome I Could Cry
The worst blues ever:
Nature sympathizes with guy
Who's missing his gal.

This song was a Hank Williams original, which
he recorded in 1949. Perhaps the defining song of
Williams's catalogue, it initially was released as a
B-side to the up-tempo number, "My Bucket's Got a
Hole in It."

I Can't Leave Her Behind
Guy follows woman
Wherever she leads. She goes.
He still wants her there.

On a Rainy Afternoon
Does he love her or
Does he not? His words suggest
That he isn't sure.

"I Can't Leave Her Behind" and "On a Rainy Afternoon"
come from scenes shot for the unreleased Dylan docu-
mentary "Eat the Document." These songs are the result
of Dylan and Robbie Robertson playing their guitars in
a hotel room. Dylan is working out the chords for these
new songs, and Robertson gamely tries to follow. They
remain unfinished as far as I know.

If I Was a King
If Bob was a king,
He would give all his riches
To this one woman.

What Kind of Friend Is This
What kind of friend would
Love you behind your back yet
Act like she don't care?

Positively van Gogh
Bob and a woman
Discuss the genius paintings
Of Vincent Van Gogh.

Don't Tell Him, Tell Me
You want someone else?
That's fair, but you should share your
Thoughts with me, not him.

If You Want My Love
If you want him to
Love you, you need to show him
Or else he won't know.

The preceding five songs are all unfinished Dylan songs
that he worked on in hotel rooms.

You Don't Have to Do That
She runs around like
A headless chicken. He says
There's no need for that.

The beginnings of a song from the studio sessions for "Bringing It All Back Home," "You Don't Have to Do That" disappeared as quickly as it showed up.

California
San Francisco's fine,
But Bob prefers four seasons
So he travels on.

This marks the official release of "California" on a Bob Dylan album. It previously appeared as a song on the second soundtrack album featuring songs from the TV show "NCIS."

Medicine Sunday
Train leaves, you're tied up.
You act like everything's fine.
Don't you want my love?

This song is an early version of "Temporary Like Achilles," which turned up later on "Blonde on Blonde."

Lunatic Princess
Princess is frantic,
She lives in the past. She's lost.
Bob wants to know why.

This is an outtake from "Highway 61 Revisited."

Long Distance Operator

Guy jumps phone line queue.
He's desperate to talk to his
Dangerous girlfriend.

"Long Distance Operator" first appeared on the 1975 "Basement Tapes" album, but in a version performed by the Band. The only commercial release of Dylan doing this song is on a super-limited edition download of live performances from 1965, in which he played the song in Berkeley, California. The download accompanied the huge 18-CD set of volume 12 of the Bootleg Series. In short: he pleads with the phone operator to let him make a call. He needs to get in front of everyone else waiting to use the phone. She's a killer of a girlfriend, and he's strangling in telephone wire.

Fallen Angels

Young at Heart, Maybe You'll Be There, Polka Dots and Moonbeams, All the Way, Skylark, Nevertheless, All or Nothing at All, On a Little Street in Singapore, It Had to Be You, Melancholy Mood, That Old Black Magic, Come Rain or Come Shine

Young at Heart

If you're young at heart,
You'll survive and thrive, alive.
Better than money.

Music by Johnny Richards and words by Carolyn Leigh. This was a big hit for Frank Sinatra in the early 1950's, and was included in the Gordon Douglas film of the same name. In fact, the film was named after the song to seize on its popularity. The film features Gig Young, Doris Day, and Sinatra himself as a depressed musician. This one falls in love with that one, Sinatra's romantic-loner character nearly offs himself and all sorts of complications ensue before he finally finds happiness just at the prospect of being alive. His character originally was supposed to die at the end, but Sinatra forced a change in the ending after too many of his recent film roles featured him dying.

What happens if you're young at heart:

- Fairy tales come true.
- You're broad of mind.

- You can make impossible schemes happen.
- You can laugh at your broken dreams.
- You live a more exciting life.
- Love is in your heart.
- You're richer than if you had money.
- You might survive until you're 105.

Maybe You'll Be There
I'm looking for you
Ever since you left me.
I'm acting like a fool.

Music by Rube Bloom and lyrics by Sammy Gallop. Gallop, who also wrote the song "You're Gonna Hate Yourself in the Mornin'," killed himself in 1971.

- I stop and stare at crowds of people, hoping you'll be there.
- I do the same thing when I go walking after midnight.
- You held me and kissed me and left me.
- I'm praying I'll see you again.

Polka Dots and Moonbeams
Pug-nose fetishist
Meets the right girl at a dance.
He likes her clothes too.

Music by Jimmy Van Heusen and words by Johnny Burke. Frank Sinatra recorded it in 1940 with the Tommy Dorsey Orchestra. Burke appears to have been the one with a thing for pug noses. The woman in this song has one, and the lyrics refer to it three times.

- Country dance in garden: woman bumps into a guy. She's pug-nosed and wearing polka dots. The guy sees that and moonbeams.
- He nervously asks her to dance.
- People seem to frown on this union, but he doesn't care.
- Now they live in a cottage of lilacs and laughter, happily ever after.

All the Way
Accept no discounts.
In love, you must pay full fare
For first-class romance.

Music by Jimmy Van Heusen and words by Sammy Cahn. The song comes from the film "The Joker Is Wild," in which Sinatra plays singer and comedian Joe E. Lewis. Lewis crosses the mob. They slash his throat. He tries comedy instead. He gets ahead, but becomes a drunk.

What "All the Way" is about:

- Love isn't any good unless your lover loves you all the way.
- Same goes for needing you.
- All the way also means thick and thin, richer and poorer, etc.
- I'll love you that way.

Skylark
A hopeful lover
Relies on a bird to find
Love that makes her fly.

Music by Hoagy Carmichael and words by Johnny Mercer. An ode to Judy Garland.

Questions for this bird:

- Where is my love? In the meadow? Is she waiting for a kiss?
- Is there a green valley where I can visit, avoiding shadows and rain? Does it have a blossom-covered lane?
- Have you heard music in the night while flying?
- I'm counting on you to help me find these things.

Nevertheless
I'm taking a chance
Loving you. You'll break my heart,
But I can't help it.

Music by Harry Ruby and words by Bert Kalmar. They also are known for "Who's Sorry Now?" "I Wanna Be Loved by You," "A Kiss to Build a Dream On" and "Three Little Words."

- In love with you, right or wrong.
- Might win or lose.
- The chances I'm taking in loving you are terrible.
- I might be sorry, but I'm in love with you.

All or Nothing at All
If I'm diving in
To this affair, the deep end
Is where I'll begin.

Music by Arthur Altman and lyrics by Jack Lawrence. A 1943 hit for Sinatra.

- No half love. Gotta be all or nothing at all.
- If you come near me and kiss me, I'll be lost, weak and dizzy.
- I'll be under your spell.

On a Little Street in Singapore
Far East, close to love,
Romancing a lonely girl,
Going back for more.

By Peter DeRose and Billy Hill. Both died young. Hill died at the age of 41 on Christmas Eve.

How we met:

- Near a lotus-covered door in Singapore.
- Moonlight on her lonely face. Embrace.
- Now I'm on a ship, sails perfumed by Shalimar. Following temple bells back to the Singapore shore to hold her once again.

It Had to Be You
Well-adjusted girls
Don't turn me on like you do.
It's a compliment!

Music by Isham Jones and words by Gus Kahn. It's a lasting favorite, showing up for the first time in 1924 and still making appearances in romantic comedy and drama soundtracks. Other big Kahn hits include "Toot, Toot, Tootsie," "My Buddy," "Yes Sir, That's My Baby," "Ukulele Lady," "My Baby Just Cares for Me," and "Dream a Little Dream of Me."

Romance ad for the passive man:

- She's no ordinary girl. He does just as she says and he doesn't know why. It must be fate.
- He's happy to be sad just thinking of her.
- Some girls aren't mean or cross or try to be boss, but who wants to be with them?
- She has a ton of faults, but he still loves her.

Melancholy Mood
A sighing lover
Wishes his ex would return
So he'd feel better.

By Walter Schumann and Vick R. Knight Sr. Schumann composed the score for the amazing Charles Laughton film "The Night of the Hunter" and the "Dragnet" theme. He died at 44 after complications from open heart surgery.

- Melancholy mood: haunts me, taunts me, strands me.
- No joy or inspiration or consolation.
- Grief and gloom until doomsday.
- No kiss, embrace or love. Love is fleeting.
- Please release me.

That Old Black Magic
You're as bad for me
As demonic possession.
Come: send me to hell!

Released as a single in 1942, the song on the other side
was "A Pink Cocktail for a Blue Lady," straight from the
David Lynch school of moody. Music by Harold Arlen,
words by Johnny Mercer.

- Black magic has me in its spell.
- Icy fingers up and down my spine.
- Spellbound eyes.
- Leaf caught in the tide.
- Set me on fire with burning desire.
- Spins me into the maelstrom.

Come Rain or Come Shine
Happy? Unhappy?
I don't care as long as you
Are always with me.

Music by Harold Arlen, words by Johnny Mercer.

The weather report:

- I'm gonna love you like nobody has loved you.
- I'm gonna love you high as a mountain and deep
  as a river.

- We're going to be happy and unhappy.
- We might have clouds or sun.
- We might have money or none.
- There will be rain and there will be sunshine.

Thanks to The Band: Derek Caney, who has been there from the beginning and provided me access to the 50th Anniversary Collection series (two or three of these haiku are his or based on his suggestions. He knows which); Anupreeta Das, who also has been there from the beginning, but didn't have the option to go home afterward and leave the project behind like Derek did; Kenneth Li for encouraging me to take this beyond an office lark; Wallace Witkowski for reminding me that writers we like often started writing later in life; Jui Chakravorty for showing me that you can finish immense projects if you apply yourself; Dan Colarusso for giving me time to work on this project; Annette MacMillan and Bill Smith for a place to write and for listening to me yammer on about Dylan this and Dylan that; Masato Kato and Effric Smith for being early fans; David Schlesinger for many things including encouragement; Sukumar Ranganathan for publishing some of these in earlier drafts; Eric Effron for a willingness to be a Dylan nerd when I needed it; Ron Chester for writing nice things in public about the haiku; Rahul Biddappa, Tresa Sherin Morera, Tony Tharakan, David Lalmalsawma and the rest of the online crew in Bangalore and Delhi; Kenneth Sean Slade and Rachel Levitt Slade for their shared love of music; Eric Martyn for his suggestions; Yuriko Kurahashi Li and Hiroko Haraguchi for reviewing the Japanese text; Jason Fields for taking the sting out of self-publishing a book; and Preeti Bhuyan, the Virgil to my Dante through the divine comedy of 1980s Dylan music. And thanks to everyone who helped or listened in the past seven years. (Including @monk1277 on Twitter. I don't know who you are, but someone who likes those Sam Peckinpah movies as much as I do must be worth getting to know.)

There are too many sources of information on Dylan and his music to mention here. I relied on nearly all of them to write this book. One which bears mentioning is "The Songs He Didn't Write: Bob Dylan Under the Influence," by Derek Barker. I've worn out the binding, which is a testament to the riches within.

I wrote most of "Haiku 61 Revisited" in Jersey City, at the Patisserie Margot cafe on the Upper West Side of Manhattan, in Bangalore and New Delhi, and, crucially, on two self-imposed sabbaticals at our home in Edgartown, Massachusetts. Writing a book while holding a job is not impossible, but it's not easy. Thanks to the tourists, washashores and permanent residents of Martha's Vineyard for providing the background banter that allowed me to dig into Dylan's world in peace.

 Robert MacMillan is an editor at the Reuters news service. He lives in New York City. He has been a reporter and editor for more than twenty years. He previously worked at the *Washington Post* and DC-area news outlets. He graduated from American University.

Bob Dylan's music has been part of his life for as long as he can remember.

Index

61750449R00345

Made in the USA
Middletown, DE
14 January 2018